Almost 5' 4"

Almost 5' 4"

Confessions of an Unconventional Model

Isobella Jade

Almost 5' 4"

TABLE OF CONTENTS

You know very well
who you are
Don't let em hold you down,
reach for the stars.
-"Juicy," Notorious B.I.G.

Acknowledgements

This memoir is truly my greatest feat and writing about my past has been one of the most emotionally difficult and wonderful things that I have ever done, and the following friends come to mind when I think about how the pieces came together during the past five years.

First I have to give a huge thank you to Jody Corbett for your honesty, support and encouragement as I dove back into my past, and I want to also thank Carol Craig for reminding me of the love I have for my mother.

Then, a special thanks to Colleen Brennan the hottest bartender in New York City with the cutest dog in New York City, Pongo. She is the girl who kept my spirits high and cracked my ass up laughing so hard for the past four years. Some of that laughter happened at Robert Milazzo's and Alex Kroke's photo studio. Thank you boys so much for making my second home since 2002 in your presence. I will always miss that photo studio and the sunlight that came through those big windows and sipping a soda on the brown couch. Another person who won't be forgotten is Michael McCabe, who photographed me being my self in Miami, during a time that I took for granted and only wish to repeat now. I have to mention Robert Haynes-Peterson at *Accent* magazine for the chance and conversations about dreams.

These next people are those who have shown up, live it with me, or listened:

My father Curtis Staub, Ginny Van Marter, Jacquelyn LaCroix, Maryam Baik, Shauna Lyons, Melissa Rodriguez, Joel

Shaw, Dan Stern, Fred Staab at NBC, and Frank Bonomo at the Apple Store.

There is no place like home, even if home is in Syracuse, and thank you to my mother and sister, for their understanding, patience and love, I wish I could have hugged you both more often.

And finally but truly never last, a warm embrace of appreciation to Todd.C. Harkrider for believing in me and caring for me so, while allowing me to take my time and when I needed to let it all out you always had a sleeve, you have the mascara stains to prove it.

Author's Note

Maybe you've never posed nude or had your little sister see you naked on the Internet, or you've never lived out of five bags. And maybe you've never written an entire book at the Apple Store because you've had no Internet connection or computer, but if the odds were ever against you, this book was written for you. Maybe you're a short basketball player, or you didn't pass the Bar Exam the first time, or you got crappy SATs scores. Maybe you are considering building a business from scratch without a trust fund, or you are coming off of a bad breakup or divorce. Maybe you are trying to become something and someone, or maybe you are simply trying to leave a mark or legacy.

Well, if you've ever strived to beat the odds, you can relate to my reason for staying in the game, for giving up stability as I slept on friends' couches, for eating from the dollar menu at Wendy's, and buying twenty-five cent bananas. Despite the sacrifice, I chose this cutthroat business, but with it comes the reality. You won't find me under the tent at Bryant Park during fashion week. Instead, I run with a different breed while trying to burn down the wall of standards. Stomping my heels and strutting my stuff, I proved I could be a model, despite being almost 5'4" in height. This memoir is about the extremes I went through to call myself a model.

While I wrote this memoir, I was living it just as I am today.

Prologue

Grab Your Bootstraps and Suitcase

<u>March 2006: New York City</u>
My clothing smelled really bad and I hadn't done laundry in about six weeks, actually more like six months. I sat on my suitcase, using all my weight to shut it, nearly breaking the zipper in the process. My life was inside that bag. It dawned on me that I didn't know where I would be sleeping that night, but what eased my mind was that I had a photo shoot in a few hours and if the photographer turned out to be cool, he might allow me to stay at his place. Or I could always rotate between my four friends' apartments.

Now, in this moment of uncertainty, I realized everything in my life had brought me to this day. Yet suddenly my life looked compact, lonely and what security I'd had was quickly evaporating—that is if I measured the items I owned against my quality of life.

A lot had changed and some days, I wondered if it was worth it. I counted back to all the places I had lived and left. Astoria seemed light-years away and forever gone were the days of living in Brooklyn Heights on Henry Street, and then 88th and Riverside in the college dorms. My days as a track runner in Syracuse, New York were even a further memory. I had spent a seven month rendezvous in Miami and then I'd returned to New York. Today, I was leaving Harlem behind as well. I didn't know what that night or tomorrow would bring. The $23 dollars in my pocket could only be stretched so far, but it sure beat the hell out of a nine to five job. Being in control of my destiny was all that mattered as I checked my suitcase zipper one more time to make sure it was secure. Something had to be. When I looked at my life, smashed and unfolded in a suitcase, I knew what I was sacrificing.

The contents of the suitcase consisted of only a few pairs of jeans, my notorious red dress, three pairs of shoes, all high heels, no socks—I never wear socks—and a few round-about tops, mostly tans and black, along with my journal that I use in moments of desperation. Add to that, random scraps of paper with dates and names I needed to remember if I was ever going to make it in this town. All I really needed I kept safe in between my jeans and my dress: my modeling portfolio.

Now that I'd finished packing, I could once again smell myself, and today it was getting worse. I had on the same underwear going on day three now. I felt gross and disgusting, but there was no time for laundry and I really couldn't afford the $4.50 anyway.

Just the act of closing my suitcase shut made me realize how much I wanted to succeed, so I ignored the smell. It felt normal to be a Raggedy Anne girl who had slept on too many friends' couches to count, and who was still struggling. I wondered what people thought of me, carrying everything I owned with me, plopping it on their floor, eating their food, taking up space in their polished worlds. I wondered if it was just my imagination or if I was really as annoying as I felt.

Everything collided with the tug of the zipper and it all became clear: You can't turn your back on things that are already gone. My stability was long past. I was especially conscious of it when I thought about the word "home." It had no meaning. To me, home was where I slept.

I added some lip gloss and looked at the little pink crusted rim of the container. Money was in short supply, and I hadn't bought anything new in months. It was impossible to pay rent and chase my dreams, too. I'd had to make the choice to either give up stability or give up modeling, despite everything I'd been through during the past four years. I figured if I gave up everything for the modeling, it would all work out. I knew I couldn't model the way I wanted to and have a part-time job. I needed to continue to focus on modeling and marketing myself. So far, my efforts were paying off and I even had a few agents calling me.

I tore another tear sheet out of *Accessories* magazine and gave it the once over. If I kept researching and hustling myself, I could continue to survive and add jobs to my resume and portfolio.

Plain and simple, having to think about rent was the demon holding me and my dreams down. However, it *did* make me nervous to know I had no home or place to call mine. As I put on one of the five coats I had once owned, I suddenly missed my old apartment in Astoria. I missed the college dorms. I missed the comfort of feeling normal and complacent, and yet complacency frightened me. My hopes to succeed as a model always won out over complacency, and it was worth it because in my hungriest, lowest moments a job would always appear at the last moment, as if to exercise my strength and patience.

I had nothing to offer a relationship or a friend, and I still couldn't pay my cell phone bill. Worse yet, I knew the bill collectors by name and my bank balance was a few cents short of zero, but today those worries were behind me. I decided that the cold air could never taste fresher as I let the door slam shut behind me. It felt good to hear it slam. I swallowed a deep breath of freedom as I stepped out of my Harlem ex-apartment. I pushed away any nagging worry that I wouldn't be able to hack it. I even left early, as a treat to my ex-roommates—two days before my April first deadline.

I tighten my signature tan bandana around my new short bob and glanced over the neighborhood as I walked down Broadway. It was a glum place, filled with people who only had one path paved for them. It made me feel ashamed to have a college degree I wasn't using as I passed uneducated people, even though City College of New York and Columbia College were just around the corner. To others, I must have looked like a passing tourist with my suitcase, as I moved quickly, eager to get out of Harlem as fast as possible or be stuck there forever.

Constant movement had made me "lighten the load," but the weight on my mind was heavy and deep thoughts were running through me. With each step in my mint colored stilettos, I subtracted what I had started with from what I had now. The loss of clothing and other belongings as I moved from place to place, couch to couch, apartment to apartment, was tiring and mind draining. Although I was confident about the choices I had made, sometimes I wondered about my decision.

Like now.

For a moment, I felt weak as I remembered the details of the past year. I had gone from a skyline view in a slightly below average apartment in Astoria, Queens, with more than sixty pairs of shoes stashed in the one closet. Over time, I lost everything, whittling it down to five bags, to then taking advantage of friends and wearing out my welcome on their couches. Finally, I had tried to manage rent in another apartment in Harlem but had failed to make the rent payments ...again. All in just six months.

Suddenly, I felt the vibration of my cell phone in my coat pocket, but I ignored it. Grabbing it and keeping my wobbling suitcase stable was a struggle. It was on vibrate for a reason; I didn't want to talk to anyone. The loud ringing could interfere and dull the faith I had in my plans. It kept vibrating.

Annoyed, I looked at the digital display. Shit! It was the worst person to call at that moment.

Her voice would kill me. I feared it would drain my enthusiasm, that I would lose the string of hope that I was clinging to at that moment.

"Hello, Mom ...can you hear me?"

Boxes of fruit, ketchups, and empanadas lined the street, ready to be shelved at the storefront I passed. It was frustrating and I was agitated that I had to zigzag through the commotion like a fright train filled with precious cargo.

"Mom, are you there?" I had my mother and my life in my hands, an awkward mix.

"Yes, I'm here, *Heather*, how are you?" I hated it when she said my *real* name, especially at this moment, when I was feeling so free, so sure of my gypsy-like lifestyle.

"I'm good. I'm going to SoHo, Mom." She had only been to New York City once before to visit while I was in college, I don't think she knew where SoHo was located.

"Oh, that sounds like fun, what else are you doing today?" Great! She sounded peppy and talkative.

Answering her with the truth would be like pulling my own teeth; I hated talking to her about modeling, about myself, about my living situation. She had given me the $1500 dollars to get the Harlem apartment that I was leaving at the very moment she called. Telling her that I didn't get that advertising job I'd lied about getting two months ago, and that I had wasted her $1500 dollars on the spur of the moment when I'd needed a place to live, would not go over well. Especially since my whole life she'd been telling me how little money she had. Telling her the truth would ruin *my* day. It would ruin this moment. It had taken enough courage already to just throw out more shirts and shoes, and one of my favorite pair of jeans.

"I'm going to do some laundry." I hadn't done laundry in months. "And mail out some more comp cards." Another lie, I had no stamps. "It's a nice day in the city. I might go to the ...Mom, I gotta go. I'm about to get on the train!" I lied again. The train was three blocks away.

I had to get off the phone. With every second it was getting more difficult to drag out the lie *and* to carry this phone call any further. Then she let me know the *real* reason she'd called.

"I wanted to see if you were alive. It has been a couple of weeks and you haven't called."

She was right. I hadn't talked to her in weeks on purpose, for fear that she would ask about my life, what I was doing and question it. Although, she never really asked questions. Or details. Maybe she just hoped what I told her was the tru Maybe she just thought it was. I quickly got off the phon a "Sorry, gotta go!" I was too close to the safety of h close to her fat belly, and speaking to her reminde cooking and I was actually hungry for it. It would be too easy to just walk back into the security of my old life. I could smell the scent of her, and I felt vulnerable hearing her voice. I had to push away the guilt and stay focused.

As I placed the phone back in my pocket, I couldn't shake the guilt, even with the pride of doing whatever the fuck I wanted. Yet, the guilt of being able to barely take care of myself melded into the satisfaction of creating my own future. It would all be okay, I promised myself again. I was my own modeling agent, my own boss, cheerleader, and "my own fruit stand." Whenever I passed the lady with her orange cart, I would think about how everyone in New York seemed to be trying to survive. Now, as I walked by her stand, she was smashing oranges into a Crush can and selling orange juice right there on 139th Street and Broadway for a buck. I admire her. She is hustling and I am, too. Only it's my skinny waist, bony hips, little curves here and there, tiny thin legs and my big brown eyes that I'm selling with a hopeful smile, and I haven't eaten an orange in God knows how long. Fruit, for that matter, was no longer in my diet. It had become more about the cheeseburger deluxe at Wendy's, where I put my daily dollar.

I had learned—more like forced myself—not to need too much. Time had flown by like all the adults in my life had promised it would. It was 2006 and I was scared as shit that tomorrow would come too soon. It felt like the beginning and the end all at once as I dragged my suitcase down the subway stairs without any help from the perverted, married, street-stalking scumbags who whistled at my perfectly shaped ass each day. I slid onto the downtown 2 train at 136th Street with my suitcase in tow and felt like the fool that couldn't afford to pay took up space for two.

me up the subway stairs and back down erred at 14th Street either. Life was about l if you fell or dropped your purse or lost e on your own. I didn't help anyone either, at you give.

ough the open doors of the subway, I swore

to myself I would start to notice things again, not just myself but my surroundings, like the smell of the day and the weather. Speaking of weather, I didn't have an umbrella if it started to rain. And yet, I soon forgot about the weather as soon as I passed a window display. Whenever I looked inside at the artist studio, I realized I had forgotten how to appreciate the beauty in a painting. I used to wonder where the artist put the first stroke. Today, I didn't care. I only cared what *I* looked like.

I strongly believed the only reason I had anything at all on my resume these past four years was because I *was* so self-absorbed and so self-serving. Admiring art, admiring anything but me, was a remnant from my past—a past I would rather forget. Now, I made up my own rules and distanced myself from things that used to intrigue me. I could be called a model only because I worked at it everyday and because modeling was something I *wanted* to do, not my only option. I wasn't running beside the tall lanky Giraffes with their fancy agency logos engraved on the front of their black portfolios. I was in a league of my own, out for myself. Just because an agent wasn't calling didn't mean I wasn't modeling. I had learned to find my own work, and fortunately all the effort hadn't killed me yet.

I was the only one who cared whether I booked a modeling job or not, or if I was on a billboard or in a magazine this month. Being self-absorbed was a competitive skill in my mind, and I was focusing more on the compliments I received than giving any to other models. Oh, I wasn't walking around like a total bitch, but I also had to keep my guard up, my winning game face on, comparing myself to everything and everyone around me. I couldn't even give credit to a talented artist without thinking I could do it better. That's what kept me sane, focused. Kept me from giving in to the despair that could have easily claimed me if I let it.

SoHo always made me feel better, calm. I was heading there now. It was the "pick-me-up" place I needed that day, and coffee was always waiting on the street corner to bring me a feeling of security. It was a high, a release, a moment to drift away from my fears: of not being able to fully understand myself; of wondering whether I was making the right choices.

Feeling buoyant, despite my ugly ass, piece of shit suitcase and a trademark bandana around my head, I made my way to the Apple Store. The Apple Store was a home to me. It had become my office during the past year and a half.

My photo shoot wasn't until later in the day, at 4:00 P.M., and even though it was with an amateur and I knew I was better than that, my need for cash was more important than my ego. So I would, with a silent, invisible grudge, lower myself to his lens for the pleasure of feeling a few dollars in my hand. I would show off my flat chest and my curvy ass.

Everyday before I went to my shoots, castings, or to the Apple Store, I would have a talk with myself, my own private religious moment—even though I wasn't religious—that involved tangling through the complexity of my knotty-haired self. The result of the talk would determine whether I was in a good mood that day or not. Although I could no longer glaze over the truth of my pitiful self, there was no fucking way I could give in, give up, now, as I made my way to an open iMac computer.

It took forty minutes to get to SoHo because the trains were running slow. It was already almost 2:30 P.M. when I arrived at the Apple Store where I would work on my memoir for an hour before heading over to the photographer's. My sessions at the store usually lasted an hour or longer, and I couldn't be late for this shoot. I was a professional even when the atmosphere or the photographer wasn't. Besides the shoot, I still needed to figure out where I was going to sleep that night. Who knew how long the shoot would last and if the photographer would be cool? I needed a back-up plan and I needed it soon.

I felt annoyed with myself and immature, like a crab or leech living off people's generosity. Even if they were my friends. These days anyone with a couch or floor space was a potential place to stay for a night or two. I excused my rudeness, calling the pursuit of my goals an obsession. I just knew that I couldn't quit. Not even with all I owned fitting in a mere medium-size suitcase; not even though I still wore busted shoes because I couldn't afford to fix them or used an old toothbrush with bent bristles; not even knowing I had a nude shoot that night and the money wasn't really very good. Still I had to model. I had to have it my way, the hard way. No other way was welcome.

All my modeling mistakes and choices blew up in my face one Thanksgiving, a few years back, during my sophomore year of college. Dinner had consisted of the usual turkey and stuffing, Jell-o, and green bean casserole. But it didn't matter how good the food tasted. When my mother called me by my *"real name,"* I knew from her tone some heavy shit was about to go down.

In a calm, collected voice she used only when I messed up, she called me into her room. *"Heather,* I need to talk to you."

Her tone pinched my ears. My sister Lara followed me to my mother's bedroom, walking proudly, acting like the Judge for "the case."

"Is there something you want to tell me?"

I thought she had something to tell *me,* so of course I said "no."

She paused, eyeing me carefully. "What is this then? Do you know where this came from?"

She whipped out the evidence. It was a printed photo of me posing butt naked with a smile and an American flag barely covering my nipples and crotch. I looked at it in disbelief.

"When did you do this?"

Heart racing, I recalled the face of that ugly, shaggy, scary old Santa Claus of a photographer and wondered why he would put my photo on his website. Why did I even sign that damn release? It was too obvious that the photo was of me, but maybe I could convince my mother that it was all a bad dream—that someone had found a picture of me and transformed it and made me naked with an American flag. Fuck! I knew that wasn't the truth. I had wanted to be naked that day. The photographer had paid me $300 dollars and I was at my prime of nude modeling, it was my first job as a paid model. I booked it all by myself, too. I was complimented and flattered at the rate he offered.

After the shoot I felt beautiful and radiant. Now everything was ruined and I was that ugly girl again—the one who wore hand-me-downs and glasses, who never fit in.

"I don't know," I mumbled quietly, but screamed bloody murder inside. I hated myself, couldn't believe I'd been caught. "Mom, I just ..." There had to be a way I could explain my need for being naked in a logical way without sounding like an idiot, without drooling on myself. Instead, I felt a flush of heat. The freedom I felt the day of that shoot, the day I left for New York as the daughter of a proud parent suddenly turned to bile on my tongue. I couldn't think straight. Shit was flying everywhere, gooey and sticky, clinging to the windows and the walls of that safe place in my mind. A place where I got away with anything and everything. My secret was out, loud and obnoxious. I couldn't shut it up. Before I could think of some explanation, my sister spoke up instead.

"Everyone knows. How could you do this to us?"

I thought of "everyone." Did she mean my friends? Did my father know? Did she mean all of Syracuse *and* all of the family, or did she mean just the family.

"Everyone thinks you're a slut," she continued without letting me say a word. "I was working at Kirby's as a hostess and one of the cooks comes up to me and says 'I saw your sister on the Internet the other day ...and she was naked!'"

When she said the word "naked," I lost my grip on the side table. With nothing to hang on to, my knees buckled and I fell to the floor. I was naked on the Internet. I couldn't take it back. The words I had spent my whole life running from, words that sting—whore, slut, loser—all those words I had tried to disassociate from by moving to New York City now jangled in my ear. I thought no one would know my secrets if they were done in New York, yet my family had seen the photo in upstate New York, before I'd had the courage to say a word.

"You know what *Heather*," my mother said.

Oh god help me.

"You are supposed to be in school!" Typical for a teacher and I rolled my eyes.

"Why are you wasting your life? I have worked so hard for you girls!" She poured on the guilt just then with all the car rides, money she didn't have, while running around to take care of our needs, and how she was without a life of her own. She really wanted me to cry when she said, "You're supposed to be making something of yourself not becoming a whore!"

She sat on the bed staring at the photo, her eyes wide and ready to rip me to shreds or kick me out of the house. It was all so predictable and that made me feel worse.

"You really need to think about what you're doing!" Her mouth twisted in disgust with each word like I was some mutant or rodent.

"You've shamed the family," Lara chimed in.

Suddenly I was my plump mother's daughter again, my alcoholic father's daughter, the below average scholar. Yet, when I thought about giving up modeling and just accepting that it was all a mistake, I knew deep inside my heart I couldn't leave that string untied. For the rest of my life, if that's what it took, I would prove to them I hadn't made a mistake—that modeling wasn't just another "*silly phase.*"

I had to find the positive in my mother's anger, to show I was smart and becoming all the things I had hoped to be.

"I'm sorry." I could hardly breathe or speak. I was in such shock I couldn't even cry, like I'm sure my mother wished.

"And I remember where I was standing," my sister continued. "I had just seated a party of people and walked back to sit down for a minute when the cook finished washing his hands and strolled over nonchalantly."

She hardly took a breath. I got dizzy and hot, as I waited desperately for her to finish.

"It made me completely pissed. I started yelling at him and telling him to shut up because I thought he was lying. I couldn't believe my own *sister* would pose nude on the Internet."

I couldn't speak past the lump in my throat, nor could I look at either of them. This was *not* the end of my modeling career, only the beginning.

"Why am I getting blamed for her ...I had several people

at school giving me dirty looks and calling her a slut to my face."
My sister was still talking as I stormed to my old room and
slammed the door shut.

Since then, that look in my mother's eyes, like I'm not her
daughter anymore, haunts me. Lara's frown, her knowing eyes,
remind me that this big sister isn't worth looking up to anymore.
Their strong, serious, and reprehending expressions were acid
pulling against my heart. I had lost my father to divorce and
DWI, I had lost my virginity to a boy who didn't deserve it,
and over the years I had many others who afterward I realized
didn't deserve me either. I had lost my track scholarship, and
there was no way in hell I was going to lose grip again and lose
my modeling too. I couldn't lose again. I clenched my modeling
dreams tight no matter if I would ever be able to fix the damage
and become worthy again when I was home. Breathing around
them hasn't been easy ever since.

After that Thanksgiving, I was *The One Who had Shamed
the Family*. I could never take that back. To repair the damage
I'd done to my psyche, I changed my name to *Isobella*. I had
thought about it for weeks after the tragedy. It would be a
spiteful tribute to my fat mother who told me I was a waste. It
would be a name that would remind me of that nerve-racking
day, every day forward, when I was confronted with the naked
truth of my actions and my obsession it brought to succeed as a
model. When it all finally became clear that I had to someway
or another be loved by my mother again. As a result, a few
years later when graduation came, I once again had the chance
to choose my own life, I chose to model. To rise above and to
become who I wanted to be. To strike a blow for independence.
But mostly, to cover my shame.

For my mother

Part 1

THE UNDERDOG
2001- 2004

Chapter 1

Disrobing my Innocence

June 2001: Syracuse, New York
My alcoholic father never gave a shit about my modeling, which
was a good thing because he was one less person to impress. I
don't think he ever wanted to be a father. He told me so a few
times when I was a teenager, but it didn't bother me. The one
thing he did give me was the gift of running. Back in the mid-
1960s he was a long jumper and a track runner. He was born and
raised in Syracuse foster homes or by his alcoholic mother. His
father left when he was two, so he didn't have a role model or
a father figure. As a result, he never really wanted to have kids,
and he has never paid child support because he could barely
support himself. When he showed up at my track meets in high
school, my parents wouldn't sit together. My mother and Lara
would be in the stands, and he was always down by the track.
Sometimes he showed up a little tipsy but he was there, which
was all I needed to know. He called me his "running rebel."

His honesty about not wanting to be a father proved to me
I could tell him anything and he would accept me; otherwise he
would have to worry about taking the blame for my life. Except
before long I became his parent, listening to his financial
mistakes and the tragedies of his "death of a salesman" life.

With each new business plan he tried to "find" himself.
Despite being a philosopher about God, politics, and preaching
"what is the purpose of life," and being a great listener, he never
gave me an example to follow or live up to. Long before I was

born, the alcohol had drained away any dream of him becoming successful. He was against having a boss and considered himself too smart for one. And yet after rehab, he'd get a job at the gas station or place an application at the Rescue Mission for ten bucks an hour—that is if he wasn't sleeping there.

I understood his troubles for the first time while my twelve-year-old hand poured a six pack of beer over the sink, watching it slip down the drain so he couldn't drink it—wishing I could make him stop. I would stay up all night and be tired-eyed in the morning walking to middle school just dumbfounded and day-dreaming about what had gone wrong in his life and how in the world I could fix it. After too many DWIs and jail time and rehab, patching up his fifty-year-old life of alcoholism was a battle he still fought and has never beat or fully mended. Yet then I thought, "*Maybe if I ran fast I could make him proud and he would stop drinking.*"

He didn't give me rules or a bedtime, so I considered him a friend. A person to talk with about philosophy and to debate the meaning of life. He inspired me to think about religion when I was ten years old and to question whether god existed. Early on, I pitied him, cared for him, tried to understand him, and even felt guilty about him. I knew I couldn't save him from himself. Later, in high school I had little time to worry about my father's life and I didn't give him much of my time, just phone calls and a few visits to the apartments he was staying at, living at, or moving to and from.

It was painful inside to say hello and goodbye to my father. His drinking meant I didn't have a constant, stable man in my life giving me attention or telling me to respect myself. As a result, I had an extreme need for attention and I got it mostly from immature boys who had just discovered their penises.

And so began my sexual curiosity.

I started to crave the feeling of being wanted and desired by a boy—by anyone who would look my way. I gave myself away too easily. The sex wasn't about deep emotions. Instead, we felt like adults and pretended we knew all about our bodies. I was more of a giver than a receiver, and didn't know anything about my vagina or what to do with it to have an orgasm. Still, I was very interested in sex. I was promiscuous, wearing short shorts and shirts without bras, even though I had very small breasts and they weren't growing anytime soon—or ever. I liked the looks and stares from boys at school, at a track meet, at a water park, at the mall, wherever.

Almost a month after I turned fourteen, I had sex for the first time.

I wrote about it on a piece of paper and stuffed it into my dresser. Then I waited a few days and took a deep breath before joining my mother who was reading on the couch. She was cramming greasy macaroni salad down her throat. I could smell its stench filling the living room air and see the rolls of her neck jiggle with the strain of her swallows. Her cheeks puffed full of the fatty salad. I shuddered, vowing to run even harder. I took a deep breath. "I have to tell you something."

She looked up from her plate. She was tired from a long week of teaching kids how to read. I sat facing her, with my legs crossed Indian style in front of her. I touched her hand, to feel close. I could smell the scent of peppermint cream on her hands.

"What is it, honey?" she asked with a smile.

"Please don't be mad." I had gotten away with a lot with my mother. I often lied to her about where I was *really* going, but now I suddenly had the urge to tell her the truth. If I could beat her to it and admit it before she found out on her own then maybe I wouldn't be considered a "disappointment." I started slow, with an innocent, careful tone.

"I had sex the other day." The house was quiet and my sister wasn't around to hear. I hadn't told any of my friends yet. The boy and I had already broken up and we weren't talking at school. Maybe he didn't like the sex, that night at the party in the tent. He said it was his first time, too. Maybe he was disappointed in me, my small breasts, or maybe he just didn't like me anymore, but I still liked him.

She looked puzzled and this time I waited for *her* to respond. She actually stopped chewing and took a deep swallow.

"Well, when did this happen?" Her calm voice made me confused, but when I took a breath to explain, she switched to a wicked witch voice making me even more nervous when she reached in front of her to balance herself and bowl of salad and gradually stood up with eyes swaying side to side. Then knowing how it happened didn't matter.

"No, forget it! You are just way too young to have sex!" She sort of stomped her foot and ran from me in an awkward run, as if she couldn't keep up with her own frustration and weight as she headed to her room.

"I know, but I am ...and we used a condom," I added in panic of persuasion, like I should be rewarded for being smart.

Instead she sounded fearful again. "Well, I don't care. You're fourteen! You're going to the doctor. Next week!"

The sound of that scared me.

That week we set up a gynecology appointment so I could start on birth control. However, I *did* have sex in the house and she caught me once, when she found an unflushed condom floating in the downstairs bathroom.

When I wasn't acting upon my sexual curiosity, or flirting with boys, or writing notes or poems to friends during class instead of doing my homework, my time was spent running on the varsity track team. It was a way to stay somewhat innocent while in my freshman year. I felt a purpose when I ran. For most of my high school career I was the captain and the top runner on my team. My yearbook was full of thank yous from my teammates. Although I felt appreciated, at the time I was really anti-authority, and even my coach thought I was unbridled. Most girls on my track team weren't talking about having sex, or wearing lip gloss. They were taking honors classes and didn't swear.

By my senior year I had run States, Empires, Junior Olympics and I hoped for a college scholarship as a track runner. My coach cared about my grades and was more of a father than my own. He never failed to keep me focused. He even encouraged the school newspaper to write an article about my efforts in the classroom and on the team. However, he could be demanding and honked the horn so loudly on Saturday mornings when he came to pick me up that it woke up the entire neighborhood. The whole team would be waiting with him in the van to pick up the *Captain* who had slept in again. Once at the track, I kept the group tireless and pumped for ten miles.

I knew running was my only ticket to become something more.

I did get out and things did come my way, just as I hoped, except I only got accepted to one college—that's it, just one—and I took it. I applied to four schools,

but was accepted to only one, based on my running.

My mother and I screamed when we opened the acceptance letter to New York Institute of Technology. I jumped on the couch and almost broke it. Then my mother and I cried because we couldn't believe it.

I was going to college. I was going to see something new, get the hell out of Syracuse and, just for sugar on top, I had a scholarship to run at a Division II school. I felt very important that day as we packed the car with tons of college supplies and goodies from Wal-Mart. It was like Christmas three months early. We drove down to Long Island a few days before my birthday, and five hours later I was free and on my own. *As an advertising major and a collegiate athlete.*

But after just one semester I quit running.

At the time I accomplished the biggest goal I had known and actually doing the running didn't matter anymore. Plus my father wasn't there to see me run. There wasn't anyone to win for. Or maybe it was the sight of the track. The appearance of the college track surpassed my critique when visiting the school but finally placing my feet on the gravel track without eight lanes made my scholarship feel awfully scammed and lame. Something just didn't feel so special about running anymore.

I thought about all the years I had run. I took a few days to acknowledge the defeat I was giving in to, and all the miles on my scrawny chicken legs. A piece of my heart caved in as I sat down at my iMac computer in my single dorm room, to email my coach. I typed in the words, "I quit." Then I felt lighter, and excited for the unknown future to come. The four letter word was a new kind of freedom I had never felt before. Overnight, my scholarship was gone. I stayed at NYIT, because it *was* the only one that had accepted me in the first place. I stayed out of loyalty. The school gave me a chance.

Running *had* done me well and now without it or a plan I didn't know who I was for a few weeks or what I stood for. Since seventh grade, running was my religion; there wasn't anything to believe in anymore. I needed something badly to live for or at least to make me feel strong again. Now, I needed to quickly make myself over. I had just abandoned the one thing that had kept me safe. Now, I needed to create a new goal.

I joined a sorority and did some of the college campus drinking and partying till 4:00 A.M. It was great not to have to sneak around. Over time, not running felt normal and I could just be me, but I hated knowing a city was so close while I was in the boonies of Central Islip. I made it through my freshman year without gaining the typical freshman fifteen pounds from beer and cheese doodles, I still looked like my skinny, old runner self.

One day, I invited my friend Audrey to my dorm. I gave her my mini photo album from high school to look at, while I flipped through TV channels.

"You know you could model," she said, looking up at me. High school suddenly seemed like years away even though it was only less than a year ago.

"You, think?"

"You look like an Abercrombie model."

Was she serious? She looked more like a model than me, I thought. She had long curly hair, and she was lean, with perfect proportions among nose, eyes, and lips. At twenty-two, she was so much more mature than me. Most of all, she was tall. For the next ten minutes, I looked over the photos with her and she pointed to the ones she liked best.

I was always posing, always making a face, a little sneaky show-off face, no matter who was in the shot: someone's sick cat, a childhood friend, or a boy I was taking to the prom. Every photo was of me modeling before I knew what modeling was. I loved to pose, to be seen, to show off, and it started when I had a hunger to feel affection from a male, when I had a hunger to be seen, desired, wanted. When my father chose alcohol over us.

Back in Syracuse for the summer, without a father figure, scholarship, or plan, I struggle to breathe and think about what's next—there is only so long you can yell the Greek alphabet. The one thing I knew was that being home was a reminder of how much I had tried to get out. The tension was building again with each bite of my fat mother's deep fried bullshit.

That summer Audrey came to mind and the thought that "I could model." I remembered the words right after my mother had offered me another bowl of her bubbling summer time chili. Instantly, I flick the bowl away as if it is poison and declared a strong "No thanks!" to the chunky second helping. It hit me right in front of the stove, that a plain, hopeless girl from Syracuse, who has no connection, knowledge or friend in the modeling world—should give modeling a try.

I did the only thing I could. I opened Google and attacked it—typing in any modeling word I could think of, while ignoring my mother's weighty feet above me stomping all over my focus. The first choices of my search showed two things: a lot of skin and tall women.

That moment could have ruined everything and it almost did. The pace of my fingers slowed from being defeated by the long legged gorgeous Giraffes and my heart rate went up when the blond smiled at me. She was naked except for the tiniest g-string I had ever seen in her butt crack. She stared at me and whispered, "You don't have a chance." I continued scroll down the whole naked and tall page and my eyebrows narrowed with doubt that I would ever be as beautiful as them.

I didn't know then but I would eventually find my chance. Of course, just my rural town luck, there were no thriving modeling agencies in this scrappy shit hole. There was nothing at all in that dusty basement to give me some hope. I almost allowed life to be greasy fried chicken, potato skins, pepperoni, and white picket fences.

I didn't tell Danny about my modeling ideas or that I was thinking about the possibility of making it a career. I wasn't ready to share my dreams with him just yet. Instead, I asked my friend Joel to help me. I met him at his house, out back by the swing set.

Even though we were old enough to break the swing set, Joel and I swung, while his little sister Angela played in the grass with their snotty, snorting bulldog that I hated to touch.

"Joel ...um, would you do me a favor?"

I had known him since I was sixteen. Back then, I'd had no license and still had no license, so he had done me many favors over the years. Now, as we sat on the swing set, he looked at me with brown eyes. His eyes always appeared a little sad though I was never sure why.

"Could you take me to meet a photographer in Fayetteville?" I asked him slowly, as I took a deep fast swing and my shoe flung off.

Fayetteville was about twenty minutes from my hometown. It would take Joel twenty minutes to get to my house from his, so it would be about a forty-five minute drive for him. It was a longer favor than usual.

"Sure, what's it for?" Explaining myself was another story— one I preferred not to tell. As I decided how much to tell him, I stopped myself from flying into the air again and so did he, by dragging our feet below us.

I wasn't sure how to respond. I *really* had a photo shoot but saying I was just going to *meet* a photographer sounded safer.

Only a couple days before, I discovered a free modeling website called Onemodelplace.com. It asked *the models* to place "five images to show your look." I didn't know what my look was and I didn't have any recent shots to put on the Internet modeling site as a starter photo, so I downloaded one of the photos from my high school shots.

My first shoot! In less than a week, I already had a photo shoot with a photographer scheduled.

The site allowed *photographers* to mingle with *models*. It was interesting to browse all the other models posting photos and to receive comments. It was intriguing and I thought to myself, *I'm just as attractive as them.*

After a few hours, I heard back from the photographer through an email. For the next few days, I waited to be contacted by more photographers who would tell me what they were interested in shooting, and how much they would pay. I didn't care about the money, or if it was a TFP, which I learned stood for Time For Print. This meant even if I didn't receive an actual print I could hold in my hand, he would give me a CD of images in exchange for my *time*. It sounded like a good deal to me.

Many of the *models* on the website were the type no one would look at twice. The websites contained an extreme amount of diversity, from younger, soft skinned, seventeen-year-old girls pushing together nonexistent cleavage, to older women in their forties who had stretch marks and yellow-stained teeth, and who posed in their lingerie. Some started with their senior class photo, like me! A few even included their friends in the photos, straddling each other and posing cheek to cheek or more at ease with cigarettes in their mouths giving a sly "don't fuck with us" look. That made me nervous and excited all at once. Most showed skin. The shots weren't about high-end clothing or makeup but more about the amount of skin you showed. The more nudity you showed, the more hits and clicks and comments you got.

On the Internet site, anyone could have a page of their own for free. There wasn't any webmaster saying "No you're not pretty enough." Any person with a photo to upload could do it. It was a new world, a world I planned on keeping a secret, a world of hits and clicks that defined "hotness" and "worthiness." It was obvious that the site was about being "exposed" and "considered hot." So many girls underestimated the seriousness of it. No one did a background check on the site users. The website only provided a list of answers to questions about how to use the site. Should you have a complaint or almost get killed at a shoot, there sure as hell wasn't a union for the *Internet model*.

The website just acted as the model's little show and tell. We were given our own personal page to decorate with photos, and a space to share information about ourselves if we wanted to share *more* than just photos.

Just by entering my information I felt the rush of being a model. The uncertainty of it was exciting. I started to analyze the size of my nose, my curvy ass, my short fingernails, how well I shaved my legs. My eyebrows looked way too bushy suddenly, and my eyes *needed* mascara.

I started to check off my "interests." I ran to the bathroom to strip to my underwear to take a better look at myself. When I was done I checked off that I was "comfortable with swimwear and lingerie."

I tried to ponder what casual meant. I feared it meant wearing an itchy sweater and being plain—I wasn't sure I want anything to be casual.

I had the choice to clicking fashion or commercial print. I hardly knew what these words meant since I didn't read *Vogue* or fashion magazines. The closest I'd been to fashion was in *Seventeen* magazine. I wasn't seventeen anymore; I was legal. I checked off Nude as a yes. "It was just skin," I told myself. Next, I ran to the bathroom again and got completely naked. Frowning, I stared at my body and noticed what happened to it when I moved and twisted and looked over my shoulder. My breasts were nonexistent compared to what most girls had on the website.

Still, I thought I had a nice body. Years of running had made my curvy and tight behind and I admired my flat sun tanned stomach in the mirror and my boney hips that made perfect cuts down along my bikini line were now something sexy. Only three photos were decent enough to show it off, so I posted those. For the first couple of moments I waited, hands folded, in my lap, for a hit on my fabulous new page. At the end of the day I received over ten comments and compliments, which were all flattering.

"Welcome to the site. I like petite girls, would you want to set up a shoot?"

I didn't know how to respond at first, so I took a few moments to think and wrote back, "Yes, I'm interested. What type of photos would you like to shoot?"

The next time I would be more accurate and know what I was looking to shoot.

I mentioned in my profile I would be coming to New York City after the summer.

I had convinced my mother to let me attend the New York City campus for the next three years of college, but that wouldn't start for another two long months. So when photographers wrote me to say hello or welcome me to the website or to plan a shoot I wrote back, "Sorry, I can't shoot now, let's keep in touch." They would reply, "I would love to be one of your first shoots in New York City, so remember me." Or with, "Ok, just let me know when you are in town."

I saved all their comments and emails. For now, I was stuck in Syracuse and the excitement of modeling in New York City would have to be put on hold. Until then I considered a shoot with a photographer in the Syracuse area. I would consider it practice for the big city.

Today was the shoot. Although the weather was unseasonably cold for summer, I waited outside for Joel. I didn't want him coming in and telling my mother where we were going.

Most of the girls on the site had, what appeared to my naive eyes, professional photos. I needed some to keep up with them. Only having a few photos against their twenty meant competition. Maybe this shoot in Syracuse would give me some shots to add to my portfolio. I needed to break the ice by experiencing *my first shoot ever*.

I didn't know what the photographer looked like as we hadn't yet met. We had only been exchanging emails. Joel and I walked around the Wedding Hall in search of him. The hall looked like a palace—all white on the outside and all wood on the inside. Joel asked questions about architecture, but when he asked about the "beautiful stained windows" I just wished he would shut the fuck up, I was so nervous.

Then, I saw the photographer. He was taking the trash out and he had a lot of it. Joel rushed to help him. He was dressed comfortably in jeans and a nice tucked-in light blue shirt. I noticed that he smelled like a fireplace.

"I usually shoot the bride on this stairway." He winked at me.

While he was setting up for the shoot, it hit me. Someone might see me and question what I was doing, because my aunt and uncle lived only a few miles away. In high school I ran track against many students who lived in the area. I prayed Joel wouldn't know anyone who could recognize me. Fortunately, he was in a daze, interested, consumed. He looked amused and stared at the artwork and vintage tables as if he were witnessing a "once in a lifetime" opportunity. The photographer and I didn't discuss payment in our emails, but he promised to give me a CD of images a week after the shoot for no charge to me. We only discussed that the shoot would involve lingerie. I didn't care; I needed photos for my profile on Onemodelplace.com and felt safe knowing a friend was with me. Besides, I wanted to feel what being a model was all about. I wanted the experience.

I went into the bathroom to get ready; I didn't know what to do with myself. My heart was racing. I added some mascara and lipstick. Unfortunately, I forgot my brush but used my fingers to weed through the knots in my hair the best I could. I splashed some water on my hands to calm down the flyaway strands by my forehead.

I had no idea what Joel was doing while I was in there, but I could hear the two of them talking and it made me nervous. I hoped to god Joel wouldn't mention that I was a track runner or that he only lived in the next town over or that I only lived in the next town over too.

When I thought I looked the best I could possibly look, or what I thought a model should looked like, I came out. The photographer had Joel wait downstairs.

I confidently stood by the railing of the stairs, where he

normally photographed brides. I wore a tiny pair of denim shorts, a gold necklace with a heart pendent on it, gold hoop earrings, and a sheer Calvin Klein bra. Next we went into a bedroom and I sat, and then lay down, on the yellow bedspread and smiled awkwardly toward him and his huge lens. The camera clicked, startling me as he captured a picture of my skin for a "test shot." He was using all these words I never heard before, and he was trying to hold the camera steady as he mumbled how he wished he had his "tripod." I felt a little weird sitting there waiting for my photo to be taken. The silence went right through me. I could hear my heart beat. I looked down and around the room, avoiding direct contact with the photographer's eyes as he fumbled with the lights again.

He said, "Are you comfortable posing without a bra?"

I couldn't say no and let him know this was my first photo shoot ever. Plus, I was there and he had already given us the tour of his huge catering hall, house, and hotel so we sort of knew each other.

I thought getting naked was supposed to make me nervous, but I wasn't that scared.

"Yes, that's fine." Speaking shyly but acting fast, I peeled off my clothing and peeled away the last vestiges of innocence. With a delicate wisp of the hand I threw the garments on the floor. I think I startled the photographer when he turned around and I was bare naked already but covering myself with the bed sheet.

The photographer said, "I have some white lace cloth in a storage closet." Then he went for it as if he had a beautiful present for me. To my disappointment, it looked like a tablecloth used for someone's wedding reception, and I didn't know whether to say "thank you" or "no thank you."

He said with my tan skin color, I would look pretty if I wore it around my head like a veil and used it to cover my body. Only then did I wonder whether I'd shaved or not and if I should go and put lotion on my legs. I was so focused on him, his movements, and the quiet between us, that I forgot I had on my gold necklace, earrings and angel ring, but he said it was okay.

Since it felt like his shoot, I followed and played as his rag doll but started to feel more like his afternoon whore as I picked up the material and wrapped it around me the best I could to cover all of the private parts. The white fabric *did* look really pretty against my skin. I felt sexy. I wanted Danny to see me like this. I felt like I wanted to be touched and caressed while I wore the fabric around me. I could feel myself getting excited over the curiosity I had and the triangle I had shaved felt itchy and moist. I wondered if the photographer was married. If he had children and when he last had sex.

We took a few shots of me looking down and giving a side profile. I felt like a Middle Eastern Princess about to lose my virginity, which was long gone already.

After the fabric shot I stayed without a bra, but put my shorts back on and went downstairs. I put on a sheer tan top that still showed my nipples and we took some shots near an ethnic inspired cloth mural on the wall. Then we went to the dining area, where I changed again, and I sat on a pink and cream carpet that looked like a quilted blanket. I faced the mirror and wore only a lace black thong and a little lace tank top, the most clothing I had worn at the shoot, except the tiny denim shorts on the stairway.

By the time we were finished, Joel still had noticed nothing. In the car he said,

"That guy was really cool. I bet it's expensive to have a place like that." He didn't know about the nude shots. He didn't say one word about the shoot; he just kept talking. "I want my own company one day."

I didn't say anything. Instead, I tried to think of each shot and imagine what the picture would look like.

I could have asked Danny to drive me to the shoot—he had a car—but we had just started dating and I didn't want to scare him off with my modeling adventures just yet. We had dinner that night and I wanted to burst from holding in all the excitement of my first naked modeling experience.

A few days later, I did tell Danny of my modeling plans but he was very discouraging. He liked me when he met me—when I was a boring waitress, not a sexy model. In the meantime, it would be a torturous six weeks until I got to New York City and I wanted an introduction to the modeling world before I got there. Waiting till then was too long. I was planning on modeling all summer and he would just have to accept it. I let Danny drive me back to the catering hall to pick up my photos, but I made him promise not to say anything to my mother or my sister about it. Then I asked him to take a couple of photos of me by the lake; he didn't know if he wanted to. In the end, I forced him to, telling him how to hold the camera, which was annoying to explain, telling him how to click it. I got pissed when he didn't know how to zoom.

Then I made dinner with my mother, watched MTV, and went out with some childhood friends to the mall, or to sit by their pools and talk about boys and my first year of college experience. Before too long, I wanted to be back in front of my computer. I told no one of my new project. I wasn't confident enough yet in my choice to tell my friends, in case nothing came from it or in case someone asked about it and I didn't know how to respond. At the time, finding a modeling agency hadn't crossed my mind. I didn't understand what it meant to be with an agency or how to get with one. Besides, they all had height requirements. I was fine with the Internet. It was making me a model. My obsession grew every day, seductive and entrapping. I barely looked at the shots of myself at the catering hall. Although I had waited all week for them, the experience was what had enticed me. Not until I was alone in my bedroom later that night did I look at them closely.

My nipples were very perky and showed in even the bra shots, but I was too embarrassed to show anyone. I took the 4 x 6 prints that screamed "nipple" and hid them in a folder, putting the ones where I was wearing the black lace lingerie in my portfolio, which was a cheap Wal-Mart photo album. When

Joel called to see them I changed the topic right away and told him I wasn't really serious about modeling, even though I was checking my email over five times a day to scope my mini-web page for an hour at a time. I would admire my page and check out other girls' images, reading their comments and comparing mine. But the words of applause, and compliments from photographers and other models, stayed with me throughout the day.

As I prepared to leave Syracuse, I compared myself to the complacent world I was leaving. It was embarrassing to try to be a model in Syracuse. I couldn't say I was a model without feeling weird or out of place. Most people I knew were working as lifeguards or at the mall or mowing lawns. No one was trying to be anything more than what Syracuse offered. New York City would be my official stomping grounds to enter the modeling world. The shoot in Syracuse was my first baby step, a way to gain some momentum towards the real deal.

I was getting rid of the girl from Syracuse. Modeling was a perfect way to do so. I hated the Plain Jane simplicity of Syracuse. I had a need to impress, and the camera aimed to please. "Sit still and smile—be a good girl" wasn't part of the plan. Through the camera lens, I could take it all off and leave it on the floor, become a woman, someone who was *wanted*.

I imagined being in the city. It would be a fresh start, a place where things would happen, and saying I was a model there would be accepted. It was New York, a place where dreams came true. I would be on my way to a new chapter in my life, *the* new chapter in my life, the golden road where every street would be mine to claim. For all I cared, everyone in Syracuse could laugh at me because I was a *model*. I wouldn't be in Syracuse doing the same old thing, like them. I wasn't boring or dusty or dull. I was making my own plans and not many people I knew could say that.

After my first shoot, Danny and I argued all the time. He hated that people could see my photos and that most photographers were men. He hated that photographers posted responses on my mini-webpage about how sexy I was, about how I had a great body and how they wanted to photograph me.

He would say, "When I met you, you weren't modeling. That's not the person I knew and liked. You threw this modeling at me."

But I would only smile and give him a big hug, then press my body against his. I *had* thrown the modeling at him, and it wasn't going away anytime soon.

Chapter 2

New York Nude

September 2001: Brooklyn Heights
I planned for my move to New York ahead of time by referring to all the emails and names I saved. For the next few weeks, I stayed busy using Onemodelplace.com to tell every photographer I could that I would be in town soon.

"Hello, I'm a petite model with a great body and I will be moving to New York City in three weeks...."

"Hello, I like your work, and I am a petite model with a lot of personality and a great body and I will be moving to New York City in two weeks...."

"Sorry I won't be in town for two weeks, but I would like to keep in touch to schedule a shoot when I arrive."

"Yes, I am interested in your lingerie shoot. I will be New York City in one week."

"I will be in New York City in three days!"

"Yes, I have a class on Wednesday, but I can do the shoot after my class."

Although I did have new classes, I didn't care about exploring and seeing the Empire State Building or being a tourist. I needed to hurry and plan a shoot in New York City, fast!

I didn't want to waste a second. I wanted to be naked again and feel the light touching my skin. The girl who once ran from life, from love, from her absent alcoholic father ... from herself was gone. Like she never existed. Unless I told someone about my running days, I suspected I would only be known as a model.

I moved to New York City on September 1, 2001, or more accurately Brooklyn Heights. Ten days after I moved, two iconic buildings crashed down. I hardly knew the meaning of those buildings, and honestly the only way their fall affected me was the lack of running subways after that day and for the following week. I wasn't from New York City and had never even heard of the Twin Towers until I set sight on the skyline.

That morning, I slept through the whole crisis in my dorm room. I thought it was just thunder or a dump truck. When my mother called at 8 A.M., I just ignored her. Afterward I walked to the promenade in my pajamas to see it for myself and tried to understand and feel something sad for a city I had just met and was so confident about yesterday. I decided to make something of the day and brushed my teeth thinking about the young men in suits, maybe their first expensive one; off to the job they worked their ass off to get. I spit the foam into the sink and made a prayer that I would live to see myself as a model no matter what it took.

I stared at the MTA map trying to let it cast a spell on me. I have hated maps and directions of any kind all my life, and then winging it and making it to class on time, up on Columbus circle, looked really doubtful. Knowing how to get on the subway and where to get off would have meant studying ahead of time and maybe even doing a practice run the day before. I hoped someone would be nice enough to help if I got lost, robbed or ended completely in a different city.

The first day I went into Manhattan I sat and listened to the train go under the water of a river I wasn't quiet sure yet of the name. The next stop was Wall Street and everyone was getting off quickly and the rush made me panicky to be clueless. They knew exactly where to go, get off. I didn't even have time to give the map a glance before I got on the 2 train, at the Clark Street Station below my dorm. Unsure of the next stop and if it was mine, I had to look at the map and get some sense of where I was heading. I leaned over a huge black women in fear of touching my tan bag against her basket weave brown one, do to so. The map looked very sexual and I took a better look, leaning further over her so my mind could get a visual of measuring how many stops were left before I miss mine. Instead of streets and subway lines and colors I see a penis. The shape of the city is a perfect shaped one. Almost planned. The Queens Midtown Tunnel even gives a shape, or a bend, to create the head of the shaft. Maybe the curve of the Harlem River making the round of the Bronx's is Manhattan's balls.

I got off after transferring from Chambers Street to the 1 train and then taking the slow elevation up to 59th Street. Racing up the hill of steps I saw the sun shining on Broadway and my school was diagonal across the street, and for a moment with the Trump Tower smiling above me, I was happy to be a student in the greatest city in the world.

My birthday was only seven days before, on September third, Danny had taken me to a shoot in New Jersey. I couldn't believe it. I was turning nineteen and on that day especially I wanted to shoot. I told him I didn't want anything for my birthday, just to be brought to a shoot. I thought he was warming up to the idea of me being a model, but the shoot only made it worse.

"Can you hold that reflector still?" Danny looked nervous, he was already getting yelled at by the photographer and we had been there for less than ten minutes.

We got lost on the way to the shoot, and we had only made up from our fight in the car a few minutes before we met the photographer in the park. I hated sitting in the passenger seat. I couldn't drive but *I was not a passenger*! Danny wore the gray, shaggy worn and torn sweater that I hated. It embarrassed me. The sweater made a statement about him. It showed he wasn't responsible, attractive, clean, *or* interesting. I told him *not* to wear his glasses either.

He smoked about a pack of Newport cigarettes and the smoke seeped through his clenched teeth. I tried not to gag. I wanted to die right there on the New Jersey Turnpike. I quickly regretted my decision to ask him to drive me to the shoot.

"Do you want to turn around?" I asked.

"We can go back."

"Do you *want* to go back?" I asked. By the time the fight started I had asked about four times.

I focused on my mascara to avoid thinking about his outfit. I discreetly tried to tell him to take it off.

"It's going to be kind of warm today. You might want to just wear a tee-shirt, because you sweat a lot." I ended with a giggle and a smile, but he didn't look happy.

We hit a bump in the road and my mascara brush hit the top of my lid and almost poked me in the eye.

"Damn, Danny, slow down!" I gripped the dashboard and checked that my seatbelt was tight.

We were so busy fighting I didn't realize until too late that we were lost. Nervously, I watched him pierce the road, refusing my plea to stop and ask someone at the gas station for help. Then in a rage he said, "I can't believe you go around meeting strangers!"

"Well, I want to model!" I sounded like I was five. "And I don't go around meeting strangers! You're such an asshole sometimes!"

He didn't like that I'd called him an asshole, so he called me a bitch. I didn't know what to say because I *was* a bitch. I couldn't stop being a bitch either. I worried about his appearance and mine, and where we were going. We were late, which made me jumpy. After what seemed like hours, we arrived at the park where the shoot was planned.

We sat by the stone wall. While I played with my hair, Danny smoked more cigarettes. I dug in the dirt with my sandal, and then reached for his hand to let him know I wasn't mad. Fortunately, he took it. We sat there, waiting for the photographer who was fifteen minutes late. Great. I had worried about being late and had freaked out for nothing.

Finally, the photographer arrived and immediately lit into Danny, barking orders, pointing him here and there. Danny thought he would spend the day smoking cigarettes and reading his flight books for flight school. Instead, he became a photographer's assistant. A very bad one. He held onto the huge camera bag that the photographer threw at him. Then, the photographer asked him to hand him the 50 millimeter lens, whatever that was. I didn't have a clue when he looked over to me with nervous eyes.

"I'm trying."

Danny really *was* trying, but the reflector kept dropping and bending and creating all the wrong shadows on my ass.

The photographer told me how he had worked with a team of lingerie designers in France, which sounded very cool.

"So after the shoot I'll show the designers the photos and they'll pick a model."

He mentioned that other girls would be considered as well.

A child with long blond hair ran by with her parents. They looked our way but didn't stare. Still, I felt like they were staring. We were in a fucking park for Christ sake, and my ass was showing for the world to see. He kept shooting me against the stone wall. About 100 meters away, I could see a bunch of sweaty soccer players. A crowd was cheering and the park was becoming more and more active as the hour progressed.

Danny went with the flow and helped to cover me with a towel when I changed into a black thong I had discovered and purchased on West 4th Street in the city. He had never seen it before and said, "That's cute." Finally ...something nice.

I felt as if he shouldn't be so pissy and that he *should* be proud that his girlfriend had a great round ass and was a model. Furthermore, I had put up with the fact that he hardly knew how to fuck me. He had only been sexually active for the two months since he met me. Still, regardless of his performance, he got to fuck me and he should have been proud and not so angry about my modeling.

When the shoot ended, Danny seemed to relax for awhile. Weeks later, when I got the photos back, I saw a huge zit on my ass. Needless to say, I didn't win the vote.

Danny hardly ever came to see me in the city. Almost every

time he did he informed me proudly that he hated New York City.

In Brooklyn Heights I lived in the St. George Hotel. I had a roommate and not a ton of privacy, but I had stability, something I always took for granted. And although it should have been comforting, it never crossed my mind it could be otherwise. I had no rent to worry about, no bills to pay. I lived in a hotel transformed into a dorm. The rooms were small since the hotel was built in the early 1900s, and the bathtub made really scary noises that made me nervous. I had a doorman, and the floor meetings with the RA weren't mandatory. In short, I was free, with only classes to disrupt my shoots. I was faking like I knew how to pose, knew what to say and what to wear, I was winging it. No one really knew about these meetings with photographers. I didn't tell my roommate even though she left me notes saying, "You're the best roommate ever!" and "I hope you have a great day today!"

She would leave the notes on the bathroom mirror and on the door saying, "You're the best!" and "I hope you do well on your test!" It was like she wanted to be sure I'd see them. She was pretty, Dominican, and had a boyfriend down the hall who was over constantly.

They were both studying architecture, and groups of other students would pile in our tiny room, sit for hours smoking pot and laughing too loud, playing sexual ass-shaking Latin reggatone.

I didn't say hello or join in. I thought they were annoying freshman.

I had only one friend in the dorms or in New York City, and I could hardly pronounce her name. She was in my Advertising class and she also lived down the hall in the dorms. Like me, she was tiny, slender, a little underweight, and had tan skin. We looked almost like sisters.

When she said "My name is Maryam" I thought she said "Mary," but then she corrected me. "No, it's Maryam." I had never heard of that name before. I thought it was weird, but we would meet up for Wendy's in between classes. Unbeknownst to me at the time, Wendy's would later become my salvation.

Maryam seemed cool enough to tell about my modeling. She approved and admired me. I told her she was pretty enough to model too, yet she never tried it. She was a bit shy about her body, but just like me she hated school.

Also, just like in Syracuse, I spent my time consumed, stuck to the Internet, working on my mini-site and adding photos every week to the page. Instead of just worrying about my page, I worried about the photographers' pages too. I wanted my ass to be seen as the number one pick by the photographers I worked with on Onemodelplace.com. I wanted to be one of their favorite models.

In the meantime, my classes were at Columbus Circle, so dorming in Brooklyn allowed me a good twenty minute commute. Because of the 9/11 attacks, the trains were all fucked up and usually I was late for every class, but mostly it was because I was planning, preparing, or returning from a shoot and I didn't care about being on time. I waited for the two train to fly me under the water and over to the land of dreams. The subway ride was where I *really* saw New York.

Mistakenly, I thought New York would show me the classiest, most dignified and well-dressed people. Yet, I never saw a Chanel or Gucci outfit on the subway. Those were names I was just beginning to learn about. In Syracuse I shopped at Deb and JCPenney. I didn't know about Louis Vuitton until two weeks before when I moved to New York City. I picked up a *Vogue* for the first time to get some fashion tips, since I needed a few, being from the backwoods of upstate New York. It was there I saw an ad for the piss-colored yellow bags from Vuitton.

I also picked up a *Stuff* magazine and a *Playboy* for sexier modeling ideas and to compare myself to the models.

School was a drag and a distraction from my newfound purpose. I couldn't get excited about listening to some professor tell me about marketing, and English without thinking, *They're full of shit*. With the city moving four flights below me, I always tried to sit by the window for inspiration. It was hard to sit still when so much was going on around me. Most of my five classes I took in the afternoon. I should have been used to my school schedule, but it was getting more difficult as time passed.

As time went on, I was no longer running track on a scholarship but I was still running a lot. I was racing in between classes to go to photo shoots, and one Wednesday, I had to get to an English class five subway stops away. The shoot had gone longer than expected and I wasn't planning on being completely nude that day, which always made the shoot longer.

After all, I didn't just show up and whip off my clothing for the first shot. Usually the photographer took a shot of me in jeans or a skirt, and then in my bra and finally nude until the whole thing was accomplished. Maybe the photographer felt better about himself, knowing we didn't only shoot nude. But it would have gone a lot faster if I just started butt ass naked from the first shot.

After the shoot, I threw myself on the closest uptown train with a huff of exhaustion, then whipped out my college ID card and tried to calm down. Twenty minutes later, I was tapping my foot and waiting for the elevator that would take me to my classroom. I rushed down the slippery hallway towards my class, with my high heel shoes clicking, and my panties flying out of my bag. I grabbed a pink pair that had slipped out and in my excitement smashed them into my overstuffed bag. Then I realized I'd forgotten my English book.

I had to share the professor's book, and he didn't look too happy about it. If anyone asked about my bag bursting with thongs and padded bras, I would just say I was at a sleepover, even though people in college don't have sleepovers, which would lead to even more questions I wouldn't want to answer.

The discussion that day was about *Lord of the Flies*, which I could swear I read in high school. I wondered why the hell I was reading it again in college. I couldn't concentrate on the book because I didn't have a bra on and I was afraid the professor would notice and somehow tell my mother. There hadn't been enough time to clasp it shut and make the subway and then class on time, so I sat there feeling exposed. My nipples shrunk with the air conditioning pounding over them. I felt naked sitting at the cold desk and looking out the window onto traffic going around Columbus Circle and the Trump Tower. I felt embarrassed for the other students who were forced to see my nipples, and scared that those who read my face knew that I wasn't really a threat in the classroom and my quick remarks couldn't quite cut down their intelligence as much as I thought it could. I hoped they wouldn't know the truth—that a few minutes before I posed nude for a photographer over thirty blocks away.

As I sat there, I grew sick of talking about Ralph and Jack and Piggie, and my thong was starting to itch from sitting so long. My eyesight was going blurry from reading and discussing the problems they were having on the island. They were on a fucking island, for God's sake. They should have been tanning and enjoying the damn coconuts, but they kept killing animals and each other. Thinking about the island made me think about being in a bikini. I couldn't stop thinking about my body and the type of shots I needed to get next.

The photographers I had worked with so far constantly told me that I should use my body and that nude modeling was the way to go since I wasn't 5'10". It was either fashion or *Playboy* in my mind. I knew I wasn't a fashion model. Now, as I sat in my next class bored out of my mind, I thought about how Coca Cola could improve their marketing.

I wanted to *be* the Coca Cola girl. When the class dismissed I didn't even say hello or goodbye to any of my classmates, I just darted for the train back to Brooklyn.

There was no time for a Wendy's snack with Maryam.

I had to get on the computer and do some research. But first, I stopped at Barnes and Noble on the way home to get inspired. To promote myself, I first needed to feed my jealousy. Before I even took off my light denim jacket and flew out of my shoes, I went right to my Onemodelplace.com page. I googled "modeling," then the word "model," and finally "New York City + Models." Then the reverse: "Models + New York City," just in case the results were different. I had to face the fact that I didn't have a chance in hell at an agency in New York City. I was dizzy with frustration.

As for Danny, I cared for him deeply, wanted his approval, and he *did* hang a few lingerie photos on the door of his dorm room. But he didn't think I was doing the right thing by modeling. He said it made me spastic and always in a rush, talking fast and about something he knew nothing about. I would bitch about the perverts who downloaded my photos and then I would be running off to another shoot.

He didn't budge in his feelings about modeling, and couldn't understand why I wanted to do something that drove me so nuts. I wasn't complaining, because I wanted to do it, but I was lonely, too. Still, I was sure I was doing the right thing, even though I didn't tell Danny I was getting naked for someone whose name I couldn't pronounce correctly, often at a home with no heat or toilet paper.

A circus was taking place in my head. When I was modeling it was as loud as cannons. When I was with Danny, it was soft delicate streamers. My emotions were mixed. I was doing something that felt, while in front of the lens, dangerous and wrong, or maybe I really liked that danger and liked that it might be wrong.

No one in my other life was trying to be a model. Most people I knew wanted to hide in their rooms partying and smoking pot. The solution to my questions was to keep shooting. I only felt good when I was in front of the computer scoping out my mini-site or at a shoot. Weekend trips to Southern New Jersey with Danny to visit his family, who had just moved there from Syracuse, were painful. I would feel lazy, bored, and pissed knowing girls would have brand new photos up by next week from the weekend shoots they were on right then. Gracing their web links were beautiful new shots for people to comment on and enjoy.

His parents' house was freezing. So here I sat, freezing my tits off, eating Jewish food, and parking my ass on the sofa. I had eaten so much challah bread I felt like I was Jewish. I tried to be friendly to his mother, who didn't approve of me sleeping with *her* baby. On Saturday, I went with the family to Temple pretending to be pure and interested. Danny didn't seem to be interested either, which was comforting. After his mother caught us having sex several times, I tried to seem eager to go shopping at 9:00 A.M. on a Sunday morning with her, to make up for being the *weekend sin*. At the store, she bought so much jewelry it was as if she owned QVC. I froze in New Jersey because I had no fat. She seemed to disapprove of my skinniness and the way I picked at the meals she cooked. As a result, dinners were quiet.

I wanted to scream from having to behave.

The entire time I was there, I wanted to be back in New York, in front of the bright lights in front of the camera and naked. I would try my hardest not to mention modeling while we visited his mother and father. The coldness of their beautiful home reminded me of the chill of a photographer's basement or apartment, the windows open to make my nipples hard and pointy. After a typical grilling at dinner, I whispered under my breath, "Fuck dinner, and fuck faking it."

To escape the pressure, Danny and I relaxed by the neighborhood pond and woods. We biked and watched HBO, something I didn't have in the dorms, and we ate mostly at restaurants on his father's credit card. With the family though, Danny kept bringing up school and my classes.

Between bites of cold steak I said, "Fuck talking about my classes and school projects, and fuck becoming a Photoshop whiz and Illustrator designer.

"And most important, fuck my Advertising portfolio altogether!"

"What do you mean, fuck your Advertising portfolio?" Danny demanded, slamming down his water. "You're not thinking about going into modeling full time?"

"Why not?" I said, tapping my fingernails nervously on the table, anxious to get this whole parent meeting over with.

I thought about the degree and smirked when I saw his mother's look of shock, but she merely continued to chew fast.

I knew she hated me and my swearing. I didn't care. I hated her too.

With a worried tone, she said, "You should really think about your future." She had just retired from being a teacher and sounded like one. Then, after a huge gulp of milk, she added, "Isn't your mom a teacher? Wouldn't she want you to get your degree?"

Big deal! In two years I would claim a printed piece of paper. It could hardly define me. In front of the camera I was more myself, more real. The grilling continued.

Will this weekend ever end?

To make up for lost time, after dinner I snuck on the computer and typed a few emails, then checked up on my Onemodelplace.com account. Nothing new. I hardly had any hits that day and I blamed it on Danny, and his mother's challah bread. I felt the pressure. How could I call myself a model if I couldn't even compete with the other "Wannabes" who were no doubt shooting at that very second?

It never occurred to me the girls in *Seventeen* and *Cosmo Girl* or *YM* magazine made more money and got more exposure, which of course led to bigger things. Or that keeping your clothes on is even sexier and pays a lot more money because of the ad campaign. I should have known this. I was an advertising major in college after all, but I didn't put two and two together. I loved the idea of creating concepts for print ads and commercials, even though my classes were a bore. Although to contradict myself I wasn't exactly gaining tear sheets or quality modeling jobs in ad campaigns, modeling new products.

I began to enjoy shooting nude more and more. It wasn't just for practice though.

It was for a feeling of empowerment—sexuality and fantasy all at once. I only felt good and confident about myself when I was modeling naked.

Yet inside, I experienced a roller coaster of emotions as I went from my boyfriend's bedroom to my college classroom to the photographer's bedroom, bathroom, living room, and kitchen. They had me taking off my clothing, running around, dancing and playing musical chairs, sitting, standing, sticking my tongue out, lounging in chairs, curling up with a pillow on a sofa, lying on dining room tables, or in bathtubs and on balconies. Then I'd run back to class. I would sometimes do my homework on the train in between. I was stressed all the time. In the back of my mind I heard voices saying, "What the *fuck* are you doing, little girl." And then, "You can *do it* little girl!"

All these bi-polar-like emotions made me very aggressive, impatient, and anxious. My heart rate would fly as I spoke to the clerk at the lobby desk and then pushed the elevator button. Then, once I arrived at the correct floor, I wondered which way I should walk. Right. Or Left. The pauses before I knocked or rang the doorbell were either quick and to the point, or hesitant, with thoughts of tiptoeing back down the elevator, out the door and back to my dorm room. I knew I wasn't *really* a model because I saw magazines and billboards every day, and I wasn't on them. I felt more like an escort, like a tease, like a present for the afternoon.

My "hobby," for want of a better word, haunted me daily. I didn't have to be with an agency or understand what one did for you to want to be a model and to call myself one. I had the Internet and modeling websites and photographers interested in shooting me.

For awhile, I decided to get serious and look up some modeling agencies by using Google. Once there, I found a list of modeling agencies in NYC that accepted photos by mail. Besides the weekly stipend my mother gave me for food, which didn't go far, I didn't have much money, so I couldn't get quality prints of my shots to send out. Instead, I used my printer in my dorm room. I spent a few hours adjusting the photos in Photoshop and cropping them, then printing out a collage-like presentation of my photos. To my surprise, they looked pretty genius and were sure to impress an agent or booker. Or so I thought.

But I never heard back from anyone.

Even my highest heels couldn't make me 5'7. It bothered

me that maybe I wasn't good enough, tall enough, but it didn't faze me for too long because I had my own little project going on through the Internet. I had a place where I could escape and be someone else for awhile. I had an alter ego brewing. I would continue to shoot with random, no-name photographers.

I wasn't looking to get famous or to be the stereotypical model or a supermodel; I didn't care about those things. I didn't need an agency to give me what I needed: I had my own little high end modeling gigs going on.

The highest I had been was past my school on Columbus Circle, my legs hanging over the edge of a roof barricade. I was trying to stay as still as possible, like a trapeze artist sitting on "a tightrope," in my case the ledge of a roof top. If I tipped a little to the left I would be a goner.

He said, "You're the only model who hasn't been afraid of sitting on such a narrow ledge in such a short skirt. Or looking down." Taking it as a challenge, I decided I wanted to be the first and did just that. I felt proud that I might be remembered for this risky pose.

The penthouse had to be over twenty stories high, but it was a beautiful view. I'd never seen a view like it before that day. The city was such a paradise from that angle, and I felt like a princess peering over my kingdom as the photographer snapped away. I willingly leaned forward to show some of my cleavage to him through my very low, denim zippered tank top.

His apartment was big and bright, with loads of sunlight. He didn't have any lighting equipment, but with the right angle, he could get a good enough shot. He was in his thirties and had a full-time career in real estate. I wondered if he was looking for a girlfriend or a playmate because most of what he shot was sexy. Naturally, he contacted me through Onemodelplace.com.

I immediately wanted to shoot with him. The girls shown on his mini-site were beautiful: flawless skin, no scars, perfect hair and teeth, big supple breasts. All were ahead of me in that sense.

Later, I learned that he wasn't skilled enough to shoot me.

Nor was he capable of really capturing a person's essence. He just wanted me in a sexy garment, which was fine by me, even though I wished I could have worn my purple dress for longer than five minutes.

Although he owned a digital and called himself an artist, he really just pressed a button as I ran around and twirled.

I didn't mind at first since needed practice on how to be natural, to give a real smile, and to show *me* in different ways. At these shoots I got to be an actress, to show emotion and to maybe even get one or two good shots out of the deal. I was like a porn star without the sex.

Later, I changed into a black thong and a denim zippered top. Next I jumped and twirled and teased in a pink dress, posing with the city as my backdrop. I felt so proud, so admired at that moment. He was on the other side of the roof, pointing. Then suddenly he said something and flapped his arms around like a bird. I couldn't hear him because the wind was whipping my earlobe, but I started spinning and let the wind catch my dress in case that's what he meant. He snapped away.

At that moment nothing mattered but the camera and me. Then, standing in between two steel poles, the wind whipped my hair and I was no longer just a girl from upstate New York.

He followed me around the apartment. Being nude wasn't a striptease. It was just what I wanted to do, and the camera followed. The third time we worked together, I sat on the stained, wooden kitchen table. Although it was cold, the sunset's golden rays were hitting my face, tinting my hair red. Sitting there nude felt right. He hadn't pressured me to do it. I had done it before. Once I was nude it was as if my body exhaled.

This time, I went to the bathroom and greased myself up with baby oil. It chilled my stomach. It glistened as I walked to the kitchen, tiptoeing and petting his cat along the way. I opened the fridge to pull out some condiments and leftovers. Then I emptied the foam ice box. I placed myself in it, sitting there with food all around me. I started speaking like I was in a cooking show.

"Then you add some mustard," I said, struggling to open

a few cans and bottles. It made for a sexy active shot of me struggling with the caps. I was on a cooking high, pouring sauces on me and laughing out loud. During the two hour shoot, I was sitting, smiling and licking my lips, my breasts looking freshly blossomed and petite, and my stomach tight, with mustard, salsa, hot sauce, and butter smeared all over it.

Afterward, we viewed the photos on his computer, then ate some chips and drank some wine. Yet, I always made an excuse to leave early. I hated being at a photographer's apartment late at night. Going to the apartment alone in the first place was ballsy enough.

Only two or three shots would come out that were worth anything. And still I went. Maybe he felt just as powerful taking pictures as I did being nude. In the meantime, I was learning more about my look. Suddenly, I knew what type of photos I wanted, and didn't just want to shoot for the hell of it anymore. The rush wasn't enough. I needed a purpose to shoot, not for a simple photo date to see what could be squeezed out of the camera.

That was the last time we shot together. He got me for free but I was getting wiser. Things were about to change.

I would soon have a rate. At the time, the thought of being just shot seemed like a bigger deal than the money. I should have started shooting nude for the cash and used the money for quality photos by a professional. Then I could take those photos to an agency. But at the time, that wasn't on my mind.

One day, on the way back to Brooklyn Heights on the two train, a group of colorful tourists asked me, "Do you know how to get to the Empire State Building?"

I must have looked like a true New Yorker. "Yeah, just take this train to 34th Street. It's only three stops away, then walk east three avenues." Although it sounded like a lot of directions, really it was pie. I felt like a champion, and forwardly asked a group of teenage boys who were looking dumbfounded at the subway map, "Do you need help?" They said no.

If only they knew—they were talking to a model.

A part of me was scared that this modeling would only be for a short time. I was in school, spending thousands of dollars in loans for an education that I didn't want. But being in school *did* allow me to live in New York City, and that alone was worth the bullshit of massive essays about *Lord of the Flies*.

Then my mother would call or a classmate would present her oh-so creative advertising project. Immediately, I felt I had to start caring about my degree. I even started to put together a design portfolio, and became efficient in Photoshop and Illustrator. I took on class projects, like creating slogans for the March of Dimes walk on Long Island. Then I would march myself over to a photographer's apartment, get naked, and the only noble needy cause I stood for was myself. I knew I would never be a tall Giraffe, but stressing over that would have killed me.

Chapter 3

Paid Model

It took a couple weeks to set up my next shoot because the
photographer said he was *so* busy. He also said in an email, "I'll
pay three hundred dollars for three hours of nude modeling
work, plus a CD of the images."

For a beginner, it was decent money. The thought of being
paid was a compliment, like I was worth paying for. Suddenly, I
was my own business and I eagerly said yes.

He set the wager, it was a gamble, and he won.

Three hundred dollars for three hours sounded right, I
figured. For one, I didn't have any credits that would put me
in the "experienced" category. Besides that I had shot with a
bunch of amateur photographers who could hardly hold the
camera properly when we shot, and who gave me items out of
their fridge to model!

Therefore, I couldn't demand too high a price so I packed
a few cute panties and tops. I was going to be nude most of the
time anyway, so the outfits didn't really matter. I kept thinking
about the three hundred dollars as I packed.

Suddenly, I heard a knock at my door and Maryam entered.
"I'm going to get some ice cream by the promenade. You want
to come?"

"I have a shoot."

She wanted to know the details. For some reason I suddenly
felt slutty telling her a photographer was paying to shoot me

nude. I just told her, "Guess what! I have a job shooting some lingerie for a new lingerie company." I couldn't stop lying. To cover my embarrassment, I quickly left.

At that time I had only been to Queens once. I dated an Italian who was from Jackson Heights in Queens, a year before during my freshman year of college. We hadn't talked in months, but it crossed my mind that at least he was someone who could help me if anything went wrong during the shoot.

I slid my subway card through the gate and sat for almost an hour on the F train.

The weekend trains were always packed. I wondered if anyone suspected I was a nude model as I sat without an iPod or reading material and listened to the conversations around me.

When I got off the train I was near a highway and a blue 1989 Volkswagen was waiting for me. The photographer was older than I expected, and no way would I have ever talked to this man if it weren't for modeling. He had gray hair, light fair skin and a beard. He looked only a little older than my father. I laughed to myself and almost felt bad for the guy. He was married with kids and shooting women half naked in his freezing basement. From the look of his clothes, he didn't make a good living and I wasn't sure if I would get lunch, the photos, or if I'd even get paid. The fact he had white stains all over his black shirt freaked me out.

His basement was his studio. It took him about fifteen minutes to set up, which allowed me little time to think of an escape plan or some way to make this shoot comfortable. I wore a new white lace-and-satin lingerie baby doll from Victoria Secret that I hadn't even worn for Danny yet. I also had black boy shorts, which itched a little but looked really sexy. As I organized my makeup and clothing, I looked in the mirror and rolled my eyes at myself.

I had way too much blush on and I grabbed some toilet paper to rub some off. It scratched my cheek a little and made it redder. *You don't even know this guy! He can't really help you; is the money even worth it?*

Then I mumbled to myself, "You're crazy, crazy, *so* fucking crazy," as I applied some eyeliner. I could hear music: "...Gimme the beat boys and free my soul." I didn't know who sang it, "...and rock and roll and drift away." It was some oldie. It reminded me of my father singing to Willie Nelson. I told myself to remember to call him later. For now, I needed to hurry up and I needed a sharpener badly for my eyeliner. I had found the eyeliner at the bottom of my purse weeks ago and it hadn't been sharpened in god knows how long. I applied it gingerly across my lower lid and hummed to the oldie, like I knew it by heart.

Afterward, I looked at myself all red—painted like some freak show, like a hooker. I thought about leaving the dirty bathroom and going home, but it was too late now. I could already hear him rattling the lights and tearing open the film. Adding a little more lipstick and mascara, flipping my hair, I whispered to myself, "Wow, you look like a twelve year old." I turned my phone off and, as I walked down the basement stairs, I had one last chance to turn around.

I took a deep breath. "How do I pose for a guy who is old enough to be my grandparent?" I muttered, peering down at my satin lingerie ensemble.

On set, I took off the lingerie slowly as the photographer suggested. Then maybe since it was only a few months after 9/11, to be patriotic, I wrapped myself in a red, white and blue scarf that managed to cover my whole body. I finally bit the bullet and posed like a 1950s pinup for the camera.

He kept saying, "Okay ...okay, yeah, that's pretty, that's pretty."

I felt awkward as I stood with my breasts hanging out and fabric through my legs so my vagina wouldn't show. Maybe it was the photographer's age, the smell of the basement, or the lack of confidence I felt in this man that made me so nervous. This time I felt like I was smaller than the lens and that I had to obey the photographer's commands of which way to tilt my head or change the angle of my ass. It was like posing for your senior portrait nude. The lighting was the same, but I wasn't wearing clothing and I was trying to give a natural girl-next-door smile.

In the basement studio there wasn't much space to work, so it was me, the pull-down white canvas background, some machinery and car tools, and the camera. Shooting nude during my past photo shoots felt more natural because I was in control, I picked the pose, I had the ideas, and I was allowed to be free to run, jump, yell, or laugh. It was ecstasy. This was different. Working while being paid meant there were two people to please and being inexperienced meant I went with the flow. He was a paying customer; I was the muse trying to inspire the perfect image.

After the basement we packed up the Volkswagen and went to the park. Quiet and secluded, it looked like a place where a girl could be found dead. The day felt like it would never end.

Before we got out of the car, he handed me three one hundred bills and said, "So, you don't have to worry that I won't pay you."

I smiled lightly, barely curling my lips. I was confused whether his statement was meant to make me feel guilty that he had to pay me or just his odd sense of humor.

I stashed the cash in my purse and started to change my clothing. Just before I had left my dorm I happened to grab my Arden B suit jacket and some dress pants. I wanted some diversity. Nude and bikini modeling was fun, but I wanted shots that would show I had many faces, expressions, and looks. I hoped he locked the doors to his car. I checked just to be safe. He looked annoyed that I couldn't trust him. But I couldn't.

The photographer wasn't paying me to be wearing a suit. We shot next to a couple of trees where I gave a more natural JCPenney catalogue smile. For the next shot, I straddled a tree branch—naked—which had fallen across a stream. The air was cold, crisp, the tree rough and scraping my legs, my insides.

After the shoot, I jumped on the F train and headed back to the dorms. I was now a paid model, not just another girl with her photo on a website. And although I wasn't working with an agency yet, I was gaining confidence in front of the camera and what better way than butt naked and making some money?

Once at the dorms, I called Maryam and told her I was

back from my lingerie shoot and asked her to meet me for some shopping. She said she didn't have a ton of cash to spend.

"Don't worry, I'll buy you something." We had a habit of stealing makeup samples at Sephora.

My sorority sisters and Maryam, the few college friends I did tell, considered me a model too, and didn't doubt anything. Just because I wasn't in *Vogue* or another fashion magazine, didn't make me less of a model in their eyes.

For the next few months, I got involved with my shoots, my "little productions." I got to be an art director. Maybe I could put *that* on my advertising resume. I laughed to myself, especially now that I was being paid by the hour. I liked to help pick out the locations, styling all my clothing and doing my own makeup. I felt secure at last!

While walking down Henry Street to take the A train at the High Street station, I saw a guy wearing a Syracuse Orangeman sweatshirt. I didn't even flinch or feel homesick. I was meeting people from websites, and I had very important dates—photographers to see each week.

Exchanging emails couldn't be more harmful than Internet dating. Time and time again I forced myself to relax before entering a dark hallway or a shabby street in the Lower East Side. I had given myself a nice new title though. It was "executive freelance model." Okay, delete the executive part, but it still sounded savvy and important.

Friends would introduce me as: "My friend the model!"

I loved their enthusiasm. I *really* loved it. Suddenly I had friends and a fan club. People I didn't even know would knock on my dorm door, asking to see my web link and modeling photos. I didn't need a magazine tear sheet or an interview with Conan O'Brien to be considered a model. They believed it. I believed it.

I was a model.

Really what I had become was a *freelance model*. It was a title I called myself more often now. As a freelance model, there wasn't much planned besides the date and time to "show up." Once at the shoot, the setup was simple: a chair, a couch, a roof, a bedroom, or a bathtub. So what if the small but obvious details that made a shoot professional were absent, such as a photo assistant who adjusted and set up the lights or checked the light meter, a makeup artist with her Mac makeup kit, and another assistant holding the reflector. Nor was there a stylist there to give the shoot a more defined purpose, while wrapping the body in fabric and "oohing" and "ahhing" about the concept and how great the colors looked. No one was there to keep everyone focused and make sure that everything was "perfect." None of those roles existed.

It was just the sound of breathing between model and photographer. The changing area was usually a bathroom or a bedroom where you would fight for space against the items scattered on countertops and floors—items owned by a sister or roommate, maybe a wife who wasn't home. Often, I glanced over at the hairspray or at an expensive perfume I'd always wanted and could steal, but I held back, fearing I might be caught and blamed. Sometimes I was tempted to borrow shoes the same size as the ones I wore, but I worried I would get bitched out for slipping my dirty wannabe-model foot into someone else's polished shoe.

Instead, I'd carefully, quietly pull out my costume of pink thongs, glitter cream, thigh highs, and a mini-skirt, and get dressed. Items I owned or had worn during a drunken night out with my girlfriends. Anything without an alcohol spill or puke on it was fair game. These items I carried to the shoot were the difference between amateur and professional. These items made me a freelance model.

Just take my picture, and make me feel beautiful.

Week after week, the sound of the camera lens zoomed and clicked, snapping and capturing the tease, the squinted eyes, the lip gloss smacked lips. Wearing yesterday's underwear wasn't an issue and the twenty-dollar shoes looked just as sexy as the six hundred dollar ones. The scent of sweat under my arms and the slight moistness from being turned on lingered long after the actual shoot. I wondered if the photographer could smell it, too.

It was our own little production. Bootleg sometimes, the lighting too dim, and the shutter speed and aperture all wrong. But it didn't matter. It wasn't about making the perfect shot. Besides Photoshop could fix anything. It was a photographer and model wanting their fix and fantasy for a few hours. Unlike before, now I got paid for *my time*.

After each shoot I was careful to pack up *everything* I brought, because running back for a forgotten ring, panty, or hairbrush only meant the possibility of being asked to shoot another time or to go for a drink and being tempted to. It was best to keep track of my shit, especially since many of these amateurs weren't friendship material.

Then I would look at myself from another perspective and feel trashy, slutty, and like I had an addiction problem. I would think to myself that maybe I could use the money from my nude shots to get some quality shots from a professional who had real ambition. The thought was always there in the back of my mind, hiding, peeking out now and then to confront me with my actions. Occasionally, guilt would slap me in the face reminding me that I was just another girl with a smile and a tease. However, it was always quickly dissolved by the thought of my being dissed because of my height, being told no by agents and bookers. At the open calls, I showed them all my half naked photos, but getting in the door was one thing, staying inside was a different challenge. I felt accepted everywhere except when in front of an agent.

No, for now I just wanted my photo taken. I was content and proud seeing my photo on the Internet, on a photographer's website, or maybe once in awhile making a few prints for my cheap bendable portfolio from Pearl Paint.

I enjoyed standing in line with my book in hand, and before that, asking in an important manner, "Where are the portfolios?"

This of course would imply that I have something worth saving and showing to put into a portfolio. And therefore I must be important. Although just having a portfolio meant nothing, I knew.

Anyone could buy a fucking portfolio and put photos in it. But having one would impress those who knew nothing of modeling, like my friends or sorority sisters who introduced me as "the model."

After all, how many people have piles of CDs scattered around their dorm room, and their photos all over the Internet and on their boyfriend's bedroom walls? Still, I needed something that at least "looked" professional. A black book with sexy photos inside must mean something, right? It had to.

Once, after I worked with another photographer in NJ, for a shoot that involved a red leathery dress and heels, he referred me to a photographer in Miami.

I emailed the Florida photographer my photos and we set up a shoot. I was to be flown to Miami from NYC and stay for the whole weekend. It was perfect and I wouldn't even miss any school. Danny would just have to see me another time. I was scheduled to shoot with two photographers who would pay me $350 each plus food and accommodations. I didn't tell anyone; after all, how would I explain this trip without someone questioning it? Besides, I felt powerful, professional to say the least, to have plans waiting for me at one of the warmest places in the country when New York was about to be blown away by a winter storm.

At first it sounded like an Internet model's dream, but with my new black portfolio I didn't feel amateur at all. I had never been to Miami before. I heard about girls traveling all over the U.S. modeling with agencies, but going on my own was more risky. I brushed away any fear. I knew this wasn't a major print job or a music video with an agency; I was a business. There was no promise of getting paid and I hadn't signed any contracts. Yet, it all felt normal, as I waited to board the plane. By dinner time I would be in Miami. On the plane I told the person sitting next to me my life story and that I was going to Miami for a photo shoot with some great photographers.

"Yeah, I model and travel a lot, but the money is good!"

I needed to tell someone, anyone, to boost my confidence and test how the trip would sound later when I told my friends about it. Really, I wasn't sure about anything. My deodorant had worn off and I smelled like shit as I sat next to this little old lady with a pretty sunflower pin attached to her pretty neatly buttoned blouse. She was sipping some herbal tea. It smelled good.

"I'm a model," I told her.

She believed me and even looked through my portfolio. I tried to show her only the conservative ones, which meant she only saw three shots. Then we had a thirty minute conversation. I hadn't talked to my own grandparents in what felt like years. She told me about the old stars and celebrities who used to excite her, like Eva Gardner.

I peered nervously through the window, wondering if the photographer would even meet me at the airport. It was all based on trust, on our emailed agreement.

When I got there, a burst of heat engulfed me, giving me a big hug hello, but Miami wasn't Ocean Drive dining, Collins Ave shopping, or the alluring Delano. There weren't women dressed in bright pink and orange colored short skirts dancing at Nikki Beach or Crobar or Skybar. They all existed, I discovered later; I just didn't see any of that during my first experience in Miami. Right as I stepped off the plane it turned into an uncomfortable hell.

I spotted the assistant photographer, who was scheduled to pick me up. He was the apprentice to the original photographer who I spoke with, the one who arranged the flight and told me what to bring. It wasn't easy to recognize this sassy guy with a pink shirt and without a sign or flowers to greet me, since everyone including him was Latino. He had a nice smile but I couldn't imagine fucking him, even though he was probably only about five years older than me. I could smell his egotistical personality and he had nothing to say that didn't include him.

"So are you Spanish?" he asked me.

I said no and was glad we had nothing in common. Again, his big-shot personality was annoying and he couldn't stop talking about all the models he had shot that past week and how busy he had been as if trying to impress me or make me feel like I was just "one of many." We drove from the airport to the accommodations, which were at his house. I only found this out once I arrived there. I was a bit nervous and disappointed, because I was looking forward to relaxing and having a moment to myself in a cute hotel.

I eased my frustration by reminding myself I was there to do what I loved. I had only been modeling for three months, and I was already booking paid-for flights and finding paid work. I was "*freelancing*," and millions of girls do it. In that sense I wasn't alone, so I sucked up the heat, the sun, the green and carried my small suitcase, which simply held high heels and a couple bikinis.

The Latin apprentice still lived with his parents, and even though I never spoke to them, I felt like some whore their son was hanging out with. They kind of stayed out of the way and mumbled something in their native language, which didn't sound too friendly. I slept in his bedroom and he moved to the living room. I mentioned that I had a boyfriend right away, as if a skinny boyfriend ten states away could really do anything to scare him. Still, some random photographer wasn't going to get near me. The distance between his camera and my body would be at least three feet the whole trip, I promised myself. I also knew how quickly things spread, and if I slept with or even kissed the photographer it would be all over the Internet and modeling forums. Even though I

wasn't a high paid professional model, I still didn't want a bad rep—to be called a skank.

There was no makeup artist or fresh orange juice in the morning. Instead, there was just some jackass Latino photographer eyeing my ass and telling me about *Playboy* submissions he had made and how he could get me in that magazine. I doubted it, but just smiled like I believed he was capable of anything.

The first day on location was Saturday and we drove to Crusted Nose's house which was one huge dusty vineyard. His nose was incredibly huge, bumpy, and crusted with warts. To make matters worse, he was clumsy, perverted and later I found he was untalented too. As a proper girl from Syracuse, New York, I put all of this aside and smiled and gave him a hug like we were old friends.

"Nice to meet cha." He had a really hillbilly voice. He kissed my cheek and I felt nauseous from both his smell and his acne.

As he got closer I prayed the zits wouldn't pop all over me.

Oh great, this is a fucking riot, I thought to myself when I looked at the two of them standing together talking about god knows what. We were quite a group. *Here I am, a model from New York, in Miami with two obnoxious photographers.* I was about to get brash and speak my mind. While at school and studying advertising, I absorbed the belief that "Image is Everything." So I knew it was one thing to have a zit; it is another to let the zit define you.

How could he not see how big and gross and puffy his zit was? I almost said it out loud because I was just so fed up that he wasn't self-conscious about it.

The first place we shot was in an upper class neighborhood. They tried to give me a tour in a beat-up rusty wreck of a car. According to them, a famous actor had lived in the house I was posing in front of, as if that would impress me, like he knew him or something.

He said, "Do you know whose house you're standing in front of?"

"No, whose?" I giggled and looked towards the huge bay window where a chandelier hung in the foyer. I wondered how many models at the big agencies in New York would have put up with their perverted shit. They probably wouldn't have even considered a job like this. Maybe I was just a loser. I just thought of the money and listened to know whose fabulous house my ass was pointing at,

"Sylvester Stalone's."

Somehow, I doubted it.

In the car, I changed into a red thong bikini the Crusted

Nose photographer gave me. Standing in the street with my hands on my hips in a confidant stance, wearing my black boots and a sexy grin, I felt out of place and cheesy. Old retired ladies stared out their windows, no doubt fainting with shock.

I stood there, my confidence shining outwardly, while internally I wanted to hide. Right then and there I should have grabbed my bags, free ticket and all, and just enjoyed the weekend in the sun and on the beach. Unfortunately, I had to go with the flow; I had no other choice. I knew no one, I didn't even know where South Beach was located or what to do if I found it.

Later I could say I had modeled in Miami. I would seem more serious, like I really get serious modeling jobs. No one would ever need to know that these guys were just having a joy ride shooting my ass.

We went to the beach, but not South Beach. We went to a deserted location with the skyline view of Miami and I shot in the water with my red bikini. It was the first time I had ever shot at a beach and the water felt wonderful. While we shot I imagined the photos and how pretty the sunset would look against my skin. I was topless in the water, playing with my bikini top, holding it up to my face, letting it hang loose — letting it dangle in the water. That's when they asked me to take off my bottom.

I wasn't comfortable with crotch shots, and I really wasn't comfortable with some person I just met getting photos of my crotch, especially these guys. I wasn't someone's little toy and I was angry they would even ask. We didn't discuss full nudity on the phone. I tried to laugh it off as a joke "I don't want to get water *all* over my body." I held my hand over my private area, protecting it from the lens.

He wasn't happy with my resistance and basically said he wasn't paying me for my opinion. I felt very alone, sick to my stomach. Feeling defensive, I started to get out of the water.

I should have expected the unexpected, but I didn't. For all I knew they could have a rope, a gun and a hard on. Again they told me they knew people at *Playboy* and that they could make me a star. As if they wanted to be the one who took credit for my resume. I rolled my eyes and smiled with an "I'm not as dumb as you think" face. I was angry at myself for putting myself in a situation like this. I promised myself I would never get caught in a situation where I wasn't in control or at least where I wasn't appreciated. I had no money to catch a cab to the airport, I didn't know where I was, and calling home wasn't an option. The embarrassment was too frightening to consider. Another 24 hours remained. The rest of the shoot was very uncomfortable and was shadowed by the argument.

After the shoot at the deserted beach I wanted to call Danny and cry to him. I wanted to call every person I knew and tell them about my horrific weekend. However, I didn't call because the thought of being told I wasn't as professional as I thought I was, and that I had made a mistake, disturbed me. I wished someone could give me advice but then another part of me liked learning the hard way. Soon I would be packing my bags for the airport. No one would have to know about my terrible, perverted, awful, no good, very bad Miami experience.

Not soon enough I was on my way to the airport, with five hundred and fifty dollars instead of the seven hundred promised, half of it paid upfront. Over a Wendy's burger, which didn't taste as good as the lunches with Maryam, the Crusty Nose photographer gave me two hundred dollars. Our agreement over the email said three fifty.

Pissed. I swallowed down the last of my burger, tasting none of it.

I stared at the face of Benjamin Franklin on the two hundreds that I had not picked up off the table yet. Something was wrong.

"Don't you owe me one hundred fifty more?" He looked shocked I would ask about the cash.

I repeated myself. "You said it was three fifty before and after the shoot!" How dare they scam me. My eyebrows bent and my lips felt suddenly chapped.

He said with a roll of his eyes, "Well...I didn't get my money's worth of nudity so I'm not paying YOU the full payment!"

That hurt. I looked over at the Latino photographer. He was sipping and sucking and slurping his milkshake. He wasn't sticking up for me. I stared at them and grabbed the cash fast.

I stood up and looked to the ceiling, then to the two idiots and said, "You know what ...in New York City ...I have NEVER in my LIFE been treated like this!"

I walked toward the door. I could hear them laughing as I walked away in a huff and one of them said, "Aww ...you're such a tough cookie aren't you!"

I went to the busted car and stood in front of it, folding my arms. I watched the two idiots tumble out of Wendy's. God, they were so ugly.

Fuck it! I was out of these fools' faces and on to New York City. I said, "Thanks!" sarcastically when we got to the airport. I grabbed my bags and didn't hug them goodbye.

Thinking about the danger I had faced only fazed me months later. I was comfortable posing nude but I was done with bullshit. At least if they'd hired a makeup artist I would have felt more professional, not an amateur, a plaything for someone to jerk off to. Sure it felt nice to be told I was hot and attractive, but all I could think about were the guys looking at the photos afterward, either talking shit about me and my attitude, or talking about all the nasty perverted things they could have done to me.

I suppose it could have been worse, but my first impression of Miami sure as hell didn't involve a *Cosmo* in hand while wearing a Versace dress at the Delano.

A month or two passed and, like ex-boyfriends that always called a few months later, the Spanish photographer contacted me by e-mail. He said he needed a copy of my Identification. When I was in Miami he took a picture of it with his digital camera to prove my age. I was smarter by the time he contacted me and I knew he wanted a copy of my ID in order to sell the photos, because by law you need proof of the model's age if you are selling photos of a nude model to magazines or posting them on a website. Since I didn't get any of the Crusted Nose photographer's photos, and the ones I did get from the Spanish boy were terrible, I wasn't in the mood to debate more with these fools so I refused to mail a copy of my ID. We debated for weeks by e-mail, and he would call me and harass me by leaving messages that threatened to ruin my modeling career. I laughed. The career hadn't started yet; there was nothing to ruin.

Using the Internet to make modeling connections was such a great tool if you could handle the upsetting difficulties. I couldn't imagine how celebrities or those in the 1950s and 1960s did it without the Internet. I thought of the old lady on the plane who admired Eva Gardner and wondered to myself, *How did Marilyn Monroe and Natalie Wood, or any aspiring model or actress do it before the Internet?*

My most memorable experience so far was in Miami again, but this time it was with a photography teacher who wanted to shoot me, to explain techniques to his class. He was from the Virginia area, and he was flying down to Miami for a week and wanted to shoot a model who was easy to shoot. He emailed me and we talked on the phone. Shortly afterwards, he made the arrangements and I flew back to Miami.

I thought it was a bit odd that he didn't contact a model in Miami, and instead paid for my flight. Maybe he just wanted a get-away from his town. Maybe he liked shooting girls on the beach. Maybe he liked the Miami area; regardless he was very professional, easy to work with. He paid for my cab from the airport. When I left my cell phone in the cab, the photographer wasn't upset or annoyed. He called the cab company and paid for the return of my phone.

I stayed in the penthouse of a beautiful hotel on Collins Avenue. I felt like royalty. I could see the beach from the balcony and I felt like a princess. The photographer had a room five floors below in a room much smaller and without a liquor cabinet or kitchen. He showed me around South Beach the best he could. He was about twenty years older than me. I wasn't twenty-one yet, so I couldn't go out and party, and I didn't know anyone besides this middle-aged photographer to party with. And *he* wasn't connected enough to get us into any great clubs.

We spent the two days eating seafood at expensive restaurants. It was the first time I had ever eaten at an expensive restaurant. While we ate we talked about our relationships. He had a girlfriend, which made the weekend more relaxed. We talked about our plans, goals, and our past photo shoots. We went shopping and he bought me a beautiful white dress which cost him a hundred and twenty dollars. I hardly knew this guy. It was a really nice gift, and I was both grateful and shocked. I felt like a famous model or something, and I hadn't even been in a magazine yet. I was waiting for

him to become a jerk, to become like some of the other pathetic photographers I knew, who called themselves photographers simply because they owned a camera. I was surprised that this photographer was paying me and I didn't even have to take my clothes off, nor did he try to sleep with me. He was the first nice photographer I had met.

This positive experience quickly dissolved when I returned home for Thanksgiving, and my sister saw me nude on the Internet.

By this time I had worked with over eight photographers. When I quickly dashed to Syracuse with Danny at the wheel and I just knew when I returned to New York I had to change my name. I could sense it.

Mainly it was because I couldn't promise I would never model naked again. I liked modeling too much. The feeling of having control over my day and life. Although I didn't know if modeling would become my profession one day, at that moment it was my life. Immediately, I knew what I had to do.

I would go to the courts in Brooklyn Heights, and fill out a "doing business as" form!

I only had to visit my bank—HSBC—and get a business account. It was the perfect plan to separate the old me from the new me. I decided to get a new name.

When I returned to the city, the first thing I did was email that asshole photographer who had posted the nude photos of me all over his website and ruined my Thanksgiving. My secret life.

He held a grudge for a few hours saying through five emails, "The shots are mine and I can do anything I want with them."

The photos *were* his, and it was rude and bitchy of me to ask him to take them down, but I had my dignity to save.

He finally said, "Okay, but I've never had a model do this to me."

For a long while afterward, I was mad at my mother and my sister. They didn't understand. They could never do what I had done. I'd like to see *them* pose nude and schedule photo shoots.

Then guilt would tug at my heart and I would feel sick to my stomach thinking about my sister having to defend me. For the next few weeks, I didn't call or email anyone from home. I had to distance myself until I could accomplish something big. Although they hadn't disowned or rejected me, I didn't feel as high on the pedestal in Syracuse as I did in New York.

I wondered, "Am *I a slut?* Did *I lose my dignity? Who was I?*" I decided that unlike a prostitute at least I wasn't selling sex physically. Only through the camera lens. And though a prostitute could go buy a coffee down the street then basically forget about the hundreds of men she slept with, I couldn't forget the look in my mother's eyes.

During the next few weeks I went to class on time and began to see how this "underground modeling world" could hurt me, and even though it was on the computer screen, I saw how it divided the old me from the person I had become.

Two years before, when I was captain of the track team, I never would have thought of changing my name or posing nude. It hurt to know that something that I liked to do could affect my family so much.

How could modeling betray me? How could something I loved make me feel like such shit and embarrass me so much? But embarrassed or not, it didn't stop me from planning my next gig. I had to get my confidence back.

In New York City, I felt safe. I could shut the door to my past. I had made a new life, and I was proud of myself for staying grounded. I wasn't into drugs or into doing cocaine at late-night parties. No, it was just nudity.

Why couldn't *they* see it like *I* did?

I was the only person in my graduating high school class to have ever done anything risky or to have left town to pursue *a dream*. So what if I slipped, made a mistake.

Let them judge. Let them call me a slut. They were still at home, eating animal crackers while I would soon be on to bigger and better things.

Chapter 4

May I Introduce Isobella

Late November 2001: Brooklyn Heights
I was blown away at how easy it was to obtain a new identity. In a matter of hours, I would have a new name. As I stood in the courthouse in Brooklyn Heights, I held my paperwork in my hand, secretly thrilled by the chance for a fresh start. It cost $5.00 just for the papered document and also another chunk of money from my weekly stipend meant for food and train rides, to get it approved, stamped and signed. That day, it was windy out, and a gust of wind almost swept the paper out of my hand but I gripped it tightly. I didn't want to spend more of my weekly metro money on getting another "Doing Business As" form should it blow away.

Isobella Jadeco. The "co" for company, because to get a "Doing Business As" name the little scruffy Italian man, who probably sold Doing Business As forms all his life and never left Brooklyn, made it very clear with a stern voice: "Either you choose to be a company, a corporation, or become incorporated."

I only had a few seconds to think, or pick. I stood there dumbfounded staring into this scruffy man's eyes. Finally, I spit out, "Co!"

Later when I was introducing myself to a photographer, agent, or new friend and I needed a last name, I would combine the "Jade," with "co" to make an ethnic sounding last name. Pronounced Ja-De-Co. Next, I used it to sign my name Isobella.

From that moment my identity changed and I had butterflies tickling my stomach knowing I was finally free.

"Thank you very much!" I told the scruffy man who didn't have a clue that he was speaking to a girl who was about to use her new identity for a career as "a professional model." One day he might remember my face when he saw it on a billboard, I thought, as I left the little shop and huddled against the building. The wind whipped me in the face but I didn't care. I could now do whatever I wanted under my new name, and I could even have checks cashed in the name of *Isobella Jadeco*. It was legal to use the name as long as I informed the bank it was my "Doing Business As" name. And yet it meant a lot more to me. This name was my shield, would protect me against any new shame that would try to bash me and my plans. I could get away with anything with this name. Suddenly an alter-ego was born and I was anxious to use it.

I forced my way through the brutal storm and dodged the piece of floating trash blowing down the damp street, focused solely on the sound of my tan boots that made me feel tall. It was the first week of December and I noticed how peaceful, quiet and sad Montague Street looked when no one was out and about. Winter was coming and that meant the semester was already almost over. Three months ago I hadn't planned on changing my name, but the fight with my mother had altered all that.

When I arrived home, at the dorms, I placed the document in a folder where I kept my poetry. It had been months since I'd written a damn thing that wasn't for school or didn't involve *Lord of the Flies*.

Once the document was safe and sound, minus a few wrinkles from the wind brushing against it on the walk back from the courthouse, I went directly to Onemodelplace.com. I was typing so fast that I had to re-type it three times before I got the website correct. Then I went directly to the members log in and typed my screen name, password and signed in. It was like clockwork. I went to the top and clicked "manage profile." I waited for the page to load and tapped my foot. Within thirty seconds my profile read my new name "Isobella Jade." I would save the "co" for later. My stomach fluttered just like the very first time I'd begun my modeling career, three months ago. It was hell waiting to get my next message or request from a photographer. I considered getting the higher membership plan and paying $14.95 a month to be a Gold member. Then I could show off more photos on my page and maybe get more messages. Finally, I did get a message saying, "Hello Isobella, I would love to shoot you for a TFP shoot, unless you are open to nudity. I can pay only $50 an hour."

And so it began again but brand new.

Only my professors, sorority sisters who I hardly saw, my family who I almost never saw, and my current college friends who knew me before I bought my alter ego, called me *Heather*. Any new photographer or friend made outside of school would know me as Isobella. I even decided to try to get some of my current friends to call me Isobella. Some of them did. Danny didn't budge.

It wasn't hard to get accustomed to; I didn't want the name *Heather* anymore. I embraced the idea of being a new person. *Heather* worried what people thought of her and dwelled on the put downs. *Heather* wore muddy running shoes and settled for being a little below average student.

As Isobella, I wore nothing but high heels, determined to become someone who was known, seen, desired, and important. All I needed to do was walk like I was Isobella and the world was mine.

Isobella would stomp and smash any fear of failure. As Isobella, I could create whoever I wanted to be and become it. My mother's damning words and my sister's accusing eyes vanished. I didn't know them when I was Isobella. And they didn't know me.

It was hard having two sets of people in my life who knew me by two different names, two different identities. It raises questions and forces explanations. It makes me look like a girl running away from her past, and maybe I was, but more then that I was trying to become the model I wanted to be. I couldn't do it with the expectations people had for *Heather*.

I was trying to surround myself with people who were creative, passionate about what they did, who took risks—people who lived to do what they loved. I was Isobella to everyone in my circle. I wanted Heather gone, dead, deceased. I tried to crucify the name.

Sometimes Heather would still appear. *Heather* played the role of my conscience while *Isobella* controlled my actions. Now, going to yet another shoot, I decided to leave Heather down on the street. Isobella rang the buzzer and headed upstairs. As Isobella I said, "Hello, it's nice to meet you" and kissed the photographer on the cheek. Then I dropped my bag and asked where the bathroom was located, commenting on the painting on the wall as I checked out the atmosphere of the studio or apartment. While there, I took off my clothing and after the shoot I picked Heather back up.

After the fight with Lara and my mother, I tried to pull any sexual photo of myself off the Internet. My sister's words haunted me for weeks and even though I was back in the city and able to do whatever the fuck I wanted, I still wanted to save face. It wasn't easy since many of the photos were posted on websites that I signed on to. A few months before my modeling obsession began you couldn't find one photo of me on the Internet. Now I couldn't control the websites where I'd flaunted my ass and body parts.

I cleared as much as I could, frantic to get in touch with the web masters of all the sites and demanding they remove me. Then for three days I missed school to work a promo event in Times Square. At 8A.M. I met five other girls on 46th Street, and after seeing who I was working with, I realized that these promo agencies employed any old average Jane or Internet Wannabe-model.

It was the fat girl's way to be a model. Or the actor's way to make some extra cash, or for the model who wasn't cute enough to model in an ad campaign. To be a promo model you only needed a somewhat decent photo of yourself and a cell phone that worked. A smile helped but didn't really matter.

A monkey could do it.

That day we were promoting a new coffee drink which had vitamins in it and which made a person act even more like they were on speed than with normal coffee. We didn't get to sample the coffee, but we sure talked about it for six hours straight for the three day duration of the boring, draining promotion. We only got three, fifteen minute breaks throughout the whole day which was barely enough time to grab your own damn coffee. It paid twenty an hour which I thought was a good rate for being fully clothed. I usually made $100 an hour to be fully naked.

When I got back to the dorms I had an email from Lara who said that the talk had finally died down at school, and she thankfully became last week's gossip. However, she mentioned that at work she was still getting harassed about it.

I didn't write her back.

The next gig I found was as bad as a doctor's visit. A photographer contacted me about an art project by email from one of the websites I forgot I was even on. The words "art project" sounded interesting. He said it would be tasteful and beautiful, capturing me "as me" to the fullest. The art project turned out to be a simple crotch shot. I said yes. Why not? I hadn't done a shoot in weeks, and I liked art.

As the days passed, I started to feel the anxiety, the doubt. I didn't have a good explanation when a few of my friends asked about my recent shoots and when I would be going on my next one. They said "they were so proud of me," and "the camera allowed me to shine." After the blowup with my mother, I needed to shine.

My friends wouldn't have to know all the details. I traveled up to the 60s on the East side. I rang the buzzer but no one let me in. A woman carrying a briefcase, looking important, with really shiny red shoes and a few matching red pimples, punched in her code and I followed her into the building. I let her go in the elevator first and waited to go alone once the elevator returned.

The elevator was huge and I inhaled musty dust, while green and yellow clumps of dust blew into my eyes. Wet sewage seeped through the cracks in the elevator walls and I stepped on a leftover Dunkin Donuts cup. When I lifted my foot brown goop covered the bottom of my Aldo flats I had just bought. I felt like I was going up slowly, almost too slowly, to the locked tower instead of the dungeon this place felt like. I definitely wasn't Jack going up the bean stock for some golden photos. No, this was strictly cash. What next? Last week it was marketing coffee, this week I was showing my pussy for cash.

The elevator made a thud and the door opened, I felt like dirty Cinderella. There was a door in front of me—a wide brown and golden burnt colored door. I was nervous to touch it, afraid I'd get some unheard of New York City rust disease. Although slightly open, there was a padlock on the door. I pushed hard with all 94 pounds of my weight. To my delight it opened. But my pleasure was short-lived. Nervously, I walked through the entryway where black-and-white photos graced the walls. It was too dim to see what they looked like, but with each click of my heels the dark tower slowly became a palace of white. It was getting brighter and more lit. I was almost there.

The studio felt huge, with floor-to-ceiling windows. I almost hoped my fairy godmother would appear to clean me up as I whistled and cheerfully sang, "Hellooooo." I hoped my voice would carry through the studio and I would receive a cheerful reply. He didn't answer. Instead I heard what sounded like a couch falling from the ceiling, another huge thud.

I walked around a corner carefully.

Finally, I saw him. His back was toward the table. He was playing with some gadget and was very focused on what looked like medical equipment. He didn't even walk over to me. Did he not hear me? I stood there quiet, watching him and then looking around the studio. From the looks of the polished wood floor the place appeared professional. Huge photography or science experiment equipment with big plugs and antennas filled the room, and thick metal and wood tables had photos scattered all over them, as if waiting to be inspected. I didn't look closely at them. Instead I decided to try the photographer again. Perhaps he still didn't know the elevator had opened and someone had gotten off and entered. It seemed a bit scary that someone could just sneak in, like I was doing.

I walked over to where he sat, where I'd heard the loud thud. I crept up behind him, touched his back lightly and said, "Hi!" in almost a ghost whisper. He jumped back and said, "Whoa! You shouldn't scare people like that!"

I talked and talked, ramping a mile a minute about how I rarely came to the Upper East Side, and about how nice it was to be in a place that was airy and white and clean. He looked bored, so I asked him about the film he would be using and the shoot.

"It is going to be very slow and you will have to be very still, okay?"

"Okay!"

He pointed over to the set, which was a table, and he said, "The camera is already positioned and ready to be used." He then told me to change down to nothing, unless I wanted to wear a tank top.

It was a sunny day and beams of light were shining against the tripod. I could almost see the camera licking its lips and waiting for the session to begin. The film was open and waiting. I swear there was a puddle of sweat below the packaging as if it was drooling. I made a quick inspection of the photographer's portfolio and a visual tour of the studio. He, on the other hand, barely inspected my flimsy plastic Pearl Paint Portfolio. He didn't seem to care what was inside. Instead, he sort of took my hands and led me to the set, which I noticed didn't look too comfortable. It was legs up in the gynecologist position on a cold metal table with big "light banks" as he called them. He fumbled with the lights, and just as I started to get comfortable with this artistic shot of my crotch, the most embarrassing thing happened. The photographer zoomed away from my vagina and said, "Would you mind cleaning up the little hairs?"

I felt like a child being told her room wasn't clean enough. After spending half the night preparing, I still had work to do down there. My Italian hair grew fast, I guess. Like a wet seal, I slid off the silver, shiny table and tiptoed to the changing area, which was a manmade moveable wall. I shaved, cut, and scissored away a few stray hairs, like I was doing my own little art project down there.

Taking a moment for myself, I finally felt calm again as I thought about the shot he was about to take. The shot I was *allowing* him to take of me. I could hear him picking up what sounded like a collection of rocks and seashells that had just smashed to the ground. So far everything was huge, loud and startled me. I wanted to peek and see what he was doing. Instead, I hurried to clean up my crotch.

Standing quietly, I looked down at it, then bent forward and tried to get underneath enough, deep enough in, feeling with my forefinger to figure out what he saw as "so much hair." Maybe with a microscope you could have seen the tiny, itsy bitsy hairs. *What an asshole!* I thought to myself as I worked away. *I'd like to see* him *clean up his hairy-ass crotch!*

I held my pink small hand mirror and I stood there trying to get all the tiny hairs I could possibly get, using my mirror as guide. It wasn't easy. I needed something to lift my leg onto so I could really get in there. I worked pretty hard, trying to get the razor at the right angle to sweep up and make it smooth down there. After the final swipe of my razor, I felt my crotch with my fingers again just to make sure it felt smooth.

"Are you okay in there?" he asked.

"Yeah ...almost done!" I said as a matter-of-factly as possible.

Moments later, I slipped back on the cold table with the feel of the warm bright lights giving a slight sensation to my bald vagina. The heat felt good. Then I thought about the camera lens zooming on my tiny pussy again, the bright lights blinding her.

I closed my eyes because it wasn't like a dentist's office, with a pretty picture on the ceiling to distract me or to convince me this shoot was a good idea. I was curious about the shots he was quietly taking, so I became quiet myself. I was interested in what he was capturing, but I also felt too awkward to speak, so I kept thinking about how it paid four hundred dollars. To divert my attention, I thought about what I'd spend the money on.

As I lay there, I decided my vagina probably did look like a flower or an interesting cave for an art piece. I just felt wide and open, like somehow I had betrayed my vagina. The image I had of myself as a cute petite package was washed away with the moistness that was forming down there. To my embarrassment, I was getting horny from the blazing heat of the huge lights. It was like my vagina was betraying me back. Letting me know she was a dirty little cunt who got off being exposed, on display. She liked the camera just as much as the rest of me. It bothered me that I was getting so comfortable with the lens focused anywhere on me, even zooming deep between my legs.

Deciding to do this shoot had been a spur of the moment decision. If I'd really thought about it, I most likely wouldn't have had the balls to do it. I wasn't thinking about the aftermath, or even the fact that I had crossed the line into soft porn. I was winging it, similar to the day I'd bridge jumped with the neighborhood boys over three stories above water in my underwear. I was thirteen, not thinking about the depth of the water, the rocks, or the fact that I wasn't the best swimmer in the world. It was just a spur of the moment decision. I could have killed myself, and wondered what the consequences of my impulsiveness would be this time.

The photographer didn't say whether I'd done a good job or not, or whether he liked shooting my vagina.

Not sure what to say when he was done, I merely said, "Thank you," then felt like an idiot.

He shot all types of pussy, I noticed from a collection of huge 14 by 16 inch prints spread out on a display table. Even girls with diseases and weird cheetah-like birthmarks on their vaginas. After the vagina shots, I then shot full body by the window of his studio. As I sat by the window, I looked down on the street, watching the people rush by unaware of the nude photo shoots going on above them all over the city, young girls with nothing to lose and living for the moment, for the rush of the clicking camera.

After two hours of work, I signed, he paid me, and then I left. I never saw the guy again and I can't even remember his name now. I only remember that afternoon my private area became not so private. It was a job I knew no Giraffe would have considered.

After this shoot, I stopped using the Internet as the only source to promote myself. It was fun to plan all these shoots and feel in control while making some money, but I was sick of the phony photographers and nothing was really moving me forward. Mostly my conscience was having a hard time finding a purpose and reason to pursue this hobby.

My life was trains, and photo shoots—and the photographers I was sharing my body with were so fucking weird. Where were the cool people, the ones who didn't have interesting art projects and who asked you to tweeze away your pubic hairs?

I needed more than just a planned photo shoot to make me feel like a model. I

wanted my portfolio to "wow" people, not just turn them on. I knew about the big agencies, the print ads and the commercial jobs, and I wanted real work, with real professionals. I didn't want to be just another girl with her photo on a website.

After that last shoot, I felt like my crotch had been violated by the camera lens. I didn't know which was worse: the photo shoot or the thought of going to the gynecologist. They were too similar.

I needed to get an agent, and with the name Isobella I knew I could.

Chapter 5

At the Back of the Pack of Giraffes Forever

<u>December 2001: New York City</u>
My dad had missed my 19th birthday three months before but that was typical. Now Christmas was around the corner and already, I was thinking about what I wanted from my mother.

What I really wanted I knew she couldn't give; I wanted an agent. Instead I was forced to spend my days thinking about my finals that were scheduled and, as they approached, I thought about all I had done in the span of the last semester. I remembered how even on Halloween I did a shoot in a cat suit, instead of going to a party with Maryam. Almost six weeks had passed and I still hadn't received the photos yet. *What would catsuit shots do for me anyways?* I asked myself.

Few photographers I met talked about agencies or ad campaigns. I didn't have an agency yet, but I craved the acceptance. That thought now haunted me daily, my height haunted me daily, every girl on the subway and walking by who was taller than me haunted me, too. What bothered me most was that I got whistled at in the streets, while wearing only sweat pants and a tee-shirt, but I couldn't get the time of day from an agent.

Once a man gave me a catcall, and I flicked the pervert off and yelled, "If I'm so hot then why the hell aren't I working with an agent?" Then the pervert said, "I'll be your agent." For a crazy moment I almost considered it. I wanted to give up and put my time and effort towards something more rewarding than trying to run with a bunch of fucking Giraffes.

On a bone chilling afternoon in December, I sat on the train going downtown as I returned from my Intro to Business class. As I watched people crowd the train with me, I started to think about why I wanted to model so badly, why having an agency was constantly on my mind, when to millions of other girls who seemed to be obsessed with the Internet could care less about an agency. I wanted the satisfaction of being in the same league as the Giraffes I admired but whom I also secretly hated. I needed an agency to give me hope, to prove I wasn't wasting my life, that modeling wasn't just a phase. That I wasn't just an Internet girl booking amateur work based on my private parts. Mostly I wanted to be able to say, "Mom, look I have an agency!" I wanted to stand up for myself and say, "Be proud, Mom, your daughter made something of herself. I'm a *real* model!" I also wanted to prove to the world and to myself that I could get an agent even though I wasn't tall and didn't look like the rest of the Giraffes I saw posted on the real modeling agencies websites. An agent was proof that I was capable of competing in the modeling capital of the world. That I was supposed to be in New York City after all, that it was my destiny to be here.

Having an agent would also ease my regrets; make me feel less like a whore or slut. I could start fresh, pretend I never modeled before, forget about the assholes I had met. Until I had an agent, I was just another body to bump into on the train. My purpose in life wasn't to be a ping-pong ball.

When the train pulled into Union Square, I headed towards an agency I had visited a few weeks before, that I felt had fucked me over. I walked through a path in Union Square devoid of snow. It was a clear day. The clouds weren't moving at all but when I looked to the sky, I wish I could have taken a picture of them. They were clumpy and gray.

As I stood there for a moment watching the clouds, some skateboarders jumped the steps. I could hear the sound of the wheels racing over the ledges. I didn't even have to turn around to know whether the guy made the jump or not. I could tell by the sound of the wheels. These kids made me feel old. They were probably in high school. Or they skipped school today and their mothers didn't care. Maybe they were embracing their youth and enjoying the day. It had been a long time since I'd done something soothing to the soul. I didn't read anymore and I didn't listen to music either. Nor did I know the hottest music video of the week. In the dorms we didn't get MTV or HBO or anything fancy. I noticed heel heights go up and each week the fronts of shoes got pointer and pointer. I didn't watched *Sex in the City* or know the names of all the cast members but it felt like rest of the world did and suddenly they all knew more about fashion than I did. I used the Internet as my source of news while scoping out the modeling websites.

Moving past the skateboarder's parade, I walked down the path, past the dog park, and just focused on where I was going. I made it to 6th Ave and buzzed the 4th floor. I forgot there was no elevator, so I tried to walk up three stairs at a time but my short legs couldn't do it. Out of breath, I finally entered the office where I met with the agent who had taken my money then had forgotten to call me. He was a Hispanic man in his mid-twenties with slicked-back hair and a somewhat effeminate voice.

I walked in calm even though inside I was bursting with rage. For a moment I was a murderer with a hatchet ready to cut something. I was welcomed by a tall blond model. Perhaps she was the girl the agent was fucking on the side behind his wife's back. Maybe she was just another hopeful model. She did have a nice full white smile. Or maybe he was just her friendly agent booking her a ton of modeling gigs when he wasn't answering the phone.

Maybe he wasn't such an asshole for not contacting me, but when I walked into his office all the rage came to me and I wanted to kick his ass. All I could think about were my slides and that he almost got away with ripping me off or taking advantage of me. I told him so. I was very spastic and speaking a mile a minute saying, "Why haven't you called?" and rushing my words without taking a breath or break. "If you were legit you would have called me!" Then I sat down to collect myself and calm down.

When he spoke, his voice was hoarse and it gave me a

chill. He was slow with his words and said, "Who—do—you—think—you—are?" His voice then got louder. "You really have some nerve coming in here speaking to me like that!"

Then he yelled at me. I was stuck to the chair, just clutching my cheap, Pearl Paint plastic modeling portfolio.

"You think you're something special. You walk in here like you're some Madonna." I couldn't believe he was actually yelling. He got up from his seat and walked to the door. He shut the door perhaps so the secretary, his mistress, wouldn't hear. I feared he would grab me, spit on me, punch me, rape me, or tell me I wasn't special again.

And then he continued. The photographer who shot the slides of me long ago was in the room, too. He was agreeing with the agent that I was "unbelievably rude and unprofessional." He walked away from the photo area which was only a few feet from the agent's desk and added, "If we called you once a year, you would be lucky!" and then he dissed my face by saying, "And your photos aren't that great anyways!"

As he continued to yell at me, my eyes began to burn; I could feel the tears coming. I tried my best to hold them in, my lips shivering and my chin trembling.

He said, "Here, take your slides, but they won't help you!"

He showed me the slides and then gave me a few since I did pay my thirty bucks.

I never heard from the little start-up agency again. They sure as hell never heard from me either.

I walked out onto 6th Avenue feeling completely fucked. Then I planned my next move. I needed to stop and get some new panties at H&M urgently, something to make me feel better. Plus I had a meeting with another photographer the next day and I needed some confidence after being verbally bitch slapped, wearing new panties always made me feel hot.

I had a presentation due the following afternoon too; it was for my marketing class final which I hadn't even thought about yet. Luckily, we got to pick a product of our choice for the marketing plan and concept presentation. It sounded sassy and sophisticated, but really it was arts and crafts and I knew most of the kids in the class would show up with cardboard and markers. I chose to create a new energy drink. I made business cards and designed coupons. Then I wrote copy for an ad campaign. I did the best I could with my Photoshop skills. The only thing I could creatively do without a struggle was adjust a photo's size and add some text. But it worked wonders. For a moment I tried to picture myself as a graphic designer or one day really making an ad for a new innovative product. I had even done extra credit and stayed up all night for it, since I waited till the last minute to start it. I was excited to use photos of myself and cropped them. Then I added text around my face and body for the advertising. I made myself into my own ad campaign. Surprisingly, it looked great. If only an agent could have seen it.

The next day I put on my new hot panties from H&M, dropped off my marketing final and met the photographer. He had been published in a magazine before and worked with a couple Giraffes who had been on the covers of Italian and French *Vogue*, which was intimidating at first. He was more experienced than any other photographer I worked with and, apparently, it went to his head.

"Oh, Isobella, look at this one; look at this." With pride, he showed me all of these photographs he had taken in France.

He had the ideas already, and he was excited and spoke in a European accent. He would spit a little as he became more and more excited about his great idea. All I could understand was "an array of colors against your skin." I also got the part that I wouldn't be paid. I would get the images and my makeup done, and I was told I would "just love the shots!" They were shots he said "I really needed for my book."

"Isobella, you have such a pretty face but your shots are not doing you justice!"

My nose did look huge in the picture he was looking at. I sat back in my chair for the first time and let him run the show. He seemed to like that I didn't talk a lot. He liked the feeling of control. I could tell he took control when he fucked a girl, too. No doubt he didn't even care if she came.

Then it was my turn to speak. He showed me pictures of himself that he took when testing the light. "And look! This is the light we will use when we shoot! Isobella, don't you like it? Wow! Isn't it intense?" The light *was* intense but *he* looked awful, posing like a fucking statue in Italy or looking like a goblin.

I didn't know whether he was showing me pictures of himself to turn me on, or hoping he'd receive a compliment from me. Neither happened.

Next he was telling me to stand up and show him how I pose. I got up and stood against a nearby wall. I spread my legs, stood tall, and lifted my arms above my head, elongating my body and giving him a sexy expression, my eyes creased and my mouth half open. He didn't like it. He made a face.

"That's it?"

I stood straight again. I let my arms fall to my side.

Excited, he jumped up and said, "This is how you do it, baby!"

He touched me, moving my body and my arms—showing me how to do it right so I would be prepared the day of the shoot. Yesterday, it seemed I was being bitch slapped and called a Wannabe. Today this photographer was telling me, "When you pose, when you *model*, you need to be the star!"

I listened. I followed his example. I moved my body, angled my neck, my wrist, my hips. I was his rag doll, just doing whatever he said. I think he wished he could have fucked me right that second. I think he wished I was his little slut. But I wasn't.

I took his control as a sign of his seriousness. I thought, *He must be good if he has such a vision.* It was in his style, and the makeup and hair was his choice. He wanted to be the one to wet me down and choose the sexy shoes. To him I was a girl he could boss around and we both knew it.

The following week when the day of shooting was done I was wet, tired, and my hair was very stringy. He had thrown me in a cab five hours earlier; it was one of the first few times I had been in a cab. I was getting comfortable with the subways, and I figured only rich people took cabs. Life on the subway was for the average person and being on the train allowed my mind to wander and for me to relax in a world—in a reality—I could create in my mind.

However on that day, the photographer took me by cab to Bloomingdales for a makeover he said I needed. I tried not to take offence to the comment and just thought of it as a little pampering for myself. I was to get my makeup done, try on shoes, then he bought me makeup and we borrowed a pair of three hundred dollar heels from the store. It was my first time in Bloomingdales and I felt awkward, messy, and inappropriate. The makeup artist could tell by my quiet, mouse-like acceptance.

I had no opinion that day, and for once I let someone else worry about making something of this shoot. The photographer and I spoke before the shoot about shooting some commercial style photos, even though that day he was more into *Maxim* style photos and ripping my shirt and pulling at it to make me look more alluring. He was telling me to tug at it and asking me, telling me, moaning to me, to "look more alive." He was getting very vocal, "Rougher, rougher!"

Of course I did shoot a few topless shots, but then when he got perverted and unprofessional, asking me to go completely nude, I felt differently.

I simply told him, "I'm tired and not in the mood for shooting anymore," but really he scared the shit out of me. Maybe it was his "whiney, little-boy-with-a-pout" expression, but I was really turned off. I told him so.

This wasn't a good comment to make. It wasn't good to make *any* comment to ego-driven photographers, I was quickly learning. He got pissed and stomped his feet, and his little pathetic pout was actually more humorous than mind-changing. I never worked with him again. Plus, I couldn't trust him. He was French, and all he talked about was sex, sex, and more sex. I didn't *feel* sexy around him, *or* powerful.

Instead I felt weak, like I was trapped in his apartment, his bed too close to the backdrop where we were shooting. The lights were off and it was too romantic for a shoot with a guy I wasn't even interested in. I wondered if the door was locked. I think the photographer thought that after buying me expensive shoes and getting my makeup done, I would do anything. That I would pose any way he wanted. He treated me like I owed him.

When I went back the next day I received a CD. I put it in my denim bag from The Gap. He acted like nothing had happened and I thanked him awkwardly, like a good little model should, then I jetted off. I had kept the makeup but foolishly left the three hundred dollar shoes.

By then, I was another week closer to the New Year. I got a D minus on my marketing plan and concept presentation and I was pissed about that. I hated energy drinks anyway. I couldn't believe that fucking professor had just about failed me. I vowed not to tell my mother that I was about to fail my class. I had to keep the mood light.

I went home for Christmas with Danny. This time my mother and sister acted as if nothing had happened over Thanksgiving. I was relieved and tried to forget about my bad grades, too. However, I couldn't relax while being in the living room again. A few dinners with the family and a visit to my grandparents, I was ready to go back to New York City.

I started to think about comp cards and headshots. I spoke to another actor I had met on the computer through American Online. I put "model" + "New York City" + "actor" and he came up in the member directory. He was signed on at that moment, too. I sent him an Instant Message right away. I typed: "Hello, I moved to New York a few months ago, and I'm curious if you have a moment to chat about acting and modeling?" He exchanged his photo with me, and although he had huge dopey ears, I didn't judge. He was really helpful. His was the first real advice I'd ever received.

One night during an Instant Message conversation he told me about the Ross Reports. It was a handy little booklet which lists casting agents and directors in NYC and LA. He said I could find it at Barnes and Noble for about eight bucks. I didn't have a headshot and comp card printed yet, but I did have some photos which could be cropped and made into a headshot, I figured.

I didn't need an agency to get a comp card. The printing company didn't care. They would print a comp card for a bum on the street with a damaged and leaking paper coffee cup. I had researched some printing places on the Internet and went to a printing studio, which was in Union Square at the time. I had them print 100 head shots for 100 dollars. It was a lot of money for me, but the quality was worth it, and while I was there I made a comp card, too. I felt professional with my headshot; regardless if I had no resume; regardless if the shot involved wet hair and a sassy look. I didn't care, being seen was what counted and the headshot was sent out to about fifteen random casting directors who dealt with TV and Films. Suddenly I was spending money on stamps, panties, envelopes, new shoes, and now comp cards and headshots, and I hadn't even booked a real print modeling job in a magazine yet. I was disgusted with how much I had already invested.

After a week I heard back from only one agency. I never met them face to face, and they didn't know me or if I even looked like the photo I sent. They didn't seem to care, from the quick conversation on the phone. I felt like I was involved in a secret mission—ordered to bring proper attire, to arrive at a time and location, and to check in with a person. It was all very cloak and dagger and made me nervous. My head was spinning when I got off the phone. I couldn't even read my own scribbled instructions in my agenda book, even though I had written them thirty seconds before. All I knew was that I was booked on the TV series *Ed* as a background actor. It happened quickly, my first exposure on TV.

I was to be on 96th Street by 6:30 AM sharp to catch a bus to New Jersey to the set of *Ed* that aired on NBC. It was awfully early for me. I couldn't even get up early for this opportunity without hitting my alarm a few times. Then I freaked out because I had slept in ten extra minutes. The agent on the phone had insisted I arrive on time, that it was life or death. Or maybe I just felt like it was life or death. From Brooklyn

Heights it would be a long forty minute commute getting to 96th Street, a serious hike.

I woke up at 5:10 A.M. and raced to catch the subway, hopefully by 5:30 A.M. Danny had stayed the night before, so he went with me to catch the Long Island Rail Road at Penn Station before returning to his school in Farmingdale. I ran, holding his hand and dragging his slow ass behind me. We rushed through the turnstile, ran down the escalator and waited. It was 5:42 A.M. Then it was 5:45 A.M. and the train still hadn't pulled into the High Street Station. I panicked. All I needed was to blow this job because of a fucking New York City subway.

I was pissed, scared, and very nervous. The minutes flew by. I begged God to slow time the fuck down, all the while swearing and jumping around like a chimpanzee. If I missed the bus that was waiting for me on 96th Street, I'd be screwed. I couldn't miss my opportunity. Like a maniac, I ran hot then cold, as I smiled over at Danny. Moments later, I told him I hated New York City. Danny was freaking out, too. He was freaking out that I was freaking out, and I was in tears over being late. Put it this way: The subway was late, and I made the bus with forty-five seconds to spare. I wondered if I was a whole minute late if it would have pulled out of 96th Street and left me crying. So far, my biggest lesson in NYC was how to run in heels, or so it seemed at times.

A few hours later, after two coffees and some stale bagels, I fluttered around the set of *Ed*, saying hello and telling anyone who asked my life story. I didn't bring a cocky attitude, but I did bring a perceptive eye. I acted calm even though it was the first time I had ever been on the set of a TV show. A part of me felt like I had really made it. After all, who would have thought I would be on the set of a TV show when I'd been in New York City for less than six months.

All day, for over nine hours, with a pathetic but standard rate of $75 a day, I was listening to other background actors complain about not being where they wanted to be with their acting. These people were acting as if they were big-shot actors when really they were just background actors like me, who worked for the same lame rate and gave a percent to the agent. When the show aired three weeks later the last scene before a commercial break featured my face. I didn't even know the camera was on me. The background actors were told by the Production Assistant to make a face like "What the Hell?" I guess my confused expression looked pretty real. After seeing my confused face on the TV screen for a full second, I promised myself I would notice where the camera was located and always be more observant of the director.

Following that gig, I was still looking for an agency or agent to represent me. I hadn't heard from the small casting agent since I was a background actor on *Ed*.

Then a promotional company based in Boston advertised on a job Onemodelplacedotcom. They sent me to Talbot's to be a technical shoe model, which meant they would measure my perfect, size six feet. Then someone else would actually model the shoes for the camera. I felt a little gypped. I wanted to be the lucky model they chose to be in front of the camera for the ad campaign, not just the model they measured. I wondered how I could be the face or foot in an ad campaign one day.

Unfortunately the girl in the current ad campaign was a Giraffe; she couldn't have been a size six.

A girl about my age helped out with the measuring. The man she was helping was the designer. They seemed to like my foot and made me stand still for over an hour. Their hands were all over my legs and their faces under my skirt.

They kept writing down different numbers and scratching their noses. I suppose they used the measurements to find the best shape for a shoe design. I felt like they should have asked me to be in their ad campaign. I left feeling depressed—hoping my check for eighty bucks would come soon.

All February long I emailed, I called, and I went to open calls at the real agencies. I went to Next, Elite, Ford, with my black plastic Pearl Paint portfolio and my new comp cards. The agents all told me the same thing every single time: "You need professional photos," and then "There is only so much I can do for you since you're so petite." And then, "I'm sorry, but you're just too short for us." Actually most of them didn't even say anything to me. They barely looked at me and my black book, as if they knew my pictures really did suck as much as I feared they might.

I didn't even consider emailing my mother back when she said "Happy Valentines Day," in an email and sent a card. It was my fat mother who had made me short in the first place.

I was now settling into the second semester of my sophomore year. My professors talked about internships and suggested we get one. I was thinking about a vacation instead.

The fall Miami trips with Wart Man and that one-time photographer, the nice one, inspired me to return to Miami. I had never gone away for spring break, and growing up my family never went on any beachy vacations. I wanted one. I had some cash saved from Christmas but really I had cash from nude modeling mostly.

I told Danny I would handle our flights and hotel, if he wasn't too picky. We stayed above Miami South Beach and below Bal Harbor in North Miami Beach, in a motel that cost only fifty bucks a night where the fan kept rustling all night long. The towels weren't soft and the bed was way too hard, but the beach was right across the busy street.

So that March, for spring break we spent a week relaxing in the sun, shopping, and eating seafood. No photo shoots, nothing related to modeling. Well, I'm lying. I made Danny take some pictures of me. Then I sent him to get me some fruit. Before he left, I turned to him with a little sexy smile and said, "Bring me back a surprise!"

While he was gone, I tanned on the beach topless, just to relax. While I laid there a man came up to me.

"That's so nice."

I thought he was speaking about the weather, but he had stopped with his beach chair right in front of me.

"I hardly ever see that in the U.S. and more often in Spain." I looked up from my magazine. He did have a Spanish accent. I smiled and said nothing.

His comment implied he thought it was cool that I was so

comfortable nude. If only he knew how awkward it really was having this guy looking at my tits. He wasn't bad looking but he looked about forty. I wondered where his wife or girlfriend was staying. I didn't take offense to him being there, but I was kind of shocked at the blunt approach from a man almost as old as my father. Embarrassed, I tried to cover myself with a towel.

It was different if it was a planned and scouted shoot, even if the photographers were perverted during some of the shoots. It was weirder to have some random man walk by and comment on my tits. He walked away, squinting his eyes, maybe to see my nipples more clearly. Then he winked. He had some wrinkles around his eyes and a little sand on his lips. He wasn't a sexy blond surfer, or someone I would like to meet again. He was pure bastard!

Shortly after he left, Danny returned with fruit and a silver necklace with an elephant pendant. I thought of my mother. She loved elephants and collected them. I took the pendant but felt like he was giving me the wrong gift. With a slight smile I place it next to my neck. It was delicate, a charming looking pendant, but I didn't feel radiant wearing it. He helped me put it on.

I didn't tell Danny about the forty year old man's comments. Instead I took a piece of melon from the container and asked Danny to lie on top of me. Like a puppy obeying a command, he did. We swayed back and forth, rubbing our bodies together. I loved how sincere he was with my body. He touched me like I was the only woman he had ever touched, soft and delicate. Then I remembered I *was* the only woman he had ever touched, been inside of, and fingered. We kissed more and I felt him get hard. Although we didn't have sex on the beach, I was feeling very sexual and loved.

For the next half hour while we lay in the sun, I almost forgot about my fake name, my modeling. That is, until I saw a girl with a great ass in a black thong bikini out of the corner of my eye.

As I lay there watching her, I checked my voicemail.

Finally I received a call from a legit modeling agency, an

agency that had been in business for longer than five minutes! I'd never heard from a modeling agency before and I was shocked that it had really happened. I was glad I'd missed the call and it had ended up on my voicemail. What if I had stuttered and sounded like my old, boring, Heather self on the phone?

I checked the voicemail three more times just to hear the words again and again. "Danny, please shut up!" He was trying to offer me a towel. Then some melon. I stood up, trying to give him a clue, waving to him to be quiet. He lay there and scrunched his lips and read my magazine. I looked up at the sky, right into the sun but I didn't mind. Sweat rolled down my cheek, my forehead, dripping like a volcano. I could taste the salty drop on my lips. It tasted good. A drop of sweetness for my anticipation. I swallowed hard.

Like a hawk scouting its prey, I stared at the girl in the black thong bikini with the nice ass. *She* wasn't on the phone at that moment listening to a voicemail from a modeling agency in New York City. "Thank you and please call us back at 212 ..." I pushed replay again. "Thank you and please call us back ..."

I took a bite of the melon and grabbed my magazine from Danny. I hugged him and kissed him again tightly. He might never understand me and my dream of modeling. I carried my excitement with me as I sat quietly in the sun. I wanted so badly to scream my guts out "YES! YES! YES! I'm finally a model!" and raise my fist and clench my teeth to the sky.

But I didn't.

We ate some more melon together. It was delicious, and juice drooled through my teeth. Our silhouettes must have looked like a painting of two lovers at the beach at sunset. Like a postcard that read: "Miss you from Miami!"

I couldn't sit still. My towel was getting very sandy from all my thrashing. I could feel small grains of sand building a sand castle in my crotch. Danny asked, "What's wrong with you?"

I didn't tell him it was the voicemail.

We watched the ocean till we got too hot and then used his father's credit card to buy dinner on Ocean Drive, like the rich.

Danny told me how good my Victoria Secret's Love Spell

perfume smelled on me as we walked around Collins Avenue after dinner.

I considered buying a tiny black thong bikini.

It was weird and ironic how the moment I'd left NYC, I'd finally received the phone call I'd been waiting for forever. I guess it's true, the moment you stop looking for success, it finds you.

Chapter 6

It's What You Know

<u>May 2002: New York City</u>
My goal after my vacation was to shock and intrigue Gene, the agent who had called me in Miami. Not to write essays about the founders of Guess clothing and how the name came from a McDonalds ad. My professor gave me a B minus. I was losing my advertising edge but it didn't matter. I had a little date set up with Gene. On the way to 33rd Street and Park Avenue I had to transfer from the downtown A train at 59th Street to the Shuttle at Times Square and then at Port Authority take the local 6 down to 33rd.

I would make it just in time.

A half hour later, I sat down with Gene from Flaunt Models at 3:12 P.M. He offered me a comfy blue cushioned wooden chair. He was a nice Jewish man who no doubt thought of me as a sexpot, from the look in his eyes. When I first got to the agency a girl about my age answered the door. She had long thick hair and a pretty yellowish tan tweed skirt. She directed me to Gene's office.

Before I sat down and ran my hands through my own long sun kissed hair, he said, "Wow, Isobella, how old are you?"

I took a big gulp. "Umm ...I'm nineteen. My birthday is in September." I sounded like a third grader excited to share my birth date. Then he looked at my teeth, my eyes, my ears, my nose, my breasts. He had to know what he would be pitching if we worked together, I guess.

"So is JaDeco, your real last name?"

Although I had looked in the phone book of New York City's five boroughs I'd found no JaDeco's listed.

"Yes it is!" I lied, as though I'd owned the name since birth. Maybe he would accept me for being ethnic with a sexy last name. I looked at the blond and stiff looking models on the wall. I couldn't mess this up; I was sitting in front of a real agent for once. Days like this were not often.

"Oh ...so is that Latin ...or Italian?" If I said Latin maybe he would consider me for Latin jobs. It was best to be balanced.

"I'm a little of both." He would never really need to know the truth: that I was your typical Italian, all-American, tree-climbing upstate New Yorker.

"Are you signed with any agencies in the city?" he asked.

I said no. Then he gladly took my modeling portfolio and flipped through its cheap pages. He bent it a few times to test its durability.

"You know you better be careful with this. It just might bust!"

I laughed and nodded. Later, after some water and some compliments on my body and my big brown eyes, I told him I would get him more commercial photos. His assistant yelled from the other room, "Gene, you have *Seventeen* on the phone!"

He yelled back, "Okay, one minute."

That was my sign to leave. Before I left, he reached over his office table and kissed me on the cheek. Finally, an agency in New York City had my comp cards and was going to try to use them, even though they were "not efficient enough" or "really selling me the right way," he said.

I hoped he would call with a booking for *Seventeen*. That would be great. Maybe he would tell the editor calling right that second that he had just met with a beautiful model that had a lot of potential, and then he would call me with the great news that I had a job waiting. I couldn't just wait for Gene to call me back.

Inspired by the meeting with Flaunt Models, I wanted

more agencies. I couldn't rely on just one agency with three employees to make my dreams come true.

I went to another agency that week. They were looking for "fresh faces." I figured I was a fresh face. I found them from a posting, an ad on a modeling forum called www.glamourmodels. com. They were located in the meatpacking district. I loved the cobblestone pavement and the vintage look of the crusty brick buildings and the warehouse garage-like restaurants. Unfortunately I would only love the agency for a few weeks.

Mr. Know-It-All with his slick greasy hair, sat behind a desk in a room with only a few posters on the cement wall. He had about twenty photos taped up with clear tape revealing his hopeful Giraffes. I foolishly gave the bastard two hundred dollars.

He counted the twenties and said, "That girl—" and pointed to a photo of a Giraffe with blond hair and nice, curvy breasts—"she was just in *FHM* magazine!"

I was mad to have to pay him. As the model, I was used to getting paid. I looked at my stack of twenties sitting in front of him, and I must have looked a little nervous because he said, "The money will be used for printing costs." I hoped he wouldn't spend it on some dinner he had planned with some Giraffe slut. I focused on the Giraffe's photo on the wall. She was lean, skinny, and had a fake tan. Her nails were painted red and her teeth were perfect.

I wanted to be her. I ignored the fact that I had made my own comp card and that I got headshots and comp cards printed for two hundred bucks myself. He rolled his eyes and huffed, "Your comp card doesn't sell you!" and "We can't use *this* comp card if you want to work with us."

Mr. Know-It-All gave me the comp card back and a plan. "I will need to shoot you. We'll shoot commercial shots outside with real film and we'll make you a brand new, sellable comp card in about three weeks."

I was confused because Gene took my comp card even though it might have looked like shit. Gene at least said he would "try" to work with it.

Now I had no choice. Mr.-Know-It-All's words went right through me. It was as if all the buildings in Manhattan would come crashing down if I didn't say yes. So I had to fork out the cash that I was planning on spending for my first real designer bag, a Kate Spade or a Michael Kors maybe. I was learning all about these names from reading *Vogue* and I really wanted something expensive that I could keep for a lifetime.

Four days later, we shot at a park on Eleventh Avenue; I met him near the highway. I snuck out early of my marketing class that afternoon. I didn't take off any of my clothing and I wore a tan knitted button down sweater from Forever 21, which I really liked. It was all very quick, only about a thirty minute shoot. I leaned against a brick mechanic shop and gave a shy smile. I didn't feel as confident with my clothing on. We used the entire three rolls of film, which I'm sure I paid for. When I posed on the corner of Jane and Washington Street, a dump truck drove by. The guys inside stared out of the windows and one Hispanic guy said, as best he could in English, "What magazine is that for?"

I felt like yelling back, "It's for *Vogue!*"

Although after the shoot, when the photographer asked for more money to get the photos retouched, I felt the guy really wasn't on my side. I didn't want anything to do with the agency anymore, so I deleted their number out of my cell phone. But before I did, I called for my images and I did get my photos this time. I liked a few of them and could even have used them, but I didn't because they reminded me too much of that fucking Mr. Know-It-All.

A few weeks later, I answered another casting I found with a few of the photos from the day with the sexual French freak. This agency had a website and it looked pretty damn professional. The models shown looked ethnic and exotic, and came from countries I had never heard of. All of the Giraffes had really good posture and they looked tall and elegant, pretty much like the fashion agencies and I was sure I would get rejected from my emailed submission. Only I wasn't. My meeting was for 3:00 P.M. and I was to bring any photos I had with me.

When I got there, to my surprise, the agency was located in a young Greek man's apartment. I doubted their potential quickly. A big painting of some Greek goddess gave away his heritage, along with his frisky hands. Even the shady guy in the Meat Packing District had a fucking office! I was already there, so I took a seat and then stood up quickly when he asked to see my body. I don't know what came over me but I even undressed to my bra and panties. He might not have known anyone at a single magazine and probably only read *Playboy* and didn't know any editors or quality photo people I should know. Still just maybe he had one connection, which would be worth my time. I promised myself I would make every encounter count, somehow. If not to excel and get in a magazine then to get some helpful information. I did a few spins and turns and bends wondering what I would learn today.

It was obvious that Gianni, the agent, liked my body and kept saying, "You have such a hot little body." It was an innocent compliment and I took it, but then he kept trying to tickle me. When he stopped, I smiled and huffed with an "I know I'm hot" face. Then I noticed how cold the room was and felt more awkward. His apartment was awfully and purposely cold, maybe. I wondered, *Is he trying to make my nipples hard?*

He said again, "You have such a cute little ass!" Then he went to smack it.

I started to put my jeans back on. For the first time I felt guilty. I was having all of these shoots and encounters, meeting random people in random places, and I wasn't telling Danny about it.

Gianni didn't even have a real name for the agency yet or a business card. He said they just went by Gianni's Models. I wondered who the other part of "they" was. When I met the Gianni a few minutes before, he spoke too fast. I couldn't remember if he was Gianni or Jimmy or Johnny. They would shoot me for free, get me a makeup artist and a stylist, and make me a comp card for free, too! It sounded like a good plan. Like the agency in the Meat Packing District, they were new, aspiring. I figured that's why they'd given me a chance so I decided to take it. I was excited. Any small interest from an agent or photographer excited me. It felt like I finally had someone on my side. I was maybe 5'2" but had a shoot next Wednesday with a fashion photographer. It seemed like everything always landed on a fucking Wednesday, right when I had class! I figured I would miss my class. I sure as hell couldn't be a model while I sat in my advertising class.

The young man who I considered Gianni requested the photographer for me, made the phone call and set it all up. I was impressed. It was the first time everything was already set up and planned. It could be a real chance. The photographer had a French accent, and it scared me that if it might have been that jerk that took me to Bloomingdales and made me get naked. Flashes of his stout and his tiny apartment came back to me. And the shoes I wish I stole. The message on my phone said: "Hey, Isobella, we're shooting next week and I want you to meet me over at the stylist's apartment on West 4th Street." I knew that area from shopping for sexy underwear; I grabbed my agenda book and quickly wrote it down. Then I replayed the message five times to get it right, convincing myself that it wasn't him.

That weekend I went to New Jersey with Danny again. This time we went to Temple and afterward made love in a park on a park bench. I told him, "Don't worry no one will see us!" He was interested, so I kept him interested by saying, "And what's the worst that can happen? We might get kicked out." He agreed it was a good idea.

It was really sexy sex. We had to sneak by a town house to get to the bench. I wondered if the owners were looking through their widows at that instant watching Danny and I fuck slowly on the bench.

It was freezing outside, but Danny's huge down jacket kept me warm. He pressed his body against mine and I wished he would say, "You have such a hot little body!" but he didn't.

The following Wednesday I met the French photographer, right on time. He wasn't familiar thank God, and was about thirty-five or so and wore a suede jacket. Before I could touch the suede of his jacket from a hug, I was thrown into a makeup chair and beat by the makeup brush for forty minutes. The makeup artist was Russian and not friendly. She told me her name was Ivy, but I doubted it. Ivy sounded like a name of a girl who brushed her hair 100 times a day. This Ivy had blond, teased, permed hair. It did look like dead ivy leaves. A chunk was dyed blue.

I think she knew it was one of the first times I'd ever had makeup put on because I didn't know which way to look when she did the mascara. She kept saying, "Up up, up," and then, "Down, down, down."

I was getting dizzy, and I was tired of being scolded for looking the wrong way.

Afterwards, I did look hot though.

Then the French photographer just said, "Mmmm ...uh-huh." He told me we had to leave and took over. We jumped in a cab and I got to see New York City again from a new perspective. I loved it when we drove by the Met Life building. We shot on the steps of the Metropolitan Museum of Art, and in the street with the traffic flying by like race cars. I had never been to the museum but now I really wanted to go. The shots were fantastic. I could feel it, and it was fashion with an editorial appeal, he said. What ever "editorial" defined, it had to be something brilliant. The shots seemed very classy, the makeup perfect. I was beautiful. And for education purposes I could consider that I was getting exposed to international people for the first time.

In the street, posing, I felt like a real model, not another Internet Wannabe. At last! Cars honked at me, and men were staring. A few cabbies yelled at me through the cab window saying, "Yeah baby!"

A couple of days later, I saw the slides and they actually looked great. I called the Greek apartment two weeks later and the telephone line was disconnected. The photographer never returned my calls and I never got the pictures. Fuck, I'd wasted my time again, and I was burning pissed. Something was damning me from above or laughing at me from below.

To make matters worse, time was ticking by too quickly. Gene's agency was the only one that would give me the time of day; he wasn't calling fast enough with castings, bookings, and jobs.

April had gone by and most of it was spent running in between my college classes and not going on one casting. I did stop by a loft not far from my college on 57th Street often though. Frances had just returned to New York City from London and he was testing models. I found him, like all the others, on Onemodelplace.com. His work was decent, but he was still testing himself as a photographer and figuring out his style. Being with him was quiet and he would make me warm delicious green tea, I would sip it standing in the hallway in lingerie. Or I would be lounging on the couch butt naked as he poured me some wine. It was a relaxing shoot.

We shot often, Frances and me. He had a nice apartment, big; it looked expensive with a doorman and balcony. It also had a great view of the Hudson River and the Upper West Side. We shot outdoors on the patio and I felt time stop. Over the next few weeks, I fell in love shooting with him. I didn't think about fucking him but he was good looking, which made our shoots more fun. Frances was pushing thirty-five maybe, but he had a young side and a beautiful smile. I had a crush on him during our sessions.

I wondered sometimes, what he would be like to kiss. He modeled when he was younger so being a photographer was just his way of testing the other side. He was married and his wife worked during the day. She and I had the same name—well hers was real while mine was fake. I didn't tell him though. He was never suggestive and never forced me to get naked. However, my attraction to him made it easy to get naked. He would play music, a few tunes I knew from Elton John and Billy Joel.

He was always professional, handsome, shirt pressed.

I felt beautiful around him. He wasn't paying me but I didn't mind.

I shot nude on his couch. It was a little rough but he showed me each shot after we took it, on his camera screen. After I approved the photograph, we would talk about our plans and how hard it all was, and I would mention Danny, and school, and where I was from. Then later, after he was more experienced, I planned a shoot with him again—this time with a makeup artist and a hairstylist, and in a studio he was going to rent.

That morning, it was way too early and I was very tired. I had been drinking coffee from the street stand and had coffee breath. I gave Frances a hug and quick kiss on the both cheeks, like I noticed the Giraffes do, and I slumped into the makeup chair without my normal spunk. Maybe it was the fight I just had with Danny that had slowed me down. He was on my mind. I couldn't get over the fact that he had a "girl" friend. Shit, I had like a thousand guy friends and now a million photographers on my list it seemed. And yet I was still upset at him after our fight in New Jersey.

He had a flight lesson at a New Jersey airport, way in the boonies. I already felt way in the boonies being in Voorhees, New Jersey, for Christ sake. It started when I was going through Danny's email while he was in the bathroom. I found an email from a girl named Stacey. I was so enraged.

"What are you talking about?"

Maybe I was crazy for asking about her. Besides, he didn't look guilty of cheating on me. Still, I couldn't be sure.

"She has a boyfriend."

I had a boyfriend but I still ended up naked at photographers' apartments, basements and rooftops.

"What does she look like?"

"She's cute. She has long blond hair, and she's a little bigger than you." He said cute. Cute! God I wanted to kill him.

When we had sex that night in the basement while his mother was reading two flights above us, I wondered if Danny was thinking about Stacey. I hoped that my long hair in his face wouldn't make him think of *her.*

Or maybe it was my mother bitching at me for spending all my cash on everything but food. Now I needed more of her money for food that week and a Metro Card, too. "Why do I have to keep giving you money?" She never could just "understand"

and give me the money I needed. I knew she didn't have it, but I did need it to get a MetroCard. She hadn't even complimented me on the photos I emailed her, and I was fully clothed.

Maybe I was just really pooped.

Now, back in the makeup chair and recalling our fight, I was still feeling ticked. It didn't help matters that the makeup artist was not the prettiest thing to look at. When I told her how I used hand cream on my face, she looked at me with disgust. Then she accused me of having dandruff and I wanted to stick the brush up her fucking ass.

She poked me in the eye with the eyeliner and my eyes watered. Then she handed me a tissue and, by mistake, it brushed against my mascara and left a black smudge across my eyebrow. Around her I became a klutz and felt greasy.

After she cleaned my face up we did the shoot.

Frances told me I looked great even though the bitch told him I had dandruff. I said with a coy voice including a little sass, "I do not!" She looked at him and then me and walked away.

He was going to shoot black and white, which would make the photos look like they were out of the 1950s. That was his goal.

To this day they are some of the best photos taken of me. I was just sitting with my legs apart, making a face like "what the fuck are you looking at?" I was wearing my Calvin Klein panties and a white wrap top, staring at the camera like a possessed alien. My legs looked very long—I could feel it—my torso high and my face serious. A simple, yet powerful shot, really model-like, which I knew would stay in my book for years.

With dark eyes, quiet expression, and strong lips, I looked glamorous. When someone doubted my modeling background, I'd have them look at my book. It was the first shot I flipped to.

Frances was starting to work with Giraffes and he was testing for fashion magazines. One on his desk was a new one to my eyes called Nylon. I felt very short around him suddenly. We didn't shoot anymore.

It was already May and school would soon be out. A year

of school had already gone by. I didn't know whether I felt productive or like shit. After contemplating the year, I decided I felt like shit. It had been ten months, and yet I had only one agent, only one real exposure on TV, which lasted one tenth of a second. Then there were the two handfuls of photo shoots that were a waste of fucking time. There must be away to get serious.

For now, I had finals. The thought of caring about my grade over my modeling was like taking my plans to be a model and pitching them to the flame, then roasting them into oblivion.

Thankfully I just needed to pass. Then I had the summer to play without restrictions or schedules or classes or professors.

Before the summer, and before I had my 2.5 grade point average and my mother bitching at me, I found a casting posted on another modeling forum site.

I said I would never consider postings like that again, but the chance for it to turn out good this time was on my mind. Plus Gene hadn't called me at all yet and it had been a whole month. Maybe it was my fault and I needed to give him better pictures? I didn't know but having an agent wasn't going to make me a model alone or maybe I just needed more of them.

On the train ride to the Upper East Side that afternoon, a man with a cane was singing. He was blind and making his way through the cars. He was singing about rubbing a girl's body. I wondered if he'd ever had sex in his life. For the way he sang with his heart, someone should have fucked him. He was a little whiney, but he was blind and most likely a little deaf too. Still, he never missed a beat. He only tripped over three people. And they were in his way. While he sang and tripped and used his cane to feel around the subway poles, he would include the friendly, "excuse me, sorry," into the song. I didn't have any dollars on me to give him a token of my appreciation for the easy-going melody, but I wished I did.

I missed my stop because I was focusing so hard on the blind man. I backtracked and got off the 4 train at the 59th Street stop. I then ran. I had to get all the way past Park, past 2nd and

1st Avenue. It was the furthest I had ever been over on the East side. I was all the way over in the boonies. On York Avenue.

I could tell by the huge tittied girl who answered the door that the agency was based on *Playboy*-style modeling. My little breasts felt out of place and seemed to shrink from embarrassment. Still, he looked past my small chest and called me beautiful the moment I walked into his room. He might have been a man with connections, a famous New York agent at one point, or a pimp or doctor, for that matter. But for now, he looked like Mr. Death-Bed. He sat there, unable to move his arms, fingers, or legs, and his head fell forward, the skin around his chin and neck was the only thing holding him together.

I felt bad for him. I had just seen the blind man on the subway and now I was facing death right in front of me. The pretty brunette, who was helping him, left the room when I came in.

Alone with Mr. Death-Bed, I watched as he tried to hold my portfolio but his forefinger couldn't hold it upright. I helped, trying not to make him feel any more helpless than he was already. He could hear and speak, but not well.

He asked, "So how long have you been modeling?"

I tried to answer him as quickly as possible saying, "I'm a college student—I was a track runner—I live in Brooklyn and I love New York City!"

I hoped he wouldn't die on me in mid-thought.

On the wall were photos of about a thousand beautiful big tittied girls, some Giraffes, mostly Wannabes and they wrote notes like "You are my shining star!" or "Thank you so much for the *Playboy* test!" Or "I hope to see you soon, xoxo."

I wondered if one day I would write him a note like that and he would put it on his wall, too. He told me I had a great body and "it's ok that you don't have big breasts."

Mr. Death-Bed wanted me to succeed, I could just feel it. He said, "You should meet Robert Milazzo. He is testing models."

Then, just as I was feeling special and like I had a chance from meeting this guy, maybe an angel who was about to face death, another girl came strutting in. She was tall, with Giraffe proportions, a bigger ass and chest, and long red hair. I gave her a glance but focused on Mr. Death-Bed who was obviously turned on by seeing her, since he wasn't looking at me anymore.

He said, "Wow, hello Red!'

I was pretty aware of beauty, but she was all tits. Suddenly, I had my doubts about Mr. Death-Bed. I didn't like how he could say the same thing to some tall, red-headed bitch he had me. I was trying to give the red-headed bitch some space on the couch, but I sat closer to Mr. Death-Bed. She would have to work her way up. Mr. Death-Bed wasn't done with me though.

Mr. Death-Bed's eyes watered, and I offered him a tissue. He said "no thanks"

and rubbed his eye with his forefinger, which wasn't working properly. I tried not to look him in the eye. It was just so gross to look at him, all red, pealing and crusted, old and sad looking.

When I left, I gave him a small hug. I hoped I would never see him again. I was off to see a photographer he had told me about. He said, "You have to go right now!"

I was thankful ...and skeptical.

Since he was sending me to see someone, compared to me just showing up at some photographer's office, I went. Getting a referral could mean all the difference. I wondered if Miss Sexy Red-headed Bitch would end up at Robert's, too.

About twenty minutes later, I met Robert Milazzo.

Immediately upon entering the studio, I considered him a pro. I could hear movement all around. Success happened here, I just knew it. I'd finally entered a real New York City Professional Photo Studio.

The studio was all his and it was unlike anything I had ever seen before. There were even drinks and food and snacks.

"You can have a drink if you want." He offered me a Coke. I took it. Then he told me to wait and handed me his portfolio to scan.

I sipped my Coke and watched him shoot away.

His work was sexy and he was very into being edgy and

each shot had a fantasy feel, he had shot plenty of celebrities and soap opera actors.

Robert was very busy and bustling around. For a moment, I wondered if I should leave. He was so consumed, seemingly uninterested in me. He was captured by a dark eyed, tanned, stiletto-wearing, skin-showing model. She wasn't a Giraffe but she had massive breasts. To my delight, he had taken a moment from *her* shoot to greet *me*.

While Robert was busy, his studio partner Alex took a Polaroid of me and then told me to call them back in a few weeks. He was legit, the first real photographer I had met. I felt honored, like I had a chance just by being in the studio. I couldn't wait for those few weeks to be over.

I saw what professional should be after I met Robert, and over the years he has become a wonderful and supportive friend. But at the time he was a master and someone I had to impress to win his attention. He wasn't going to shoot just anyone.

He didn't intend on shooting me right away, I could tell, because I always called him. He never called me. Finally the day we were supposed to shoot I canceled.

Danny and I were arguing about how much time he spent smoking pot and not making out with me. He was standing in my dorm room saying, "I'm here, in this fucking dirty place!" He was pissed, too. "I'm here in New York City and I hate New York City!"

I didn't want to go to a photo shoot that day all frustrated and pissed. I especially didn't want to disappoint Robert. So I rescheduled. I felt like shit. Very unprofessional to let Danny ruin my shoot.

Robert later told me he was surprised to get my call to plan another shoot. He said "Most people that cancel never call back." But no one in New York was as aggressive as me. Danny might have fucked up my shoot but I would always come ringing, running, and begging to reschedule, especially with Robert Milazzo—a real photographer.

We did reschedule but he didn't plan to shoot me. I wasn't worth his time yet. He wanted Alex to shoot me. I reluctantly agreed. I just wanted to be back in the presence of that photo studio with the cool refreshing Coca Cola waiting for me.

He said, "It will be a test shoot so bring whatever clothing you want. Bring some lingerie." I wrote everything down and when I was about to hang up and say, "Thank you," he said, "One more thing. There won't be a makeup artist so you'll have to bring your own, but we do have some makeup here, too."

It was only a test shoot. He obviously didn't even know if I knew how to model. All he had was a small Polaroid of my cheesy face to judge. I would have thought I sucked too, from that photo. I felt like I was getting the shaft when he said Alex would shoot me.

Fortunately, that day Alex was working on a project on the computer, so Robert grabbed the camera and we started shooting. Robert was vocal and I was by then used to photographers being vocal. So when he yelled, "Yes, yes, more, more, turn your head over your shoulder," I knew just what to do.

I had on a mesh black tee shirt which showed my nipples. I'd found it in the box of "sexy stuff" Robert offered me to look through. He didn't say I could keep it, so I put it back in the bin when we were done. I wet my hair with a hairspray bottle and added some dark black eyeliner. The rest was my natural self. I had a thong on and that was as naked as I got.

Afterward, he downloaded the images right away, and we sat together and looked at the photos on the computer. He handed me a CD of the images before I left and before the elevator door closed he spoke fast. "You did really well. Call us after you've viewed the photos on your own and let us know which ones you like best."

I had pleased him. I took the rickety elevator down three floors and pushed the door open onto 29th Street. It was a really sunny day and summer was coming I could just feel it. I knew there would be many shoots to follow.

Over the next few weeks, Robert became a friend, a confidante, a person who could give me his honest opinion and answer my silly questions about modeling. Over a few months he helped me find my strengths, and forced me to focus on what I had instead of what I didn't ...height. He soon became the only photographer I was comfortable posing nude with. I didn't know how I had been willing to bare it all so nonchalantly before.

Suddenly I needed to be comfortable, feel comfortable, and I was aware of my feelings at a meeting or a shoot. My instincts warned me when a photographer was being an asshole.

I needed to be able to trust the photographer more often, so I stopped using Onemodelplace.com like an obsession and instead took Robert's advice and mailed my shots out to a few commercial print agencies he suggested.

Now I had a place where I could go to get creative. Robert at one time was an art director at an advertising agency before he chose to live a freelance photographer's life.

We would discuss ideas and plan shoots. Girls, Wannabes, Giraffes, girls of all kinds would stop by Robert's studio. I wasn't worried though. Most of them would come from Mr. Death-Bed's office. A few came from other agencies that I'd heard of and had only dreamed about. Alex would greet them. I would stare and offer them a drink like a waitress and then listen to them say, "Oh I just want to model. I just want to be in *Playboy*."

I wanted to puke.

Most came in with big, massive tits and no ass. They were sexy, and Robert of course, as a man, liked that. If I was him, I would have shot them, too. Although, most of the time I only saw these air-headed Wannabes and Giraffes, once or twice and that's it. They came in, planned a shoot, and then they shot and left with their CDs, even Robert knew they didn't have a chance beyond the Internet. I liked that we were on the same page, that I had someone who I could debate my own chances too.

I only had to take one class to stay the summer in the dorms. I convinced my mother it would help me to graduate in four years and stay focused if I stayed in Brooklyn Heights for the summer and took a painting class and an astronomy class too. I didn't have a lot of friends in the dorms and Maryam went home for the summer but spending it in upstate New York was a very mind-numbing thought.

As a loyal girlfriend, I would sit shotgun on the weekends with Danny to New Jersey to eat more Jewish bread. Then as soon as I could escape I would meet up with Robert and Alex wherever they were and soon feel accepted again. I spent time researching other photographers too, since I still needed practice, diversity, and more shots for my portfolio, and Robert wasn't always available just for me. I figured every three months I needed a new comp card to mail out to agents and try again and again and again. Gene had recently sent me out on a shoe modeling job for Calvin Klein, but the shoe didn't fit. It was the first time I had seen other models at a casting. The Giraffes stood all together in a herd. I stood behind them towards the end of the line.

A few of them shared their latest tear sheet and giggled over how easy it was to get. Or maybe they were just giggling about the weather, but I felt like shit with my flimsy, cracked, black portfolio. When it was my turn, three Giraffes were standing behind me. The two who had just gone fit the shoe perfectly, and the women who was fitting each girl's foot smiled and said, "Thanks for coming!" as if she really meant it. Then she turned to me and took my black portfolio, gave it a very quick glance and held the shoe up. She asked me to place my foot in it.

It was my chance to be Cinderella and I failed. There was no prince charming. My lack of a pedicure might have been the reason that my foot didn't fit into the fucking shoe and the reason why every Giraffe there seemed to fit it perfectly.

After that casting, I didn't hear from Gene for awhile.

I told Robert how upset I was. He said, "How about I take some photos of your feet and hands so you can be a body part model?" I wondered what he meant by a body part model.

Around this time, Danny and I got in a massive fight. He was basically on his last branch and barely hanging on. He was fed up with my attitude, my itchiness, my constant need to talk about myself, and even though his dorm room walls were covered in photos of me, and even though I had been a model for almost a year, he still hated my modeling.

My chest hurt, and my stomach fluttered. I felt like I lost everything when Danny told me we were over. It happened when we were waiting for the A train again at the High Street train station. He was visiting me and he couldn't stop saying how much he hated New York.

I snapped back, "Well maybe I hate you!"

I had to meet my astronomy class Uptown at a museum and I was late. Danny was coming with me because, even though it was a college class, he was studying to be a pilot at his school so what was the difference? My professor said I could bring him along.

I always got cranky and felt out of control when I was forced to be still. When the train wasn't coming quick enough, a wave of panic would hit me.

"Calm down," he said.

"Well, you're fucking annoying, and you've never supported me and my modeling in the first place!" I wasn't done.

He started to walk away and didn't turn around. He was headed to my dorm room, but when I caught up to him I refused to open the door.

He just stood there and we argued again. "Please don't leave me," I told him over and over, crying because I knew what was coming. I knew if I opened the door, he would run in, grab his bag of clothing and pot, and be out the door in a flash. He did just that when I did finally open the door while holding his sleeve. He dragged me part way down the hall. My heels couldn't dig deep enough into the carpet to stop him. I let go.

I didn't follow him until a few minutes later. I thought he would come back, say he was sorry. Then I would say I was sorry, and we would make up and have sex.

But he didn't. I walked all over Brooklyn Heights trying to find him. Later that day, I found him by the promenade reading one of his heavy flight books. He looked peaceful. I sat down next to him, saying nothing.

He said, "I don't want to talk to you for a few days."

I said, "Okay, well ...I still want to talk to you."

Danny didn't make eye contact or take my hand when I touched his fingers. He brushed my hand away like I was a fly, and continued reading. I felt like a fly. More like a rat.

For a few days I didn't eat or sleep, and I was so upset by his abrupt words. After the third night without a "goodnight," I had to talk to him. When I called for—no joke—the seventeenth time, he finally answered and said I could come the next morning. I didn't sleep. I hadn't been sleeping for days. In the morning I forgot about my afternoon painting class and caught the 6:00 A.M. train to Trenton, then Philly, and then another train to Southern New Jersey, Cherry Hill. It was a two hour train ride.

I only got as far as Trenton. I got sick on the train and had to be hospitalized for dehydration and anxiety. Modeling had never put me in the hospital, but my crushed heart did. I couldn't believe he had hurt me so much. While I had been holding up a shield against all the perverted photographers who won my nudity as an afternoon pleasure, I had forgotten that I was insecure without Danny. I needed him to feel alive.

However, I was stuck to a tube pumping sugar back into my dehydrated body and I had to pee. When I finally got out, Danny read books about instrument flying and he had a flight lesson. The routine was murdering me and my creative juices. Although we made up, he seemed pissed that he had to drive from Southern New Jersey all the way to Trenton. Still, we made love in the basement. I didn't cum but he did, and when he grabbed my ass tight as he came, things seemed back to normal. Unfortunately, as if I didn't feel out of place already in New Jersey, I was the talk of the weekend for the family. The talk was about "my health and how I couldn't take care of myself." Everything I didn't want to hear.

Each hour of that weekend I hated his mother more and more. She was fat and kept giving me tips saying, "You really should learn to cook." As if I was going to make a pot roast in my dorm room.

To ease the tension, I went to Temple, with Danny and

his mother and father. We acted as though we were prude, but when Danny's mother wasn't looking, I rubbed his crotch. Also, when he wasn't looking, I prayed to god. My own god. Under my breath I mouthed, "Please keep me focused. Please don't let me get sucked into the bullshit of being normal, bland and boring. God, please help me become more of a model!"

The next two days in New Jersey almost sent me back to the hospital with a heart attack from pacing the town like suburban dorks. I had to get back to New York fast.

A week before, I had planned a shoot with Robert at the beach. Fortunately, when I returned to New York, he had a rental car waiting.

Only a couple days before, I'd had tubes and a piss pan near me at the hospital. Now I felt hotter than Pamela Anderson just thinking about being in a bikini at the beach.

The summer was almost over. I didn't have much to show for it besides a hospital bill and some paintings of trees and the lake near Danny's parents'. I guess if you judged me based upon my modeling credits and my college credits, I was more of a student than I was a model. That would change though, in the middle of August.

Robert told me he was working with a magazine called *Women's World*. A thrill of excitement raced up my spine. My eyes widened and got wet. I had shown my ass and every body part, even my insides, for the past year and the clock was now striking for me! It would be my first tear sheet and I would be turning twenty in a few weeks. He warned me ahead of time that it was conservative and that I would have to keep my clothes on for the shoot. He knew and I knew that might be a little weird, but it would be for a national magazine. If only Danny were here to share it with me. Maybe I could finally convince him after the shoot that modeling was a good thing. I had an agent now;(even if he never called), I had successfully met a quality photographer, Robert. Now, all I needed was Danny to care.

It was a year since my first shoot in Syracuse and I walked

into the hair salon with my heart racing. I felt hot all over. I figured I must be hours late, but it was only five minutes or so. Queens was a mess to find again.

There was hope for me today though. I forgot about my mother, my sister and my father who, last I heard, was buying and selling old bicycles for fifteen bucks, as I waited for Robert at the salon and my chance to finally be photographed in a national magazine. Funny, all it had taken was meeting Robert. I had flipped through three hair magazines when Robert appeared. I felt like I had rushed for nothing. I hated sweating over nothing.

I noticed the wrinkles on the faces of the women sitting next to me also waiting for Robert. They were not models at all, with their double chins and wearing baggy jeans that went up to their ribs and over their bellies, looking desperate for the "makeover," that they really needed, but it didn't burst my balloon. This was the day I had been waiting for all along, even before I knew I was waiting for this day, it was waiting for me. First my photo was taken. The scary "Before Shot." I looked at myself in the mirror afterward. I tried to duplicate the smile I gave Robert a moment ago, to imagine how it would look. I decided it would look really scary, despite the fact I was the prettiest, youngest one there.

I was told I would get bangs and a haircut. The stylist said, "I want to correct your big forehead." I tried to feel good about myself, but she was making it hard.

She kept saying, "It's big, it's big, and you have a long face."

I told her I was Italian, as if that would explain my big forehead. I felt self-conscious like I did around the Giraffes or any tall women. Then I agreed that bangs would make my eyes more of a focus. I looked at my eyes and they were my best feature after-all. She gave me an "I told you so" look. I remembered back to all my photo shoots and thought, *"Maybe all the photographers thought I had a big forehead."*

I hadn't had my hair cut in over a year. As a result, I had split ends galore. I had grown up with my mother cutting my hair. The hairstylist played with my hair. She told me she was, "feeling the texture of my hair," whatever that meant. She stroked my hair ends and my scalp. It felt good. She started cutting slowly. Wow, I didn't even see her get the scissors, and here she was already cutting away and making my bangs a masterpiece, like in the movie, *Edward Scissorhands*.

I got a nervous feeling as I watched my forehead disappear. Then she asked, "Am I hurting you?" I knew she was cutting more than I wanted on purpose. As I watched my hair fall to the ground, I wanted to say, "A lot."

I thought about my mother braiding my hair in elementary school. She would work so hard on making my French braid perfect, and if I saw one bump I would rip it and yell at her. Even then, I was a terrible daughter.

After my bangs were cut and my hair was trimmed I did feel better. Almost like a goddess, but not quite. I was still bummed over my big forehead as I checked out the other ladies. They were looking better—younger, too. I felt the opposite: older and more mature with my new look.

I wished I was in a commercial for Herbal Essence and the voice-over would say, "Doesn't she have beautiful, luscious, voluminous hair, isn't she's radiant!"

Next my eyebrows were attacked and shaped. Robert took a few photos of the hairdresser also tweezing my bushy eyebrows. After the comment about my forehead, I didn't feel so special. I felt dirty because I thought models were supposed to be perfect.

I wondered if Robert would think less of me and my bushy face and big forehead.

Then before I got on set to shoot the headshot for the magazine, the makeup artist applied red lipstick to match my shirt. The shirt was mine. I was given nothing to wear but Robert told me that the magazine might "say" the clothing and jewelry were from Lerner. I never shopped there. Old ladies shopped there. I started to wonder what type of old lady magazine I was involved with.

He took a few more shots of my eyebrows and told me it

was for the editorial. He told me they would add a story that would show "how to make eyes appear more vibrant." Oh god, I really felt gross then.

As if I was once again posing in lingerie with the French asshole who took me to Bloomingdales, I obeyed Robert's every word with a smile and a nod.

After watching the other women's makeovers, I knew I wasn't desperate for a makeover. I accepted my flaws. Besides, I had a greater purpose for being here, even though I didn't tell anyone how much I was bursting inside, imagining the tear sheet. I was so absorbed in the excitement of finally knowing what a professional shoot felt like, that I could ignore everything else. Even if I *was* with the ladies of the neighborhood sewing club.

When it was my turn for the "big makeover shot," Robert put together some extra rolls of headshots for me to keep. I felt like he secretly gave me the royal treatment as if to say sorry for being beaten by the tweezers and hairdresser. It wasn't a paid job, but it wasn't about the money. It was about becoming a model in a magazine.

I now could say I really was a model. I would have a tangible way of proving it to my friends and to Danny. More importantly, I finally felt like one and I would have something to show my mother.

Chapter 7

Will the Tiniest Model in New York Please Stand Up

October 2002: New York City
For a photographer, Robert seemed to be getting me more gigs than anyone, even if it was just one. My junior year had been in session for a month and now on Tuesdays I had History from 11:10 A.M. to 12:35 P.M., which usually made me think of my own history and what I was doing to be remembered one day. Then to calm down I usually met Maryam for lunch or to feel productive I went to Barnes and Noble to look through magazines around 65th Street, or I went to Robert's Studio. I had to go there today. It was the only place I ever felt honest. I had to rush whatever I had to say though because I had Business Writing from 2:30 P.M. to 3:45 P.M.

Robert kept telling me I should be an actress too and use my personality. I wanted to sign up for an acting class. I wanted to be the next Guess girl too. Then after another photo shoot I mentioned how hard it was to find something sexy to wear that fit my tiny body. He had a lot of cloth and fabric at the studio used for backdrops and suggested I make a bikini myself. I thought about it. He wanted me to be so many things. I was working as a sandwich sampler girl at Cosi, a few times a week and I made sixty bucks each shift. It felt good to do something normal. Next door to the café there was a women's clothing store and I was thinking about modeling for Casual Corner. Everything all around me was somehow inspiring and

I contacted the corporate number; I considered mailing some shots that looked like their catalogs. I would wait until I had some though.

Robert thought I was a genius to call the corporate number myself but I shot down his idea about an acting class. It would cost over $100 dollars and that was money I didn't have. Besides, I was an actress everyday trying to be a model. I didn't need more classes or teachers in my life.

It was difficult to find a modeling job that equaled *Women's World*, which hadn't even come out yet. I had been hunting for it every week at Barnes and Noble.

My visits to the magazine section had inspired me to think about Robert's words about making my own bikini. Since it was fall, the magazines at Barnes and Noble didn't have any bikini's inside so I looked into my older collections of *Vogue* and I even read through some of the *Victoria Secret* catalogs to get inspired.

I started creating one design that night in my dorm room. I figured a bikini or a thong would be best to make. I grabbed one of my oldest cotton panties I never wore anymore and cut it up. What was left appeared to be just a triangle piece and two pieces of elastic. It seemed simple enough. I looked through my clothing deciding what would be good to ruin or distort and destroy to make into a bikini bottom. I cut and ripped up my old jeans. I started with no skill and no sewing machine but I needed something to keep the pieces together so the next afternoon I went to Pearl Paint and bought a glue gun. It would help to keep the pieces together that evening when I had measured myself but without a measuring tape, just by using my fingered width to figure out how long a thin piece of denim should be to cover my crotch and in-between my legs. I put the denim up to my bikini line, then to my ass, standing on my small stool and looking in my bathroom mirror in my dorm room. I measured with my fingers how long the elastic waist of a pair of panties I owned was. I didn't have ruler. I didn't want to buy one. I wasn't trying to be Chanel. By 2 A.M., I had a beautiful denim bikini bottom with glued on sequins and beads.

The next day I excitedly called Robert and even though he was shooting someone else, I begged for an hour of his time. After the shoot, with a CD of images in hand, I rushed down to Canal Street to get a portfolio book for my bikini design photos. I would make a separate book for them, because I was multi faceted now.

Then I jumped on a train going back uptown to Penn Station to meet Danny for the weekend. I wanted to badly print up some of my bikini design photos but I couldn't do that trapped in between another tortuous visit surrounded by his mother. That weekend, out of the phone lines of New Jersey, I received a call from a casting director I met through mailing my photos out to random casting directors. After convincing Danny to drive me, I met him at Barnes and Noble. I was getting used to meeting strangers in random sketchy places and Barnes and Noble was innocent enough. It was the first time I met a casting director face to face.

Danny looked up flight books and held a grudge for making him wait while I met with the casting director in the Starbucks coffee shop.

He asked, "So how long have you been acting?" I had no experience besides that background work on the TV show *Ed*.

"I haven't been. I never have." Shit. I should have mentioned that small feature of my face for a tenth of a second on *Ed*.

"Well you have a very diverse look. You seem to have a lot of range!" He was speaking seriously and I left him a few comp cards and a headshot.

I met Danny afterwards and he scowled, "Was he flirting with you?"

A week later the casting director called to tell me a student at NYU needed an actress for a short skit the next morning. He said urgently, "You need to meet with him tonight."

I was the actress chosen for the part. I got nervous. I had never acted in my life (besides everyday to photographers pretending that I was the next supermodel).

He said with excitement in his voice, "I already sent him

your photo but bring a couple anyways." I wrote down the phone number of the student in my pink agenda book and forgot about studying for my History test.

I met with the student only a few hours later and I rehearsed with him the lines and then I was back to see him again at 8 A.M. I didn't have a lot of time to prepare and I was very nervous. I was scared of the real cameras, a real script. At NYU. It seemed like Paramount couldn't have been better at that moment.

The student had said, "It's a three minute comedy skit, similar to something on *Saturday Night Live*." That sounded easy and interesting.

"You'll be the lead and the only actor. The character is a loud and angry girlfriend confronting her cheating boyfriend. Except the boyfriend was a bobble head doll."

It sounded a little like bullshit. I said to myself sarcastically, "What an opportunity this is ... I would be yelling at a doll?" Still I figured, *What the hell.* It was a role.

The next morning it was just me screaming and yelling, pulling my hair out over this bastard, and banging on the table, in a rage, screaming, "WHY DID YOU DO THIS TO ME, HOW COULD YOU?" as my lover's head bobbled up and down. NYU had really kick ass equipment. It felt as if I was on my own TV show, I actually thought I was on *Saturday Night Live* for a moment when the lights turned on. They were bright lights and the laughter from a few camera guys encouraged me. They filmed it at different angles and I had to fake cry a few times. It was more difficult than I thought. And I think I did a terrible job. I felt like a bad actress on a soap opera but it was a learning experience and it tested me against pressure. Before I left the student said, "Don't worry. You were supposed to be a bad actress." I didn't know whether I accomplished my goal or not. I didn't think yelling at a doll could be credible.

Unfortunately a few months later I would be screaming those words at my real life boyfriend.

That week I thought I killed Danny's mother. She called

Danny's room and I massaged his balls while he spoke to her. The conversation on his end was, "No she isn't here."

"Oh really."

"What does it look like?"

"What is she wearing?" Danny voice was serious.

"Okay, I'll tell her. Thanks, Mom."

I thought she saw a naked photo of me on the Internet. She was always in front of the computer when I visited in New Jersey. She already thought I was too skinny, couldn't cook, and was lazy because I slept till noon. I knew if she saw me nude it would give her a heart attack. During the phone call I imagined her looking at my naked skin on her computer screen and then her heart would stop right there from the looks of my little titties and my ass sticking out.

When he hung up I found out she called about *Women's World* Magazine. It was October 8, 2002. It was the best day of my life!

She was the first to see it. Even before my own mother. I had no idea it was out, I couldn't believe I was such an airhead! I was sad that while I was stroking Danny and kissing his shoulders she told him about my first tear sheet. I should have been hunting for it instead. I should have beaten her to it.

We jumped in Danny's car and I made him run lights and almost get into an accident as we raced to the nearest grocery store. It wasn't there. I was so pissed. I worried that plenty of women in their thirties would snatch up every copy before I got a chance to get just one!

I found a few copies left back in New York City. One had a rip on the cover but I mailed my mother a clean copy with a note saying how much I loved New York. She seemed proud on the phone. I wanted her now to tell her friends at work, "My daughter is a model!"

The magazine wrote that my shirt was from Lerner, I was pissed about that but I felt like a famous model showing Maryam and flaunting it around Roberts's studio.

I couldn't enjoy my feeling of being a real model for too long. Two weeks later Danny and I were drinking and playing beer pong at one of Danny's flight friend's apartments. It was a mess, beer on the floor, loud, yelling, "Oh man! Damn you almost had that!" The game of beer pong was life or death. I wanted to die when I wasn't being stared at by the flight boys. There was Rich and Adam, and Rob, and a few others who eyed me up and down. I wanted them all to think, *Danny's girl is hot!* Maybe they would convince Danny that having a girlfriend who is a model was a good thing. One guy at the house, Rich, even printed up a picture of me off the Internet and put it on the wall.

I was so amused that I didn't hear my phone ring. When I went to the bathroom I saw I missed a call from Danny's father but I ignored it.

I didn't check my voicemail for two hours. After we were all drunk and Danny was really stoned, I remembered to tell him his father called. He left the room to call his father back. When he returned all the color had drained from his face. He mutely handed me the phone back.

His mother had died.

Danny and I drove back to NJ in the dark and I thought about how she was the first person I had known personally who had died. I missed a few days of school due to the funeral plans and I wrote a poem for Danny to read at the funeral. I bitched at Danny for making me buy an ugly pair of shapeless black pants at The Gap and a huge gray sweater.

"When will I ever wear this again?"

He stood by the doorway of the fitting room. The next day I felt like an unattractive conservative, preppy, bitch at the funeral.

A few hours after the funeral he said, "I want to be alone and the only place I can think is in my car." He walked quietly away from me.

I felt like we were breaking up all over again.

His mother was dead but she was still tearing us apart. I felt that she died on purpose just to ruin my life. She wanted me to feel guilty for my modeling, for taking her son away from her, for taking his virginity, for being thin.

That night Danny sat with me on the couch and hugged me tight. I looked up to the sky and said to myself, "See, he is mine!"

He laid his head in my lap. I rubbed his head and kissed it like a mother would have. I felt motherly and I thought about us having kids one day. I planned to keep my modeling to the minimum for the next couple of weeks. I whispered in his ear, "I am not going to model anymore." He looked up at me and at that moment I knew I was a liar.

It was a lie to ease his mother's voice in my head. We both knew the truth, I had my own life and I had to shoot. Besides I wasn't dead yet, and nothing not even my boyfriend's mother's death could distract me. While I was in NJ, watching his mother being buried, and when I wasn't comforting Danny or making a collage of photos in remembrance of his mother and writing poetry, I was busy planning my own projects in my head. I was making a list of things to do when I got back to the city.

The first moment I had near a computer I took it. I told Danny, "I'm just checking my email to see if any professors wrote me about homework."

I couldn't believe it, the girl from Robert's studio, the Miss *Maxim* Wannabe girl had a higher hourly rate. Her Onemodelplace site said, "Lingerie $150 an hour." I felt immediately behind. I had a tear sheet from *Women's World* but I felt invisible to the Internet world. I was scared there was something I was missing by not trying to be the most sought out Internet model on Onemodelplace.com.

No one else was calling me and I was starting to think no one ever would.

In Danny's room a day before the funeral, I had quickly submitted to a modeling casting. Then after the funeral I checked my email again in hopes for a reply.

It was there. I was scheduled for a week later on Friday November eighth at 1 P.M. sharp for an interview.

When the date came around I arrive at the showroom for Intimo.com, an undergarment company, with a feeling of possibility waiting inside. A tall corky man with glasses and curly wizard hair told me that the women's division was growing and they needed a new underwear model. I hoped it would be me. The interview was simple since I already had plenty of photos in my book of myself wearing lingerie.

I worked my personality and showed them all of my body shots and got the job. I left knowing I got the job, I just had this feeling. Another Wannabe was waiting in the hallway, I wanted to tell her not to bother but I just strutted away clicking my heels and smiling inside.

A few days later I was back and I was excited, it was my first paid legit modeling job and I booked it myself. I would be on the company's web site modeling conservative underwear, bras, tank tops, boxer shorts, and sleepwear. They were a well-known brand and it made me feel like I was actually making it as a model.

After Intimo, the following week I mailed my photo to Stuff magazine on a whim; I waited desperately for a reply. To keep my self busy I made some new goals for myself. I tried to mail every week to ten different places, agents, magazines, casting directors. I hadn't signed onto my Onemodelplace account since that first session with Intimo, now I was planning another session again, and even though I didn't hear back from many of the casting agents or magazines from my mailings I was learning to be my own agent. I understood that hearing back one out of twenty mailers was lucky. Still I was in college and there were classes, and grades to blow over, teachers to please, Danny to please, my mother to prove myself to, but with modeling instead of trying to get in with the agency, I wanted to get in with the magazine. I called it "skipping the middle man."

Danny wrote me a little note that same week in the shape of a heart and put it in my checkbook, it read, "I love you." The next time I saw him he told me, "You are like a wife to me." Maybe my lies about giving up modeling were working and he was falling in love with me.

Then I found notes in his closet from a girl.

I asked Danny about her. I thought he was worse of a liar than me when he said, "Oh ...her.... We're just friends."

I confronted the girl one night when Danny went to his car to get a forgotten lighter. I knocked on her dorm room. She inviting me in and instead of bitching her out, I tried to be her friend. I almost liked her. I sat on her bed. I wondered if Danny had sat on her bed before. She liked to draw and scribble stars and circles, and she listened to Dave Matthews. She was a hippie and she liked to smoke pot. She got Danny really high. My stomach got butterflies when she said, "Really high." I wanted to kill her. I eased myself with knowing I was prettier.

Then Danny chose the ugly girl.

He dumped me, on exactly our year and half anniversary, right before Christmas. I felt my world collapse. I almost couldn't breath. I defiantly didn't eat.

He felt that my "cocky attitude is growing and my nonchalant- nude- lifestyle wasn't disappearing and it was inappropriate."

I agreed I would never just be the waitress or the girl studying advertising again. I had been a nude model and the deed had been done. He couldn't change me or my past.

I didn't think we would ever be over though. Even, after I imagined him having sex with the hippie girl and her screaming over it. I still thought we would work it all out.

I couldn't catch my breath when he said, "It's over. I mean it. We are over." He must have had to say it to me ten times. I just couldn't believe him. Modeling had ruined us. I was unable to walk, sit, sleep, or open my eyes. I ranted and cried. I howled, I panted, and I almost fainted. I threw out my Victoria Secret Love Spell perfume that Danny had loved and I put all of his pictures slowly into my drawer. Days went by; I stood by the elevator in the dorm about to go to class and just couldn't press the button to go down. I had to stay in my dorm and die. I didn't accept phone calls but I jumped up every time thinking it was my prince returning to my arms and throwing the coke whore into the dudgeon.

I tossed and turned and flipped my pillow a million

different ways, I left mascara marks all over my bed sheets. I didn't know how to live in New York City without him. Even though he hated New York City and hardly visited me he was still with me, in my mind, most of the day.

He was right, I was selfish and I wanted him back. I sat for hours in my bed, crushed, I could feel the blood spilling from my heart. I was disgusted and unwashed, unshaven and distraught. It was finals week and I couldn't even try to pass my class. I didn't give a crap about anything but love.

Our memories stayed in the pit of my stomach but then I wished he would die when I thought about them fucking. Then I would wish she would die or have an overdose from smoking too much pot. After I made my wish my conscious took over and I always asked God to forgive me every time I said "fuck them" before I went to bed. It stung to be left for the coked out, pot head.

What kept me sane was the interview I had with *Stuff* magazine for a column called "The Powder Room." It had worked! I had simply just mailed my comp card to the magazine with a cute little note signed *Love, Isobella*. Now I was walking into Dennis Publishing on Sixth Avenue in my highest heels. The column was where girls talked about men, sex, and relationships. The columnist liked the idea that I was dating a pilot and that I had jerked him off on the plane once or twice. Then I got the call and I had done it!

Even without Danny as my true boyfriend, I still could fake it for the column.

The columnist had set up a little dinner and drink fest and I was to meet her at her apartment with three other girls and we would talk and she would record us.

Only two other girls showed up. The sassy little columnist in a perfect little black dress; she was engaged to probably a rich handsome broker and their apartment was small but it looked very expensive. She was so mature to me. So pretty and sophisticated. I felt like I talked too much during the interview.

"I like it when he touches every part of you during sex,"

one girl said. She was blond and curvy and had a boyfriend for two years.

The other girl, a brunette with an oval face and quiet eyes and lips full of gloss said, "Yes! Make me feel like I am not some slut you have in your bed!"

I agreed with, "I love it when I get my butt kissed literally!"

Everyone laughed. I did, too. I mourned Danny.

We all talked about how much we hated catcalls. The brunette clung to her Gucci bag said something about how she "might experiment with sex toys if it was given as a joke!"

With a sip of wine, I added, "I like wearing sexy lingerie and giving my man a little private fashion show before we go at it."

It was a lie. Danny had never seen that and by now I was almost sure he never would.

Chapter 8

The Amateur Runway

<u>January 2003: New York City</u>
I didn't expose anything about Danny during the actual Stuff magazine interview that would have offended him. I could have embarrassed him in a national magazine about how much harder I wished he penetrated me, but I let him keep his inexperienced dignity this time.

The New Year was here by the time I got back to New York and since three was my lucky number I thought of it as my lucky year. It really was too, and on Tuesday January seventh, at a Japanese restaurant on East 85th Street, I had the photo shoot waiting for *Stuff* magazine. It was the next step for "The Powder Room" column and it was the next step for me to have tear sheet number two.

The night before the shoot, I was anxious and couldn't sleep. I kept waking up in fright, not remembering whether I told the editor that I didn't have class on Tuesdays and now I was a liar in her eyes when I said, "I can't show up till noon, I have class."

Never a morning person, I had to sleep in, even with a *Stuff* magazine shoot scheduled. I knew if I got a lot of sleep the shoot would be even better. In the morning all I needed to do was get coffee, slip on my favorite red thong, and look great with fresh wide eyes. Unfortunately I woke up that morning feeling like I didn't sleep at all and my lie that allowed me to sleep in wasn't worth it. In a daze with puffy eyes at 11 A.M., I took my time getting dressed putting on whatever wasn't in the flooding laundry basket.

The red thong was dirty. Of course. Maybe there would be a pair of sexy panties for me at the shoot. With this thought I decided to hurry and get there as fast as possible.

I walked energetically to the A train, first grabbing some coffee. As I said, "I'll have a small coffee, no milk, just sugar," I ignored the voice of my mother wondering why I was walking to the train without underwear on. As I slide my MetroCard and graced through the turnstile, I heard the train coming and I sped down the escalator. I dashed onto the train just as the doors closed behind me.

When I got to the Japanese restaurant, the paper coffee cup that read "Happy to Serve You" was stained from swaying coffee dripping down the sides. The makeup artist smoked in my face as she hurried to make me into model perfection. I figured she was a bitch right away and as soon as I put my coffee down, she ashes her cigarette right into it to prove me right. I coughed a few times through the smoke and then apologized politely, while she added blush to my cheeks and laughed like a fucking hyena with the other makeup artists.

Later hiding behind a curtain, I ended up adding more mascara and my own sultry lipstick. I was so pissed she didn't make my eyes really sexy and I couldn't believe that *this* was the makeup for such a well known national magazine. I still said thank you to the makeup artist and glanced around the restaurant, there was a buffet but the food was cold. I had missed a delicious lunch. I was hungry. The coffee in my stomach wanted a bagel badly and I now regretted strolling in late for cold leftovers.

I had my excitement to chew on instead. I watched the assistants and the editor run around debating the next shots while I sat next to the hairstylist who was curling one other model's hair. I was quiet and forgot about posing with all those amateurs and embraced this day, another professional day.

Who would have thought, just by simply mailing the magazine my latest comp card I would have this shoot. I knew that card, with my deer eyes and coy expression peering over my bare shoulder, would get me another tear sheet, I just knew it. That was all I needed, and sitting here now with editors and photographers from a real, live, known magazine, it was all proof that I could actually model and without an agent.

Next it was my turn in the hair chair where the gay hairdresser fluffed my hair and put it up in a messy pony tail. I hated it but just let him pull at my hair and thought about what I was doing at this moment.

A few months ago *Women's World* was shot with my mother in mind—maybe that job would help her one day forgive me for my nudity. But she would never understand there was so much more I wanted to do that involved my sex appeal. Right now was a perfect start for an upstate girl like me. I would now maybe have the diversity I needed to get ahead in this business. I would be seen in a sexy men's magazine that millions of girls would give up their left breast to be in but I could also be reserved, sit straight in a red preppy shirt for a women's lifestyle magazine for my mother's eyes. I was on a career roll and as he tugged and yanked at my head I prayed, *Please make it last!* Maybe I could now try the modeling agencies again after this tear sheet came out?

Then, I showed the stylist, who was a cute little Indian guy, my book. I told him, "I'm not just a model." Trying to impress him I added, "I also design bikinis and sexy lingerie." After some flaunting and flipping through my design book which I kept next to my modeling book, I got his number. He dressed me in a sexy skirt and gave me a tan mesh pair of panties, which I kept and later felt guilty about. The Indian man tried really hard that day to make my cleavage appear for the shot. I knew how difficult that was and I thought he was real sweet and considerate, even though the corset left a red mark under my breasts.

When it was my turn I stood still trying to understand the photographers directions, I was balancing on the restaurant booth seat, standing by a Japanese themed window and hinged to it like squirrel. I kept thinking, *This is* Stuff *magazine! This is* Stuff *magazine!*

I thought I heard him mumble that the test shot was a major close up and I gave my best sexy little grin, but after seeing the Polaroid I quickly fixed my pose to make it more about my stomach and legs since the real shot was going to be obviously a full body shot. I adjusted and noticed the scar on my arm suddenly; it seemed huge and I faced that I was full of imperfections.

The two other girls from the interview were there at the restaurant staring at me, they looked like sleepover buddies, giggling together and I smiled their way. There was also a new girl, with long black hair; like a witch, with curvy hips and huge breasts. She had confidence that came out of her humungous chest and she was giving me her death threat eyes, full of vanity and experience. The three girls stood together and I was sure they all had bonded over lunch, while I was a sleeping liar at the dorm. I should have been the first one here, they had exchanged numbers by now and emails; they all watched as I crouched down against the railing and tried to make them jealous somehow with an awkward jelly-legged stance.

My eyes were on the new long-haired girl, who had hardly said a word to me yet. She wasn't at the interview dinner. She was the Queen, I guess, as she flipped her long black hair after my turn was over. A true seductress, she only needed a whip. With a smirk she said, "This is my third time posing for *Stuff*," when I asked her if it was her first time, too.

Then the photographer asked me to join the black-haired snot and I had to compete with her huge D cup breasts. Oh great. Next it was us battling for attention, sitting together, giving sexy smiles at the camera, and smelling each other, side by side in the booth. Her plastic breasts kept bumping into my arm and for a minute I wished I had fake ones, too.

I thought she was a real show-off, a real slut but a smart one. I wondered how she managed to get so exposed and be seen three times in *Stuff*. Was she fucking the photographer or an art director? I wanted to be her, or be better than her, so I whipped out my modeling portfolio book and showed it to everyone there in hopes I might get hired again. Even the catering workers saw my book whether they wanted to or not.

When the April issue hit newsstands two months later, my young look made me appear like a twelve-year-old trying too hard to look sexy. But I didn't care; I had four copies and the beautiful shiny page in my portfolio book. The tear sheet glowed in the plastic sheets.

Maryam bought a copy, too. I emailed everyone in my contact list and bragged about it on my Onemodelplace page. Later the magazine mailed me prints from the shoot. I had done it! It had only cost me a stamp to mail in my photos. Still with all my excitement, I didn't know how to make the column not scream "inappropriate," to my mother's teacher eyes and ears. Maryam and I celebrated with a bottle of wine she bought and she showed everyone in the dorms her copy. She led the way and was becoming my best friend. If only the counselor in high school who told me to go to a community college could see me now.

I brought a copy out to Long Island to show my sorority sisters. I figured, I might as well keep the friends I had who were supportive of the photos of me in *Stuff*. One shot was of just me, giving sassy smile and my pony tail bouncing on top of my head; my legs did look jelly filled. The other shot was with the long haired, big breasted snot, we sat side by side. The sorority girls all gave me "Oh!"s and Wow!"s and I was known from then on as "*Heather* the model." I wished they would have called me Isobella, but I forgave them when they hung the magazine on the sorority dorm wall and showed all the frat boys. There was a small parade around the dorm and a party for me.

I was a celebrity.

Then I was a loser when I past the Farmingdale station on the way back to the city. I was fine on the way out to Central Islip but on the way back, I lost it.

I had to cry. By then I had Joel, we had started dating and he proudly put the magazine on his wall up in Syracuse too, but I missed Danny. I missed his sweat stained tan hat. I missed having my boyfriend a quick train ride away. How could he have left me at such a glorious moment of success? Did my hard work mean nothing to him?

I wanted to leave a copy by his door with "FUCK YOU!" written on top of it in huge black marker.

I sat on the train with a sad smirk and looked over the magazine and huffed at it. Thinking of Danny, made the credit a simple thing and my name looked even smaller now.

It was just two small two-inch shots surrounding the interview. My title was printed:

Isobel

model, designer

I kind of wished it read " Isobella," and not " Isobel," but the article did include my blunt opinion on men, sexual positions, and lingerie, along with the other girls, and I convinced myself that I looked the best out of all four of us. I stared at all the details of our faces and bodies printed in the magazine. Then it struck me. They weren't Giraffes or agency quality models, just more sexy girls. As I past Farmingdale, it occurred to me that I couldn't be sure how much quality it would give me if I showed another modeling agent the magazine. Or, if Danny would ever congratulate me.

I felt embarrassed about the statement I made about how, "I love it when I get my butt kissed literally" as I looked out the window of the L.I.R.R train. My emotions were rolling fast and the sound of the train was in sync with my mind, changing again—*Maybe I don't need an agent anyways.* I eased the heartache from Danny and the two months we had been apart with this accomplishment, because I *had* gotten the tear sheet myself. I could make it as a model without the assistance of anyone or anyone to prove myself to.

I didn't know which was the victory—the accomplishment of getting in *Stuff* on my own or being another girl in a sexy magazine showing her ass. After seeing the faces of my sorority sisters, Joel, Maryam, and the random people I showed it too as well, I considered it impressive either way. Of course, deep down I knew that it was impressive only to those who knew nothing of modeling, agents, and the entertainment world. Knowing this and being realistic always ruined the glossy shot of me. It all became very clear and as the train pulled into Penn Station, I felt in my chest that there was more waiting for me. As I got on the 2 train heading back to Brooklyn Heights I wondered what it was that was waiting out there for me. During the ride, I didn't know if I could seriously make it without ever having an agent calling me every day. Gene, at Flaunt, probably had thrown out my comp card when I didn't book that shoe job. I didn't know if I could model in an advertising campaign without an agent. No one legit does that, do they? I had to forfeit my self earned tear sheets and get one that called me more often. Then I would truly feel my worth as a model.

When he visited the following weekend, Joel didn't ask a lot of questions about the *Stuff* shoot. He didn't ever ask about my nude modeling past either but he seemed to respect what I did with "good for you's" and "that's cool's." I took his quiet nature as respect; I should have recognized it for "dorky, unthoughtful and unable to give me an orgasm."

The tear sheet was like a Grammy to me some days but most days that followed I knew the truth, more would only equal success. So when Joel's family even chimed in telling everyone that stopped by their house how I was their son's *model* girlfriend, I again saw how small the world was in Syracuse and how big the world was in New York City and how much I needed more tear sheets.

In a month no one would care about the magazine anymore and I needed something new and fresh to expose me. I was searching for what was speaking in my gut. I could feel it on the train, buying accessories at H&M, and while staring out the window in class, before I went to bed, in my heart beat, and where ever I was I heard, "You haven't made it yet little girl."

There was no one to confront about these thoughts, besides Robert, who hugged me and gave me some ideas to take my designing of bikinis to the next level. He suggested I try to get them seen in magazines as well. This cheered me up for a second and I knew there was a ton of potential inside of me, but that word haunted me and it also reminded me when my track coach in high school said it. It meant you hadn't made it yet, it meant you were still trying and below the norm.

My next plan was to be even more aggressive on the Internet while keeping my bikini design options in the back of my mind. Soon, my goal was that every website known to the modeling world would have to become known to me. If the word model was involved, I had to know it. Be on it. Or be using it. I had started to accept that "Freelancing" was my title and with or without an agent my eyes and ears were always open for new opportunities and venues to market myself as a model. I kept this in mind at a promotional job for Sketchers; while a Spanish girl and I handed out fifty percent off flyers she mentioned a new website Craigslist.com.

My ears perked up.

This website would become my fortune during the next three years. With school still on my schedule, I first used the website to gain some small magazine tear sheets and later, my first lead role in a music video too, along with pretty much every item on my resume to come. Right after searching on the Art and TV and Film sections, which also advertised modeling jobs, I shot for an editorial for *Mass Appeal* magazine, an urban magazine published in Brooklyn. The shoot wasn't paid, but it would be a tear sheet the ad promised. I knew I didn't always get what was promised but I had to try anyway.

The magazine editorial was basically a story about a photographer's apartment and how many girls walk through it in a week. It wasn't *Stuff* but the thought of a tear sheet clung on my mind, even though apart of me felt I would be portraying his afternoon escort.

Later I could always say that it wasn't me if my mother somehow sees it. The ad also said to bring something sexy or something that showed your personality. I thought instead of wearing some lingerie or some swimwear, I would make a bikini design, something special, and grabbed my glue gun and another pair of jeans to cut up.

When I walked into the photographer's apartment for the

shoot and revealed my design, he absolutely loved the steamy mixed media bikini bottom I created. I didn't have time to make a matching top. He said it was ok and directed me to the bathroom. There, I messed my hair up after adding some black eye liner. Then I quickly leaned against the white hallway and put my thumb into the rim of my bikini bottom, the rest of my fingers touched the wood and beads that were glued onto it. I gave some attitude but no smiles, and I squinted my eyes to look even sexier. Then I covered my breasts with my other arm hugging myself, my nipple or two might have showed. He was shooting quickly and didn't care either. Apart of me wasn't too sure the magazine would like it though so next, for a different effect, I ran to my bag and pulled out a colorful pastel piece of fabric I brought with me. Placing it evenly across my chest barely covering my nipples again, but trying too. It would act as a perfect top for now. It all took about five minutes and then I knew I was done when another model walked in.

I could look forward to this tear sheet in about six weeks. I *was* getting some modeling jobs but nothing ever seemed like enough. They always found a way to appear lame and amateur when I thought about them after.

I was frustrated and burning with hopelessness whenever I saw Giraffes in another ad campaign, in magazines, on billboards, walking by me, sitting down next to me on the train. I gawked at them when they weren't looking. Their books, filled with tear sheets, probably from magazines they didn't submit themselves to. In their presence I didn't feel so proud. I was confused by our differences.

There had to be away to rise above, and one day be equal. Maybe I had to meet more people, hustle harder, listen better, ask more questions, but to whom? Robert could only offer all he had, which was wonderful but I pined for more knowledge and ideas of getting either with a bigger agency or skipping the middle man all together. It was information I was sure these Giraffes didn't need.

There were Giraffes seen on the subway advertisements too, modeling the skin care laser surgery services. Then there they were, in real life only a few inches away, holding their black modeling books in their bags. So close I could smell their shampoo and skin cream; they weren't using the Internet to get places.

It all reminded me of all I wasn't. Yet.

I looked around and it seemed there was always a tall woman in my face, pushing a stroller down Broadway, there was another tall sneaker wearing Giraffe coming out of Duane Reade, then a few standing together, probably coming from a casting I would never know about, waiting on the subway platform. There was always a more beautiful long-haired model to compete with me.

That semester, to feel like a tall Giraffe, I strutted for over five boutiques on Orchard Street on the Lower East Side. Apollo and Cherish were my favorite boutiques. The shows were amateur and mostly held at a lounge on Orchard Street called Bauhaus and we also did shows at other clubs called Eugene's and Dorsia's. The most well known brand seemed to be Body Hints Lingerie and Bang Bang clothing which had a huge store on 8th Street. Those particular shows made me feel very special. The rest of the time I worse the most ridiculous outfits.

Each week there was a new location for the show and a fitting at the store. I was told to most of the time wear a black or nude thong. First each week I got a phone call from the girl who ran the whole show. She got the clothing. The models. The location. She was The PR queen. I was asked again and again, "Isobella, I am just confirming the shows this week. You are comfortable in a thong right?"

"Yes, of course." Little did she know wearing a thong was old news to me.

"Okay, well show up with a nude-colored thong and some black heels."

I usually didn't have any fresh thongs so I would spend money at H&M or Victoria Secret buying some.

"You are okay without payment?"

I wondered how many Giraffes would have said yes to no payment what so ever.

"Yeah, of course," I repeated. Every time, I accepted the job I felt busy and taller.

Then I'd get the location and the time to meet, which was usually in the lower east side and around 6 P.M. She made it sound as if the world would end if the "models" weren't on time. But then other times she didn't give a shit if we showed up and she was usually drunk before we hit the stage anyway. Every time she stressed to stay afterwards to enjoy some Vox Vodka in our V.I.P area of the club.

"Isobella don't forget your free bottle of Vox!" The bottle was supposed to make us feel better for being the free models of the night. Her drunken voice annoyed me and I took the bottle because it was easier that way. My legs usually hurt by the end of the night and the bottle seemed to weigh as much as a bowling ball.

By the end of the first month I had over three full bottles in my dorm room.

Maryam came to a few shows, too. She was my little fan club. She was hot in her Miss Sixty Jeans; she should have modeled with me, I told her so. She'd bring some of the guys from the dorm and her boyfriend Johnny. As I walked and showed my stuff, I had a fan club screaming "Yeah Isobella!" Maryam and the guys said it as a joke most of the time because they all knew me as *Heather*. But what the hell. They were usually too drunk to care. I'd hear a few "*Heather*"s as I showed them my entire ass in a blue furry thong with a blue feathered top that barely covered my nipples or the top was forgotten all together and my chest was just splattered in hot pink body paint. The next day in the dorms I wore my biggest sweaters.

Sometimes Joel was in the crowd but he didn't scream my name or whistle. He'd take photos with a disposable camera like it was amusement for free. He was making only $30,000 a year so it was a wild time for him being around any type of models. Eight of us Wannabes came out, one by one, in thongs, in stretchy spandex, in black tight dresses, in sequined gowns; we were hotter than the strippers at Scores.

Once the routine started to get boring, I suggested that we spice up the show.

"Maybe we can walk down the runway in groups of three or four. Like this."

I grabbed the wrists of two other Wannabes and showed the PR Queen just how we would do it. Soon I felt like I could do her job. I thought about what it took to put together a fashion show at a club like she did. She said she had her own PR Agency. She might have been a model before her cellulite and over-brushed hair. She was helping the club bring in traffic and she was helping the boutiques get exposure. I wondered how much she got paid for it since it didn't seem like much work to me. But she had a hair salon involved and makeup artists. I observed her connections.

As I rocked it in ripped tee shirts, I question if that was even fashion but I wore it anyways with pride. The only difference I felt was that the girls working Fashion Week were paid and were seven inches taller than me.

"How do you get free photos?"

"Where do you print your images?"

"Who shot your comp card?"

I was suddenly the queen of answers for these girls and it made me realize that even though I was wiser than these girls, we were still on the same runway, at the same pathetic mold infested club, drinking the same vodka week after week, and wearing some skanky or barely there outfit and none of us had real agents. We were all Wannabes gathering together to bitch and it was starting to make me feel like my old self, the girl Danny couldn't stand.

I wasn't shooting nude and instead was looking for actual jobs, not afternoon photo shoots. I had given my body a break from constant hard nipples. I was becoming hateful even, of the word nude, too. So I took the job as an "Afternoon Sandwich Girl," at the Cosi café more seriously, it was a good gig and quite the opposite of my racy fashion show strut. With my plate of sandwiches I wore a conservative long skirt and tall boots. The sandwiches were hot and heavy for my small wrist trying to balance the silver tray, I occasionally miss-pronounced and said, "Would you like a Punani" which I think meant pussy in some other language. I got a few weird looks and phone numbers I never used from midtown business men on their lunch breaks.

I worked a promo for Levi and it paid a huge sixty bucks but it was only for an hour at the new flagship store in SoHo. I had to fork out money just to do the promo and buy a pair of Levi's to wear. So in the end, I only really made twenty bucks after buying the jeans that made my ass look flat. Then it took six weeks to finally get paid by the promo agency. I submitted to more promos off Craigslist.com and I missed being on the set of *Ed* and craved a moment with a photographer at *any* magazine again. Since my phone wasn't ringing for castings at *Vogue*, I worked again for a new Nautica clothing store for three days for over thirty-six hours, handing out ten-dollar coupons and T-shirts in Times Square and Rockefeller Center.

I had handed out *Us Weekly* magazines at movie premiers and after parties for events I only dreamed of being invited to. During one of these gigs I got a call from *Latina* magazine — again my mailing worked and the photo editor asked for a meeting. Yet to get to her desk, I had to lie on the phone that I was Costa Rican. It worked, but in front of her I don't think she bought my thick American upstate accent and my born-and-bred American-backyard-dream smile.

It was a good feeling though, being in the photo editor's presence. It was a reminder of *Stuff* magazine and *Women's World* and how they came to me. It did feel good to know as a short model I had magazine credit and I had worked over twenty promotional events that semester. Shortly after the meeting with *Latina*, I walked with ten other girls; I stood the shortest in my four-inch black heels, for an Alloy catalog fashion show at the Bridgewater's Catering Hall. Too bad we didn't get to keep the clothing. It was uplifting to stand with the tall Giraffes again, to be considered again, to get even a face-to-face meeting with an editor again. The experiences would all lead me to greater things to come, I just knew it.

Chapter 9

The Last Lap

June 2003: Syracuse, New York
The summer had started with the thick, mushy macaroni salad stench of Syracuse clogging up my nostrils. I would stay for as long as I could stand it, I told my mother. My ass, in short denim shorts, was sticking to the crumb-stuck couch again. I was feeling almost as green as the fabric.

The food permanently stained on the carpet made my heart rate climb as I sat, and when I walked across the rug, it had lost its softness and felt stiff and icky to tiptoe upon. The scent of last night's dinner clung deep in it and the smell wafting through the whole house made me dizzy walking to the kitchen for some veggies and dip. Even standing in front of the refrigerator, hot flashes came, and the usual mild summers of upstate New York started to sizzle in the living room. I felt cooked; inflamed unable to breathe, while slurping another water bottle.

I missed my dorm with its frigid air conditioning.

I wondered *How did I live without it? Better yet, how did I ever live in fucking place?*

After a week of trips to Wal-Mart, afternoons of barbequing in Joel's backyard, and shopping for things I didn't really need at the Carousel Mall, I had to rebel. Submitting my body photos through email to a few castings from Craigslist made me feel like I had a purpose in life again. I had to get back to my model self. I was losing it every time I wasted hours on The Fat Couch in front of the television listening to my mother chatter and stuff her face. I started wearing my bikini all the time and felt a little better.

I sucked on some watermelon and relaxed as I slide my fingers across the keyboard of my mother's computer. Then calculated how many websites I appeared on when my name was googled. Over twenty! The Internet really *had* made me a model. Afterward, to keep my secret, everything was deleted. All my modeling photos—gone. God forbid my mother witnesses my ass flashing across the screen again.

If I had to stay any longer in the house I might never have gotten the stink of greasy food out of my pores and hair. Fortunately I got an email. This time it was from the pre-teen clothing line I submitted my photos to. They were looking for a fit model for kids sizes. My flat chest now was a blessing. I replied quickly, "Great! Yes, I am a size 10 kids!"

I was done with the upstate, and I grabbed the next Greyhound bus back to the dorms early, before my summer classes began.

Right away, back in New York, I was ready for my plans on 37th Street. I started working with this aspiring clothing line that paid $100 an hour. It didn't matter if I only tried on three skirts and a denim skirt in fifteen minutes, I still got paid for the hour.

In a small studio space with five sewing machines, and three windows, I watched and saw how a real pattern-maker worked. I would quickly disrobed down to my thong and bra and she would be touching my waist softly, asking me to turn and lift up my arms for the measurement around my chest and then around my hip bones. It felt good to get a job where being short and petite "counted."

It was an awesome job that ended to soon. It all ended over a paycheck. I had worked for three hours one week and only got paid for two. When I proved I was right they never hired me again. It made me kind of wish I didn't complain about it. Maybe I could have worked a few more times and made some more cash. The easy one hundred bucks was nice since I wasn't going to spend my summer as a waitress and my mother wasn't planting a money tree.

Without the fit modeling job to look forward to anymore, I worried unless I met some photographer's soon the summer would contain only my summer classes. Things really looked bad when Joel came into town in his muffler moaning piece of shit car. After a cheap but delicious Indian lunch, we went to the Meatpacking District. He complained about the subway ride now costing two dollars instead of a dollar fifty, even though he didn't even live here. We headed downtown; he always looked so awkward holding the pole and was not a New Yorker at all.

Being on the cobblestone street again reminded me of that Mr. Know-It-All who had dissed my comp card then charged *me* two hundred bucks to shoot *me*. Today I was hoping for a better experience when I met a handbag designer named Jac. The week before I had a random encounter on American Online Instant Messenger and I found myself chatting to a person who knew this handbag designer who had just moved to New York City. My AOL profile did say in my Occupation: Model. He had told me that his friend was looking for models to model her bags. It might have been fate. At that moment I grabbed my nearest purse and went right to the mirror and stood on my tippy toes and practiced. I couldn't believe how random life was, luck could happen anywhere.

Working with Jac was the first time a female took my picture. She shot the shoot herself on a little digital camera; she brushed my hair and then told me how to hold the bag. Jac, made these handbags in her bedroom, she was a do it yourself kind of girl, and on the way to the terrace I saw her sewing machine. It looked serious, along side a weird tough looking metal brace and hammer.

I was happy to meet someone who was under the age of thirty too. After shooting with Jac I felt kind of pathetic with my glued together scrappy bikinis, but she got me thinking. Suddenly now, with only two classes to worry about and blow off, it seemed like the perfect time to think about doing my own fashion show one day. First I needed more practice scrapping

my designs together and some more quality images for my
design book.

I got busy. I was, of course, looking for something for
free; I would be the best one to model my own work, since I
figured I looked pretty damn hot in my designs. So with Robert
busy shooting some soap opera star, I started exchanging emails
with a photographer named Joey, telling him all about my bikinis
and hoping for a meeting. His posting for "models that need
new shots" hooked me and regardless of the height requirement
I submitted to his posting, crossing my fingers that being honest
about my height wouldn't interfere with the chance. Then he
called.

With my modeling portfolio by my side I walked carefully,
slowly, into the Houlihan's restaurant in Penn Station to meet
Joey and his wife, a makeup artist. I was nervous and late,
they were already there. They were from Arizona or some hot
Midwest town but with their laptop ready and notebooks full of
sketches, they were serious and they didn't fuck around.

I sat down and then clumsily handed off my portfolio
book to his wife, Ali. I was glad to show it off to anyone these
days. I was tired of being a promotional model in Times Square
and promoting products I didn't give a crap about. Ali flipped
through the coffee stained pages only stopping at three she liked.
Nervous about her opinion, I stared at her hands, admiring her
ruby ring. She didn't look older than twenty five and Joey was
maybe in his early thirties, but they had their shit together.
A perfect cute couple. She said she was model when she was
younger and when she stood up I felt short again. However,
they must have liked my idea when I said, "I want to create
something that would show off my artistic side!"

At the first shoot I would wear my own bikini designs. At
a mansion. A week later I took the New Jersey Transit to meet
them. I got off and the New Jersey air still smelled the same,
when a plane flew by I thought it was Danny.

At the shoot, it felt good to finally not be asked to reveal
my breasts by the photographer. I pranced around in my sexiest
design that looked like an Arabian Queen's underwear with

shimmering beads, lacey dangling fringe hanging around my ass, and even wood pieces hanging below my crotch. It took three hours to make. It matched the vintage rug and the elegance of the mansion's golden tables and chairs. I felt very tall in my Steve Madden stilettos and I arched my back and elongated my neck. Ali had curled my hair and swept it up. She had transformed me into a mix between a soft, red-lipped Playboy Bunny and an edgy black eye-liner, take-no-shit fashion model, almost like the Giraffes in *Vogue*.

For the next shot, I left all my bullshit modeling fears behind, and posed in a fairy tale ballroom with a chandelier. I stood between two French doors, touching the handle and my reflection, the beads, the dazzle, the rapid camera clicking felt right. At noon I was even offered water and lunch. Soon it was a routine; I would come in the morning and stay till about 8 P.M. It would be an all day event of hair, makeup, pizza, shoot, break, set up the lights again for a new location. It was wonderful and new to get the kind of royal treatment that I imagined only Giraffes got.

During the next week, while en route to a little quick test photo shoot for a new television network called Fuse, I had discovered a print shop on 18th Street. They were quick and a day later, I had prints for my design portfolio.

Now I had a great new asset to myself besides my perfect ass. I wanted to see my sexy bikini's in magazines too. I thought of the little Indian stylist from the *Stuff* magazine shoot and searched my notebooks for his phone number. I was glad he remembered me and my designs. We met a few hours later downtown near the World Trade Center site. It was the first time I saw the crater of construction and when I handed him one of my sexy tiny panty designs I felt a little guilty to be revealing such a sexy item in front of such a horrific construction sight. He liked the pink jewels on the front of it a lot and I really hoped he would use it at his next styling job at *Stuff* magazine, like he said he would.

Almost two months later, as I crossed Broadway and headed

for the train after one of my summer classes, I got a weird phone message. The male voice stated his interest in my pink panties in *Stuff* magazine. He wanted to purchase them. I thought it might have been a prank. Some pervert or maybe that Crusted Nose photographer. In case it wasn't, I went directly to the closest news stand and picked up the magazine and there it was in 10-point print, it said "pink panties" and my name. Isobella Jade. I couldn't believe it! I was in the designer credits.

The little Indian stylist hadn't been returning my calls lately; I had wondered what happened to him and my pink panty design but he really had used my little creation after-all. I flipped and studied each page of *Stuff* magazine about ten times, searching for the photo of a model wearing and flaunting my sexy pink panties in the magazine, but there wasn't one shot of the actual panties. I bite my lip as the jumble of by passers hit my arm while grabbing newspapers and Kit Kat bars. I really wanted my panties seen in the magazine not just my name. After another few seconds of debate I bought two copies. Regardless it was *my name* mentioned in the magazine. That counted somewhere in my world.

The summer was almost over but I had something to show for it in print. Even if it was just my name. I brought the credit directly to Robert's studio, highlighted my name with a pink highlighter and waved it around. After my parading, I sat on the brown couch that pretty much every model who I had seen walk through the studio sat on. I could smell all of them all over it. My tiny legs fit the full length of the couch. I was a perfect fit on that couch.

Then I curled myself into an S-shape lying in a sexy pose, waiting for attention from Robert and when I didn't get it I picked up *Us Weekly*. I flipped through the gossip for a few minutes and picked up another magazine off the stack called *Talent in Motion*. It was sitting there looking lonely like no one ever flipped through it.

"Hey Robert!" I yelled to him.

"Yes, Isobella?" He was busy at the other side of the studio mopping.

"What is *Talent in Motion?*" It was cheap looking. Flimsy. It could have been stapled together in someone's living room perhaps. It felt breakable but I had seen it before at the news stands in Penn Station so I figured it must be legit. I noticed that the editor of the magazine was in almost every shot with huge hair and a thick red lipstick smile. In her 30s, maybe married a few times, and she loved to drink.

He yelled to me, "Oh …that …it's a magazine about aspiring talent in New York." The people inside the magazine did look aspiring. Then his voice got serious. He thought for a moment and then yelled over to me with excitement, "Maybe you should submit your designs to them. Maybe they will feature you."

"Really? Ya'think?" I yelled back and I tried to picture my story in the magazine and then got really excited about it.

It was a small circulation trade magazine based right in New York. Robert was right; it would be perfect since it gave exposure to aspiring singers, artists, and designers. I found the editor's email in the front of the magazine and I emailed her some photos.

Then about four weeks later I was working with the magazine and editor, at a club in NYC called Vue, giving my first debut as a designer. I was so nervous that I couldn't eat or sleep for days before the show. I didn't invite too many people because I was scared it would be a flop. I asked Jac to help and I told her I would introduce her and her handbags to the editor too. She liked the idea, of course.

Joel wasn't in town to give me a hug or some sort of boyfriend support so I didn't tell him much about it. Instead I rushed off the phone with him whenever he called in the days leading up to it. I stayed up all night in my dorm designing the last minute details on the artistic swimwear designs. My eyesight was getting blurry. My hands were sticky with clumps of crusty glue from my glue gun.

Each design was glued, tied, or simply stayed together with elastic, which I bought at Pearl Paint. It was truly art with no plan at all, using only denim that I cut from my own jeans or leather pieces I bought at the Mood fabric store on 37th Street. The leather was the base, my canvas, and then I spent hours decorating them with fake jewelry, glitter, bottle caps, anything that looked like it would stay on.

I picked all the models. I told the editor I wanted them ethnic, petite, and sexy. She said she had a few in mind. I told her with a little force in my voice, "I WANT NO GIRL OVER FIVE FEET SIX INCHES TALL!"

There was no fitting. The models had to be a size zero or very small. No exceptions. I was using my own body as a pattern and I was my own fit model so the girls had to be tiny. For once, the modeling world was going to conform to my standards, not the other way around.

When the night arrived, I looked like shit at the show with tired eyes. Giving a fashion show was a lot of money and strain for me that night. Considering I barely had enough money to eat now that I spent so much on buying shoes and supplies, new comp cards, stamps, and envelopes for modeling I had to get something out of this fashion show that would help me down the road. The magazine was not a huge one but it would be a nice tear sheet for my designs.

I was so overwhelmed that I even gave to the models any garment they wore. That was foolish. I spent hours working on these creations. I worried I could have sold them and made some money.

Everyone was so proud of me or maybe it was the alcohol speaking and congratulating me. The models did a great job and no one killed themselves walking down the runway. No one's design fell off, no breast was shown.

One of the models looked drugged out, I swear she was shooting up in one of the bathroom stales before the show. Her arm was all puffy and swollen. Jesus! I thought this was *just* a small fashion show. I knocked on the door quietly. "Are you OK in there?" I yelled over the music. I couldn't believe it. I must be something special if girls were already shooting up before my show to calm their nerves. I didn't say anything rude to her, I

felt a little flattered by the whole thing. I listened to her friend
say, "Take it easy, do you think Jason will come?"

I hardly cared, it was her turn, she had to get moving, I
banged on the door with my fist and worried the drugged out
chick would passed out any minute. I would have to then just
pushed her friend out of the way, and peel the beautiful creation
off the girl who was passed out and thrown it on and strutted it
my own damn self. I banged harder.

A second later, the stale door opened. She appeared. Her
eyes hazy, her face all red, I considered it blush and as if the
New York Post, *Women's Wear Daily*, and *Vogue* magazine were all
waiting. I dried her eyes with a paper towel and threw her out
towards the runway. I was praying she wouldn't rip or ruin the
design before she got out there. I couldn't believe it. Drugged
out models were already appearing at my first fashion show.
The models danced on the runway and shook their asses. The
crowd loved it. I told the models to go wild and be an animal
out there. It worked, and some of them looked like real live
strippers moaning and playing with their bodies, fingers in their
mouths.

Three hours later I went home alone and sober. My bag
that was first full of designs was now empty. It looked kind of
sad carrying it. I was so out of it that I told the cabbie all about
the night, as if he cared. I dragged my dehydrated self to bed,
but not before checking my email and browsing the new section
I found on Craigslist called "talent" and typically scoped the
"TV and Film" section too.

I passed out knowing I had accomplished the goal. Even
if the magazine was a little lame and printed on what looked
like glossy construction paper. At least I have photos I thought
to myself as I turned my cell phone to silent. I had something
in print, again, to remember all this insanity. I went to sleep
thinking about the girl's face that almost OD'd in the bathroom,
and was too tired to return the missed call from Joel.

When Joel came into town the following weekend, he
fucked me really hard as soon as he walked in the door and I

needed it. I had been so stressed from the fashion show the week before and I had to wait another few weeks before I could pick up the issue of *Talent in Motion* at the news stands. I could hardly wait for the day when I would stop by the newsstand at Penn Station and then bring it right over the Robert's.

While he was visiting Joel followed me to the fashion district. I was looking for a mannequin. It might save me time if I ever dare to have another fashion show. The price of a hundred dollars was a little high. So I decided I would ask my mother for an early birthday present: a mannequin.

My plan with my own designing was: it would be a leverage to keep busy and make contacts. I would pitch myself as a model and if I was turned down, I would pitch myself as a designer. I had to have *something* that no Giraffe would be able to bring to the casting or job.

I imagined how fake fur panties would look and feel as I got my grades in an email from my professor. With all the cutting, sewing, gluing and swearing over the fashion show I had forgotten my summer classes. Now it was the end of August.

I failed Biology.

Somehow, I passed my other class, Direct Response Marketing. It didn't matter when I called my mother; a heavy brick of fermenting guilt and grades hit my head over and over. As she proceeded to yell at me I felt guilty, but what I hated more was that I was taking a class on something that I could fail in the first place. I hated how everyone in my class loved their college experience and wanted an A. I hated how she bragged that my younger sister was applying to colleges already and included throwing it in my face that she was sure to get into the college of her choice.

I was reading the book *The Ugly Business of Beautiful Women* by Michael Gross and I called my mother to try to impress her about the history of modeling. She didn't care about Lauren Hutton's gap or Suzy Parker, and instead my Visa Buxx card which I spent more on glue gun sticks and clothing than food and MetroCards was the latest topic. I hung up on her pissed and threw my phone across the room; it landed somewhere on the floor over by the heater and window. After a few deep breaths, I felt bad for hanging up on her. I found my phone under the refrigerator and called my mother back to apologize.

I cried into the phone, "If it was such a good place than it would have distracted me from my modeling. School should have pushed me to care more about Advertising. It should have grabbed me!"

My mother didn't see it that way and gave no leeway for my excuse instead she gave me another bitching about how I was wasting her money. She snapped, "You are not going to be a model, you need to focus on your degree!"

How could I though? I didn't appreciate the degree I was going for. It bothered me I would have loans for a place I hated so much. There was no fucking way I was going to graduate with flying colors. Never. My goal and revenge towards her was now not to.

I knew deep in my soul I wanted to excel in modeling regardless of not being the typical or a normal tall Giraffe. I knew I had to find away after college to still model and I was willing to give it my heart, all of my strength, and every hour if I had too. If I had to even wake up early for it, I would. I knew I could at least get in one more magazine before I graduated college.

I was freelance but I could be professional if I had the chance to do it full time. I already passed the first test of marketing myself when you aren't the typical 5' 10" Giraffe, wasn't that more impressive than passing Biology? But even my father, who hadn't worked a job in years, pushed me down. I didn't want to call him ever again when he said that Modeling 101 is a very rough business to enter but I didn't care. I hung up on him too.

Fuck them. I'd prove them all wrong. I would make it as a model.

The summer ended with the Black Out just before I moved from Brooklyn Heights to the dorms on 88th Street and Riverside Drive in Manhattan. I was alone and checking out a commercial modeling agency during an open call on 22nd Street, near the Flatiron building. It had been a very long wait in the hallway and finally I was about to show them my book, when the lights just went out.

Everyone at the agency laughed and thought it was an electrical failure, trying to keep their classy image. Outside the streets were flooded with too many people. Something was wrong. I was wearing a short denim skirt, standing on the corner of 23rd Street and 5th Avenue and trying to think of my next plan. I didn't know whether to start walking back to Brooklyn or if the subways were running. I didn't have cash to get me all the way back to Brooklyn and the cabs weren't stopping anyway. Standing there puzzled and in a daze, confused with the other millions of New Yorkers, unsure of how to get home. The only way seemed to be by foot. In my heels I was slow, with my bag and my modeling book smacking me against my thigh. I was bruised and battered by the time I got to the Brooklyn Bridge. I would take the longest coldest shower when I got back to Brooklyn Heights. That is if I ever got there. There were hundreds, more like thousands of people surrounding me, it was almost pretty when I looked behind me to see everyone walking, cramming together, and whining about the heat, shoulder to shoulder like prisoners, some walking with the traffic aside cars. I hoped the bridge wouldn't crack, split, fold, and break below me. I suddenly became religious and said a prayer that it wouldn't. It didn't matter who was a model and how many tear sheets you had, whether you were a dentist or a construction man, or even a Giraffe, nothing would get you home sooner.

I made it off the bridge and was welcomed to scattered clothing and books, and sponges to clean the bathroom and the room *was* a Black Out. I had been packing for the past two days and now I had to pack in the fucking dark. It was too hot to try. The noise outside sounded like more fun. Brooklyn was melting and the ice cream stands were just giving it away. The liquor stores weren't even asking for I.D.s. I took my ice cream, hot dog, and cup of wine and walked to the promenade for my last glimpse of the skyline. It seemed everyone in the neighborhood was there, but I didn't know anyone. Some kids were playing with glow sticks, and people were strumming guitars and singing. It was an extravaganza. Sitting on the benches I was cozy and didn't mind when the guy sitting next to me started talking about the economy. I listened to him and watched the dark gray skyline. I told him I was planning on getting my Advertising Degree and work as a full-time model. I was excited to tell someone my plans. I spoke fast, explaining to him about having my own clothing line. "You will have to pick one," he said. I noticed his zits and bad breath. "I'll do whatever I want," I snapped back. I wanted to be capable of being everything.

It seemed even strangers were now tearing at my modeling dreams too. When he asked to keep in touch and I huffed at that idea before I stormed off pissed and hating Brooklyn Heights. It was dark and The St. George Hotel looked haunted. I had the doorman walk me to my room. I took out my contacts in the dark and put my face under the facet. I went to bed laying on my clothing, books, and sponges because it was too dark to finish packing. I found a little comfort in knowing that Joel would be here soon to help me move. I was moving to a stuck up, clean, bitchy marble stone area of the city. I would fit in great after talking to that asshole on the promenade. Even if I was, most likely, the only girl on the block who ever posed nude just for the hell of it way back when.

Chapter 10

The Piece of Paper

September 2003: 88<u>th Street and Riverside, New York City</u>
Having spent the summer completely absorbed in myself, I forgot
that my sister was getting ready for her own college experience
while I was just glad to get mine over with. A few weeks before
she wanted some advice for college, I had no tips to give her and
I wasn't in the mood to be a big sister either.

It was too much to take calmly, she being a freshman only
reminded me of my defeated track scholarship and what my life
would have been if I kept it. I would have never posed nude. I
liked my result status on Google more, I told myself.

School had started and of course to damn me, right on my
21st birthday and another try at Biology greeting me. On my
birthday, the phone didn't ring much and I counted my friends.
I didn't get many cards and emails saying "Happy 21st!" I had
lost my friends. I had been trying so hard to be Isobella that I
had lost touch with my sorority sisters too. I purposely kept my
distance from anyone who had ever known me as *Heather*, they
were pretty much out of my life for good. Beside Joel.

I only heard *the name of my past* at school now, and I liked
it that way. I was proud that I had done so well with marketing
my new name.

The day after my birthday I finally got some good news. I
managed to set up a meeting with the agent and owner of Parts
Agency. This time there wasn't a height requirement, it was for
body parts. It was what Robert had been talking about all along.

I met the agent at her beautiful apartment on the Upper East Side and I tried to show her only my classier nudes. I hadn't heard from Gene in months and I needed some representation. And it's not like the opportunity to be in front of an agent was a regular chance I had. I might as well not blow this either.

She must have liked my proportioned body because she sent me out the next week on shoe modeling castings for Tommy Hilfiger, Stewart Weitzman, and Franco Sarto. I couldn't believe the brands I was writing in my agenda book. I walked into each showroom putting my nude past aside and acted as sophisticated and clean as possible. I painted my toe nails over and over to get them just right, yet after days of running around to shoe showrooms, nothing fit right. Since agents live off of percents, I was useless and she soon stopped calling me.

I stuck to promotions for *Clean and Clear* and during a promotional event in Times Square for Nokia I met my now best friend, Colleen. At the beginning of the day one hundred promo models wore blood red tee-shirts. I handed her a tee-shirt out of a huge cardboard box, we were both a size small. It was a dragging day; I was tired of screaming in the streets about Nokia's new three way calling. It was an edgy little promo asking nervous tourist, "Would you like a threesome?"

Soon Colleen and I started bitching about the pathetic promo and we talked about ourselves instead of screaming. I learned she had moved to New York City from Milwaukee to be an actress. It sounded a little cliché but I was still impressed. I immediately admired her will to take a chance. I needed a friend. We exchanged numbers and we were still unsure of each other but I was excited to make my first alcohol purchase with her. I whipped out my I.D. and proudly paid for the four dollar bottle of chardonnay at Gristedes. I was an adult. There was no turning back now until at the register when Colleen asked to see my I.D. I guess I could have lied and given her an excuse not to see it and reveal my past. My real name, but she had already begun to reach for it.

Colleen with her long dark hair, almost black, and her blue bird-colored eyes would continue to call me Isobella, even though she knew differently. I finally felt okay about letting someone new know my real name. That night Colleen and I drank the cheap chardonnay after first chilling it in front of my air conditioner. We laughed over my shoes, the mound it created. I gave her a pair since we were about the same size, and we were becoming best friends.

I started to submit my headshots and comp cards to casting directors again from a new issue of *The Ross Reports*. There was a new website I used sometimes called Nycastings.com, and another called Actorsaccess.com but I needed a new headshot and comp card first. I found a cheaper but slower new printing place from another Google search and discovered CK Designs, based in West Bloomfield, Michigan. Now I would have my new headshots and comp cards in two weeks for half the price. It was a good deal for a girl in college. This time I tried to make the four shots on the back as commercial friendly as possible, like Gene had said he wanted me to be. Even so, I couldn't help but put the *Stuff* magazine photo my main image on the front, praying it would *wow* someone.

I hoped that with my small experience on *Ed,* I could get more, this time with what I considered a better headshot. I knew it didn't take much to be a background actor and soon was involved on *Sex in the City*, and the TV series *Ed* again, then *The Jamie Kennedy Experiment*, and an HBO movie called *My Sexiest Mistake*. I listened to all the background actors complain again about their sad lives and I wondered how to get a lead role one day.

Finally, I don't know what hit him but Gene from Flaunt models called. He had a casting for shoe modeling with Brown Shoe. It sounded ugly but I went with high hopes it was something beautiful.

The day Gene called I was working as a cafe promoter, this time at Pax Café, but it was the same routine of handing out samples of panini sandwiches again, for twenty-five bucks an hour. Fortunately, the cafe was right near the showroom so I ran over after my shift to make the 2 P.M. casting. I was wearing a skirt, which is needed no matter what the weather is for a shoe modeling casting, or so I was told by Gene. He had come through; he had remembered my little size six feet.

I raced to 5th Avenue, but without socks my bare feet had been standing in my tall tan boots for over three hours by now, they reeked and I wondered if the director of the showroom could smell it. Even worse, my feet were black from the insole of the obviously cheap boots. Embarrassed by my dirty foot and the smell I slipped my tiny foot into a beautiful evening wear shoe, as elegantly as possible. I smiled at her meekly, and said in almost a whisper, "I am so sorry, I should have worn pantyhose, next time I will."

I felt like a dirty prissy air-headed bitch ruining the expensive shoe. I was only in there for a few minutes. I looked and was an asshole as I thanked her a million times and rushed out like a neurotic tweedy bird, "I am so sorry, I am so sorry." *Did I blow it again?* Shoe modeling sure wasn't the easy job I thought it would be to get. The castings were always full of pressure and guilt. Still, surprisingly, the lady must have been impressed or just needed someone desperately, she called Flaunt and somehow I had the job.

I wasn't sure if I could consider shoe modeling a true modeling job since any girl with a perfect size six foot could do it, but I was glad for a job either way. I was booked with a real modeling agency, Flaunt Models and Talent, even though they were small the agency *was* located in the best city in the world, New York City. I truly was a model.

I was booked to work five days, showing off the new styles for the following season for a company called Naturalizer. I couldn't believe it; it paid $350 a day. I really couldn't believe it, just to show my little foot.

I ran to get a pedicure after I hung up with Gene. I slide into the nearest pedicure chair and the little Chinese lady scrubbed and pealed so much dead skin off my foot and then scrapped and cut and filed my toes. It hurt whenever she braised the corns and my rough, dry skin. I had never understood, until that afternoon, how much work it really was for these ladies to give a pedicure. I wouldn't have wanted to do it, smell it or see it all day. I gave her an extra three bucks because I was about to make over $300 a day, I could splurge a little.

At the show, the shoes were the nastiest, roughest, brownish shoes I had ever seen, fitting the name of the company Brown Shoe. Still I pointed my toes when needed and showed the shoe like I enjoyed wearing an old lady pump. I worked with three other girls, they were models too, but talked more about acting and they were not tall or even glamour girls—defiantly not Giraffes. But I was nervous and comparing myself to the girls of the Perfect Shoe Model Clan, everything was so damn perfectly tucked in; even their skin glowed without foundation. I took note of their weight, if they had acne, how they smelled, I measured their height against mine. I would never be as clean as them. It was difficult to resist from swearing or from saying, "Fuck, this shoe hurts!"

I knew, just from looking at them and listening to them speak they never showed their crotch to a photographer in their lives. I sunk into myself as I listened to them speak about the last episode of *Gilmore Girls*. I was quick to observe their bland comp cards, the photo of one girl holding a puppy and another sitting sweetly on a park bench, and then I saw their flawless and clean portfolio books.

I only shared the first few photos, I felt like the *rebel shoe model* with lingerie shots and half naked photos hiding in my portfolio book. I sat, a little embarrassed, while they had tear sheets from pregnant mother magazines or sweater catalogs. They fit the personality of the sturdy, brown loafer they wore. I was the bad ass anti-sweater and no underwear girl, who was still in training to never have a rotten, dirty foot again. I pretended to be polished, sitting with my back straight and crossing my legs, brushing my hair down flat, all that lacked was the book balancing on my head. I had my hot tea and clean socks. I was as quiet as I could be.

I felt scammed when I saw other girls who lurked out of the other showrooms, they wore colorful greens and bright orange and some had short skirts and urban outfits. Girls who modeled for teen brands like *Hotkiss* and sexier shoe lines like *Carlos Santana*. I was jealous of the pearl crocodile stilettos on their feet. I wanted to wear that hot red sparkling shoe.

Then I remembered where I was, and how far away the nude shoots seemed, I had seem two spectrums and today I was a professional shoe model. A job, a good job, I was classy and would receive a huge paycheck, *just to show my little feet*. I argued myself that I was glad for the job no matter what the shoes style was. What mattered was that I was modeling. I knew being booked for this job would convince Gene that I could be booked for other jobs. Maybe a print job for an ad campaign. This was just the starting line. So I held back from talking about sex, men, or making silly remarks or jokes. The girl I was paired up with was married and conservative; I wanted to appear professional and be admired so I acted like I enjoyed wearing the itchy prude white Anne Klein outfit that I was forced to wear. We held our teacups steady, not spilling a drop, and chatted for days about diamonds and home furnishings, which I didn't know shit about.

All day long my foot went into and out of those damn ugly shoes probably over eighty times, and by the end of it all my foot, my whole foot was red and blistering from shock and damage and my ears were bleeding from the conservative conversations. I went to the bar where Colleen worked and got my usual cranberry and vodka and swore loudly about the whole damn tea party.

My feet were really bruised from then on, from racing from the last of my college classes on Columbus Circle to the Graduate Center down on 34th Street. It was nuts. Joel now wanted me to take a Spanish class too, to be more cultured like *him*; I thought a tear sheet in *Latina* magazine would have been better. *Who the fuck did he think I was?* I grudged but he said, "It's only once a week ...just for an hour." I grudged more. I hated learning things I didn't want to learn. I was already writing and researching for the school newspaper *and* working at Henri Bendel's as a product manager for an elite bath product. I was tired of that job and I hated standing around bored at the ritzy store. Mussing around, I didn't get to use any my creative skills at all. Sometimes celebrities would come in to buy Henri Bendel bags, all the sales girls would squeak. I couldn't help but laugh. I didn't give a crap. I was pooped from standing still. I wanted to run the streets. All I could think about as I stood there with those ridiculous aggressive "live or die selling" sales women was: *I will never again work for someone.*

I quit the stiff job at Henri Bendel's, I was glad to prove to myself I didn't need an internship. Something wasn't right though; I could feel the pain in the middle of my chest building as I packed a small bag for Christmas vacation. Joel picked me up and every time I inhaled it hurt. Something was constantly punching me in the chest. Maybe the pain was from putting up with those stuck up sales girls or something I ate. Or that damn Spanish class, it could have been the shoe modeling or not doing one damn photo shoot, any of them might have been the reason that I unfortunately got pneumonia that Christmas. Or it could have been stress.

On the couch, gripping a heavy blanket for dear life, I let my mother massage my back and put Vick's chest rub on me. She fed me creamy clam chowder soup. I didn't move from that couch for days. No one believed that my chest pain was much more than a simple weak cough. It was only after lying on the ground at the hospital after three long days of hacking up my lungs and spitting all over the couch that they finally listened. I was frail and unable to breathe without moaning in front of the nurse, crying for air and a pillow. It was a terrible Christmas. I was hoping Joel would propose to me and he didn't. I got just more lingerie. My father only gave me trinkets and used books he got somewhere, maybe a garage sale. My sister loved her first semester of college and I wanted to just run away but I was bedridden.

I recovered in a few days and I was glad to be Wonder Woman again whipping off my blanket and racing around the house to grab all my things. I could be on my way and back to New York, to the dorms on 88th Street, to my real home. Most importantly I could still take on the "lead role," in the music video I recently had submitted for on Craigstlist.com. I didn't even have to meet with the director before hand. I was booked just by my photo. I felt alive again. I had a gig, something I live for, I was refreshed, I was a warrior and pneumonia couldn't even defeat me.

It sounded sketchy, being shot way out on Long Island, for a male alternative band that I never heard of called Coheed and Cambria. Also when the director said other girls would also pose as leads, I debated the benefit of being one of four. The money made me curious, it paid $150 each day for two days and it was a lead role, and would be my first.

I didn't even watch MTV and in my college dorm I still didn't get cable, and I didn't know what was hip and new with the music industry at all. The band members just looked really stoned and scruffy to me. I was just glad to be paid and glad to be able to put on my resume "Lead Female," regardless of being one of four. There was a whole production crew and they even had a makeup artist, and a stylist who let us keep the clothing and too small red shoes. Plus there was lunch and a paycheck too. I didn't care who the band was.

At the musty bar on Long Island we four girls laughed and shared modeling experiences, even though only one of them really looked like a model. The other two looked like groupies and I was the tiniest model they all probably ever had seen. The four band members played or drank from the bar. My role was to portray one of the bitches at the bar, sporting in 80s gear and sassy lipstick and earrings, a side pony tail, a green mesh tank top, and each one of us lip synching a line of the song. That was our own moment. It was best not to ruin it. I was glad the director was giving us our own moment with the camera. Being a bitch was easy for me.

The job of being a bitch and getting our makeup done the same each day, same outfit, shoes, and lipstick, would separate us from the twenty horny female background actors who showed up for free. Probably, local Long Island girls, happily there to just watch the band perform and hope to be the lead one day, like us.

When it was my turned, I mouth the lyrics and the word "Sniper" the best I could and pointed at the camera with a little gun shot smile. Of course later my part had to be edited out because of the war in Iraq. I was pissed because women can shake their bare ass on TV, but I couldn't mouth the word "sniper." I didn't worry too long, I got a copy of the video with the actually unedited version I could use if I wanted too.

The video shoot introduced me also to the manager of the band who ironically had bought his motorcycle in Syracuse. He mentioned the band might be on MTV and I doubted they would appear on it, but maybe. (A few years later when the band was featured on the cover of *Rolling Stone* magazine, I almost shit my pants.)

Then out of the blue, about a week after the Coheed and Cambria gig, I heard back from The Parts agency, but as soon as I did I had a horrific accident. An afternoon of innocently roller skating with Joel turned into an accident involving me and a trash can. I lost control of my skates and flew down Riverside Park and right into a sharp metal trash can. I got a painful, bloody mess of scratches on my stomach, elbow, hands, down the sides of my thighs, and a terrifying silver dollar size scrap on my left knee. It happened exactly a day before I was sent to a casting for *GQ* magazine for a leg job. It was a terrible day showing the casting director my band-aids and still asking for the chance. I swore after this let down to never roller skate again because it could cost me my modeling career like it did with a chance for this job. I had been through too much to just throw it away from attempting some trick on my fucking roller skates.

To finish off the semester I took it easy standing as a mannequin for three days during the Famous Footwear store opening on 34th Street. I worked at the Beauty Expo at the Javis Center doing things like getting sprayed over five times for California Tans. I was really ethnic looking when it was all done.

I hadn't forgot my designs and I mailed a few magazines and now I was also going to meet the stylist at *Playboy* on 5th Avenue, regarding my designs; I had found her name in the front of the magazine and sent her some photos and called a few times. A few dozen times. The stylist finally called me back asked if I had something for their "Back to School" issue. It sounded promising but my designs wouldn't work out for the issue. Still, I was glad to walk into the offices. The meeting would train me once again the importance of being assertive and what it meant to take charge and make a phone call.

The best part about my last semester of college was that the video for Coheed and Cambria came out in early May, and without MTV to witness it myself, Colleen told me. She called me to say, "You're all over the music video!" I was happy to be on TV again even if I couldn't see it myself yet, and this time for longer than a tenth of a second. It was the perfect timing because I needed a smile, I was getting the last of my college credits done—thank god the bullshit was almost over—and now regretted leaving math for my last semester, like an idiot.

There were no plans for interviews or even research of ad agencies in New York City. I was not going to get sucked into that. Buying a suit wasn't on my agenda. Modeling had to go on.

I had done New York for three years, I was apart of the rat race and I looked back on all the apartments I had seen, the offices, the piles of CDs I had acquired, I flipped through my modeling portfolio and my tear sheets still looked fresh. I had gained a modeling resume on my own in the toughest city in the world. On my own. Even if it had involved some ketchup, American Flags, glitter, and ripped thigh highs. I now knew the subway map like I invented it. Over time the loud tourists had even grown on me, and I knew the entire blind bum's songs on the train by heart, and I was a graduate of accomplishing the New York City hustle, but something in me needed a change. A new map, a new coffee stand, or city. Suddenly graduating college was a perfect time for a sabbatical from the pavement.

I knew what I was going to do.

Part 2

THE SURVIVER
2004- 2006

Chapter 11

Preparing for the Perspiration

<u>Late May 2004: Syracuse, New York</u>
I had to move to Miami. The ad on www.destination360.com
read, "The place to see and be seen." I pictured myself dancing
on the beach, shooting for a Miami magazine in my bikini. It
sounded good.

I continued to pack up my dorm room, my comp cards,
photos, and all of my shoes. I called Robert and said goodbye. I
called Maryam and said my goodbyes. I called Colleen too; I felt
she would miss me the most. I kept staring at all I owned boxed
up. When I slowly unplugged my iMac from the socket in my
dorm room, college was truly over and I couldn't remember one
damn thing I learned there.

My modeling portfolio reminded me of where I had been,
what I had learned and told me where I was going. I could feel
the future waiting to come out and surprise me with a new
thong bikini. It wasn't the fucking corporate world. I had tried
to model for three years and I wasn't ready for that life. I had a
lot more modeling to prove to my mother and myself. It would
be serious this time. It would be for a new life, a new chance, a
new me, without shame.

I boxed up the last of my boxes and shut my dorm door
for the last time. I walked down the bottom step and when I
did, I couldn't even remember any names or faces of the phony
photographers who had shot my breasts and inside my crotch a
year and half before.

Before the freedom to do whatever the fuck I wanted began, I had to visit Syracuse. Mainly because I hadn't found an apartment yet in Miami and I needed a pit stop. So on The Fat Couch one more time, I sucked on a red popsicle in the living room while studying the list of things To Do in my hand.

My boxes, summing up all I owned, would soon be transferred into Joel's non-air-conditioned hatchback and we would venture off to Miami together like Lewis and Clark. I looked forward to a new city, a new place to model, a new place to take a chance. The way the word Miami vibrating off my lips was thrilling. Escaping New York fast left no room for questions or a debate of my choices by my friends, by Robert, by my family, and this month in Syracuse would fly by, I hoped.

The idea of controlling my own destiny and being able to say, "Nope, I don't want to—fuck off" to the corporate world was an orgasm I could feel with each suck of the sticky, red iced juice. I was free from hauling across Columbus Circle to class. I took another lick of my popsicle and felt the cool sensation of having no boss, no teacher, and no 401(K). The only plan was to be available every day, anytime, anywhere as a full-time model.

I skipped graduation. I didn't want to walk and pretend like college was something other than what it was for me. Plus, I had walked enough in heels for three years. I didn't want to reminisce about all the school projects; I was my own project from now on. I stood strong against the idea of throwing any cap and having a piece of paper defining me. Screw that, and I grabbed another red popsicle.

My mother offered to buy me a suit, and told me how wonderful it was that I had graduated in just four years. That first year on Long Island seemed decades away now, and the past three years in the city had really crafted my plans to now make sure that whether my mother knew it or not, modeling would not be *just a silly phase*. It had to be more; it had to become my professional full time career.

The first thing we needed was an apartment, so using Google, Apartment.com, and even Craigslist.com, I made a list of possible homes and called Joel. I had recently found an apartment in North Miami Beach! The "beach," part of it and the $650 rent sounded good. Right away Joel mailed a check for the first month, last month, and the deposit. It was a huge investment for him without anything in savings. The confusion with the Spanish landlord over the phone questioning, "You pay check?" made me realize that we might be the only New Yorkers to have ever lived in North Miami Beach without seeing the apartment first *and* who spoke English as our first language, my only language. I hoped the apartment wouldn't end up being a shit hole.

Still for now, we had a place to live and call our own; it was only a fifteen minute drive to South Beach and we were right below Bal Harbour. Right on 78th Street, perhaps just five blocks to the beach, like the map showed. It all sounded very rich and glamorous. We would be there in 17 days, no matter what it would end up looking like or not looking like.

All I needed now was to make myself known in this new city where I knew no one, as a model who was meant to be hired for your next gig, job, editorial, and commercial or ad campaign.

To start the marketing of myself as a full-time model I made peace with my brash opinions about the Internet modeling world. I really needed my Onemodelplace.com account to get the marketing rolling. I decided it might be a good thing after all to sign on more often and to update my photos. I didn't know any quality photographers in Miami yet to launch my welcoming so I had to change my profile a little and adjusted my city from New York City to Miami. After a few hours I had a few referrals from Miami photographers, but no one looked that great. Suddenly now being a member from the New York City Internet scene seemed like an elite society compared to Miami. I didn't get too upset about this because a bigger disappointment was an email about my online English class; a class I thought was over, gone and could be forgotten now.

The email brought an early hurricane on my Miami plans for a moment, when *Frankenstein* threatened my graduation status and freedom bell. It would be fucking *Frankenstein* that wouldn't allow me to graduate. I could see math or economics getting in the way but *Frankenstein*! Online classes had killed me now twice. My mother would flip out, maybe throw something. When I told her, she did.

It was brutal to be beat by the education system and in despair I begged my professor through emails and voicemails to "please let me still submit my three week late final and let me pass and graduate."

I had already gotten a few hundred dollars in graduation money and I didn't want to have to return the cash. I waited. The next few days were nauseous for me. While I waited for my grade, Gene called with a job shoe modeling. I thought I was done with New York City but here was a chance to make some cash, and since I was going to be paying rent soon, I could use it. I thought of Joel—I knew for sure he didn't have any dough for Miami saved anywhere. So I took a Greyhound bus for the five day show and as soon as I got back, there was an email waiting. I got a C- on my paper but it meant I passed, by terms of the required curriculum. I had my 125 credits and now I truly had my Bachelor of Science in Advertising but there was no time to care or contemplate, when our new apartment was waiting in Miami.

The day Joel and I were leaving, my father arrived in a loud Oldsmobile. I wonder who he borrowed it from as I greeted him in the driveway. He looked older, his Velcro shoes and baseball cap, baggy jeans, rescue mission clothing at least twenty years old. He was a mess of wizard hair with crooked eyeglasses and his eyebrows needed some taming too. He wished me good luck and handed me a crumbled five dollar bill. I wanted to give it back; he looked like he needed it more than me. A part of me wanted to ask him if he was happy, healthy, or hungry but feared the self inflicted guilt it would involve, already knowing he wasn't in a good state. So I didn't ask; I just hugged him tightly goodbye. When I hugged my mother next she let go slowly, and my sister gave me a half hug, half pat on the back. She looked as if she didn't know whether to be happy or sad for me. I wondered if she forgot that I shamed the family and changed my name and if she knew I had plans to be in another magazine hopefully soon. I couldn't stay to understand any of them or their expressions. Joel's car was waiting and I ran down the driveway yelling back to my mother, "I will learn how to drive in Miami!"

I was ready for a Florida tan and I pulled out the map. What the hell did I know about all the hurricanes, roaches, and sweat that were to come?

With my name sounding sexy and ethnic I was bound to fit in, especially in a town where I had no past, where I would never be known to pose nude, and no mother could easily be heard chomping last nights left over's. I figured the further I was from home the better my modeling would be too.

When we got there it was dark and the realtor office was closed. Sleeping in the car wasn't exactly the way I wanted to start our Miami life so we actually stayed the same motel that Danny and I had stayed in a year before during Spring Break. It was the only place I knew of spur of the moment that was in our feeble budget. Go figure—the grubby motel was only a few blocks away from our new neighborhood.

We were way too anxious to sleep until we drove by our new apartment. As we navigated around the complex, Joel was already bobbing his head to the Spanish beat outside and I was already rolling my eyes at him and scoping out the danger of our new neighborhood. I counted the numbers on the hideous apartments and there it was, with the streetlight shining on it. A huge garbage bag sat in front of the door. I jumped out of the car and rang the doorbell to test the sound but it was broken. It made me a little nervous, but we had a home. And we had a mailbox! We had six windows! And three bushes in front of the windows! Things like that were luxuries based on the sounds and smells of poverty polluting the air around us.

Our landlord was Sixto. I could barely count to six in Spanish and he knew little English. Just as he barely did a background check on us, we barely did one on him and he barely made sure the apartment was ready for us. We got the keys and confirmed the first month rent as PAID. July was PAID. It was June 25th and we had gotten five days for free. I considered this a bonus, and it made the rusty stove, the rattling toilet, the windows that wouldn't fully shut, and the broken door handles something I could try to ignore. My heels didn't click so beautifully on the unpolished wood floors either. I accepted that but then when I casually plugged in the air-conditioner and sparks flew, I lost it. *What kind of hazard apartment was this?* I felt very poor and ugly with sweat dripping down my back and into my ass-crack. Joel was anxious to blow up the air mattress and settle in. I feared we would sweat forever; maybe even die from dehydration in a day or two.

It was hotter than hell and I even proposed that hell was cooler than Miami in the summer. We had no furniture to sit on. No television. No tables or chairs. Just a knife set and our clothing and shoes, mine mostly boxed since my last day of college, the lamp, along with a few rag towels to wipe our wet faces on. We had no friends. Calling home already and bitching was childish. I considered writing an email once we got a connection. I realized we were the only English speaking, educated people on the block when we wanted to get an Internet connection. Without it I couldn't start my chance here at all. I prayed tomorrow would be better as we climbed into our leaking air mattress bed and tried to sleep through the loud salsa and meringue music played outside by people who surely didn't have a job to wake up for.

When we finally got some glamour—the Internet, three long days later—I figured Joel would get a job right away like he hoped, he bragged about being Bilingual and starting a career as a graphic designer, maybe at a Latin Advertising agency. Then we could move to a nicer part of town or get a condo maybe, he said. It sounded like a hopeful career and plan since he did speak Spanish very well even without any advertising agency experience by his side.

One of us needed to start making some money. Joel had recently left his job working as a legislative assistant for the New York State Senate so it seemed logical he would get hired for something quickly. But I refused to waste time. I launched into hustling up some modeling jobs to help bring in money.

I held back from calling my mother for an emergency supply of granola bars and juice boxes, just incase. Opening our empty cupboards I saw how precious money could be, money that I spent on thirty pairs of shoes in college. That fifty bucks I spent on those stripper platforms, I wore only a few times at a shoot, now would have made our kitchen full of fruit, bread, chips, beer, and maybe even some ice cream. There was at least three months until I had to start paying my college loans so I could exclude all responsibility there until then, but I could feel my heart rate heighten from the worry of a gas and electric bill added to the monthly rent payment. Then the Internet bill hit me. The phone bill, too.

"It isn't a silly phase," I wanted to yell when Joel asked, "Do you have any modeling jobs coming up?"

I flipped him middle finger. "Like I whipped them out of my ass."

That was when shit started to go down. When out of Joel's mouth came the daily, inevitable, "What have you done today?" I breathed heavy hot air, as I walked around the apartment, struggling to lower the air conditioner. I wondered how much it was costing us to stay cool.

When I couldn't stand the sight of the apartment anymore, I grabbed my handy notebook; I had the addresses of all the modeling agencies in Miami South Beach inside. I was going to figure out the Miami bus system and get an agent and headed for the stop which was around the corner. Only a dollar twenty five, it seemed an advantage against the NYC MTA system and I took a seat in the way back.

Once I got off the bus, I guessed my way to Ocean Drive from Washington Street—I smelled my way towards the ocean. When I crossed Collins Avenue I was catcalled and hustled for cigarettes from the usual array of men and on the extremely opposite end, mostly tourists were eating at cafés and laughing way too loud. The sun was tiring and burning me, making my eyes squint and trying to force wrinkles. My armpit stench was dripping down the sides of my denim dress. It might have been hottest day in the history of Miami. I forgot for a moment that I was suppose to look freshly powered, like the "new face" this new agency was looking for, so I added some foundation to my forehead and along my nose.

Today would be my day, I could feel it. Maybe afterwards Joel and I would make up from our fight and we would celebrate with some macaroni and cheese.

I had on my extra inches; I was at least 5′6″ today. Except when I got there,

I tripped up the stairs and kind of fell inside the agency door, sweat glistened on my neck. I strummed the sweat out of my hair and grabbed my confidence while welcoming myself when no one else did, "Hi, I just moved here, from New York!" Their doubtful eyes and silent response didn't worry me, like they know what New York looks like anyway.

I forgot about Gene and Robert for a moment, and pretended as if I was new to this modeling game, another airhead ready to learn and be fluffed. Today my stories of being tussled with amateurs wouldn't be alluring. I would be more appealing to be assumed as pure and a virgin to the lens perhaps, as I nervously handed off my portfolio book to the gay Darth Vader agent.

I took a seat like I was asked. The white sofa was comfy and the room was airy, the first clean thing I had seen in Miami. I inhaled the scent of ocean near by; it smelled fresher down here in South Beach.

I was feeling at home, picturing my comp card on the wall of the agency, reading a magazine I wanted to be in, and waiting to be called. I leaned back into the sofa and I pretended to be in a furniture advertisement for a moment, crossing my legs with my fingertips grazing the sofa cushion. I was a small, tight, and tanned package. I was bound to make me some money in this town. A few Giraffes were waiting for approval too—only their skin didn't look nearly as nice.

When my name was called, I thought his frown was some

sort of a psychology tease and it would form a welcoming smile, but no.

I was dissed when he said, "You're just way too short for the commercial board," and was dismissed by Darth's finger pointing me towards the door. I fumed. I slammed my book on the coffee table.

"In New York City, no one ever cared!" Darth didn't look impressed.

I walked out, snatching my portfolio book. Deep down, I knew I was full of shit; my height was always a discouragement in New York. Fuck, to think if I had been born to thin tall parents I would have no problem walking up into Ford, Elite, and even this damn agency on Ocean Drive would have welcomed me with open arms and a cool refreshing water bottle.

I tripped back down the agency stairs; I was surprised at myself for being so vocal and aggressive already and so early. It wasn't even yet noon.

On the sidewalk, I set down my bag and my modeling book to adjust my skirt. I didn't even look at the ocean. I also wasn't in town to notice the art galleries or pastel art deco architecture, and I just didn't give a shit about anything but me and getting something out of this day.

So I rushed by all the cafés, all the motorcycles, all the store fronts, everything. The sun through the palm trees was making my skin browner by the second, my mouth was parched but I ignored it as I opened my notebook. I kept walking as I crossed off the agency that had shot me down, scribbling over the name like it never existed.

There were six more months of our Miami lease. I was only in the middle of week one and I headed back to Collins Avenue, focused on the schedule I made for that day. Making every minute count, the "seek" of seeking out representation continued.

I crossed Washington Avenue after saying no again to a cigarette panhandler and continued on Lincoln Road, walking down a promenade of pastel colored shops and green and yellow organic cafés that Joel and I most likely could never afford to dine at. The pink shoes in the window teased me and then smelling the restaurants I passed, all with good food inside, in a pretty row made my mouth water with jealousy. I took my hunger and put it towards getting a damn agent and walked right up into Wilhelmina, and five minutes later I walked back out with my ego beat up, my denim dress reeking and soaking in sweat.

I guess I didn't expect it to be *that* easy anyways.

The voices of my friends walked with me towards the bus stop, "You will find a lot of work in Miami. You should easily get an agency in Miami." Even Robert saying, "You *look* Miami!"

Then out of the corner of my right eye I saw something ugly and familiar. The Crusted Nose Photographer. It was terrible. My mouth dropped. Fuck. This was perfect. We had almost met eye to eye again. It was strike three of the day. We were only a few feet away from each other but I didn't give him the satisfaction of seeing the look in my eyes.

I don't know how I could have forgotten the chances and odds that I would sooner or later run into him. A few hours later I was greeted with an email in my AOL inbox that showed me how small this damn town was.

He wrote, "I know you. I know your real name," cursing me with *Heather*, I could see his clutter of warts and smell him all over again.

Being that close to him was being close to *Heather* again. I couldn't be dragged down. I didn't move ten states away from New York to have this crusted, ugly, untalented jerk dampen all I was trying to be. So I didn't write him back. A week later when I had my first photo shoot in Miami scheduled, I would really be able to start a new and I would never run into that asshole again.

At the shoot, I was giddy and girly meeting a photographer who I supposed by his smell might have been a fisherman before he picked up a camera. He had some tear sheets, but nothing really that impressive and *Cosmopolitan* magazine was not on his resume. But he had been a professional for fifteen years so I got into my bikini, wondering why he hadn't gotten more tear sheets in the past fifteen years. Then I flipped through his portfolio book before we started shooting.

I had almost said no to his email in the first place, but as the first two weeks went by and I had nothing else lined up, I caved. I just needed to shoot. To feel useful in this town. The girls he shot were not all Giraffes and maybe he'd turn out to be a friend, like Robert was; I sipped the soda he had offered me and settled into his cream colored couch. I tried not to wonder about the plant that was dying in the corner; I just kept turning more pages of his portfolio. I was almost through his whole book when on the next page of the portfolio smiling at me was a picture of that cocky, sassy, son of a bitch Latin Apprentice. That guy who worked with the Crusted Nose photographer. It scared me. I almost dropped my soda can. For a moment I thought I was being set up. I had no idea that cocky Latin phony photographer was a model too but I never let the fisherman know of my past. I was alarmed, first seeing that Crusted asshole on Lincoln Road and now this shit. *How did my luck turn so sour?* Forcing me to remember all the faces I didn't want to remember. I tried to act normal as I added some more lip gloss.

After a few minutes my nerves were calm, the more shoots I did, the further away my past would be. I was waiting on his balcony, ready for the shoot. He fixed his suspender strap and I stood by the railing, fidgeting with the strings on the side of my bikini and looked out to the Miami River. He asked me to bend and show my ass. "Sweetie, just a little bit more," he crooned. After the third time it was starting to get annoying listening to this huge, suspender strapping fisherman make small talk while trying to keep me bent over.

I kept my cool since I didn't have to get fully naked. He mentioned the photos he was taking would be seen on an online betting website. I didn't know if I could trust his intentions or what an online betting website was. When I signed the photo release I did wonder if this fishy photographer would later make money off my ass. Money I would never see.

Now I wanted to leave, I was starting to worry he was

another scam, and just the thing I swore I wouldn't get into again. I started to collect my bag and portfolio but he then mentioned a bikini designer who was on her way over. So I stayed in my bikini and settled into his messy apartment, keeping my high heels on, taking a seat into the cream colored couch again next to the mile high newspaper pile. I took another soda too. He sat in front of his computer, and kept mumbling about a girl he shot, who wasn't much shorter than me, she just booked a job with Sally Hansen Nails.

I looked at my own nails and considered growing them out.

My ass was starting to stick to the leather couch and when I stood up to greet the bikini designer I had some couch-lines on my thighs. The women gave me the tiniest bend of a smile. I looked towards the photographer for some help. He made a point to first mention my sad flat chest. I stood the tallest I could but rolled my eyes at him, and then he put an extra emphasis on what I did have. I tried to rub the couch imprint out of my thighs. I took his cue and arched my back, pushing my ass out, when he admired it for her. The designer seemed pleased enough.

I would be a model for her next online catalogue. I understood that she didn't have funds to pay but that was okay. I put rent and Joel aside; it was a swimwear job, a catalogue, I needed the opportunity. It would do for my grand entrance into the Miami modeling scene.

I didn't think my chest was *that* flat, but at the swimwear shoot, the blond girl with C cup breasts did fit the bikinis better than I did. I looked at her plastic paid for breasts and then tried to find her flaws. It was her flat ass. Now I knew why I was hired. She was a total flake and outside of her perfect perky breasts, I couldn't figure out how she got jobs. At one point the girl mentioned an agency called *Los Olas* in Fort Lauderdale. I could hardly pronounce it, but I decided I would send them my photos. If she could with her huge chest. I could with my nice ass.

Shortly after I had a meeting with the agency in Fort

Lauderdale, which Joel drove me too; it felt good to get a smile from an agent for once. Even if they weren't on the South Beach row of elite agencies I wanted to be with.

After my meeting, in the car, I counted our nickels and dimes and we headed to the Salvation Army to buy a couch.

The next day, right after we had positioned our newly bought but defiantly old—eighty—dollar—and—one—stop—short—of—the—dumpster, maroon couch against the wall, I got a message. From the agency. Already! I was sent on a casting for a Burger King commercial. It sounded like *dinner money* to me. So I took the bus because Joel finally had an interview. I sat anxious on the bus and pushed away the pick up lines from the Hispanics, who just could not give up for one second. I thought of the condo I would buy, the ocean view, and pictured myself in the commercial.

At the audition everyone was Hispanic too and the lines provided to read were all in Spanish. I should have asked the people on the bus for a quick Spanish lesson and instead looked dumb trying to quietly pronounce the simple greeting with the right diction. In front of the casting director I was ragged with a flustered tone, "OK, then just say it in English," he finally offered.

Joel's interview went really bad at the Spanish Advertising Agency. He blamed it on our rotting mailbox. His resume had sat at the edge of the executive's desk, but it was bent and water stained. I thought his scratched eyeglasses and his khaki attire was the real reason we were still eating Rice-A-Roni.

So instead, he took on the job title as my chauffer. It was nothing new, he had done it in the past and he might have had to do it forever since getting my own license cost money. With just my modeling keeping the roof over our heads, things were depressing. We began to see how long one loaf of bread could last and how appealing applying for food stamps might be after all. We were capable of making ten food items stretch us through the following week, or I hoped. With food in short supply, I knew I couldn't be picky about who I worked with anymore.

Before we went to bed Joel whispered into the dark, "I

think we should go home." It had been barely three weeks! I got pissed at him for even thinking of giving up and I pushed him off the air mattress saying, "Fuck no .... No. No ...I didn't move here for nothing!"

Hearing Joel worry forced me to be strong and I grew survival instincts. To live my dream I realized that my dignity might have to be sacrificed. And if it meant posing nude with some scumbag, I would do it. I wasn't going home.

Chapter 12

The Deed Was Done

July 2004: North Miami Beach, Florida
After I blew that Burger King commercial, the agency in Fort Lauderdale wasn't calling anymore. So far I had researched all the modeling agencies in Miami, *Arthur Arthur, Stellar Model and Talent, The Green Agency, Michele Pommier, Latin's, World of Kids*, and even one called *Lipstick*. There were a few meetings but nothing had worked for me. So without representation I had begun to rely on Onemodelplace.com more and more for networking and a potential paycheck. The website seemed to be the only choice. So I added some new swimwear photos from the Fishman and a few old ones of my bikini designs to my page as well.

To feel better about myself, while knowing I wasn't going to get an agent in this town, I quickly planned a shoot from a referral on Onemodeplace.com. This photographer had said he liked the photos I had posted of my artistic bikini designs and I accepted his idea of posing with a tiger to maybe make something of Miami. At the shoot, I hung onto a thick silver chain attached to a real, live Golden Tabby Tiger. I was feeling quite special that day, proud of myself, the same excitement as I imagined a shoot with *Sports Illustrated* would be. Only the fur top design was mine and I let the suede skirt fall below my left hip while giving a "Jane of the Wild" stance with the live beast in-between my legs. I stretched my torso high, shoulder up, stuck out my chest, and stood as tall as I possibly could for the photographer and tiger trainer.

I was told by the photographer that some of the animals in the shoot were used in films and commercials. It sounded special but the shoot was a trip and a little bit of an investment. In the car Joel almost ran out of gas and we fought about having to drive to the jungle when I wasn't even getting paid for it.

After I had sat on the tiger, walked it, ran with it, petted it, I was beat, sun soaked and running on adrenalin. I knew I might be the only model in Miami who had posed with a Golden tabby Tiger. That had to count for something, right?

That didn't really matter to our landlord though unless it paid the rent. The next day I unwilling accepted my fate as a Miller Light spokesmodel. August 1st was coming.

The promotions for Miller Light would start before the MTV music awards in September and I would be making twenty dollars an hour as a Miller Light Girl. This Miller Light job was bound to feed us, but a few weeks was actually long time, and until then I had to get some sort of other income flowing to keep us afloat. Luckily, the check for that last shoe show in New York would arrive just three days later and August rent could be paid. To celebrate we shared a six pack of beer and Joel felt revived too, he even put a membership to Netflicts on his forbidden credit card that was only meant for emergencies. We rented a movie using Joel's credit card. Our little party of popcorn and beer only last about two hours but I was grateful. Maybe one day we could get some sea food on Ocean Drive.

The pleasant memory of our little party would soon fade because that was the same night the roaches destroyed our maroon couch. We had a few roaches occasionally appear on the couch or poking around the apartment, but when eight ran out and four were found dead underneath, we left our popcorn and beer and dragged the piece of shit couch to the street. Within fifteen minutes a car pulled up, and we could hear some huffing and we knew our roach infested couch was someone else's business now. It was a little sad though, that couch made our apartment look like an apartment. Without it we only had objects that spread out around the apartment. There was the air mattress, that had to be re-pumped every morning, three plastic shelves with my jeans and tank tops folded on top, the computer, a folding chair and table from Wal-Mart, and the pink chair we got at the Salvation Army.

Surviving on nothing with value meant my Internet obsession grew. The computer was the only nice thing we had besides Joel's terrible car, the Sweat Mobile. I went to bed praying to myself that everything would work out.

Joel didn't join me in bed for long; neither of us could really sleep. He spent a lot of his time day dreaming about getting a job and spinning on the Salvation Army pink reclining chair. That action of spinning might have been his only joy lately, besides the Netflicks. He spun another round; while I panicked for just one modeling job to appear on the screen. It appeared that Craigslist was worthless in Miami.

My fingers were to my mouth. Terrified of not meeting the right people, doing the right thing and gaining more work. Of fucking failing. I ruined another fingernail chewing on it. I spit the torn piece at the sandy wood floor; the floor was basically the trash anyways. Our apartment never felt clean, even with nothing in it. It was still full of sand and roaches. I stared at the screen searching for something to submit too. I could even hear a family of roaches running across the floor, I had to kill one just to let out my anxiety. Joel kissed my neck when he walked by, but sex wasn't even on my mind and doing it on the air mattress wasn't that appealing either.

I was busy waiting for Miami to give me something. Anything. Something, that would get me paid and get me out of this damn apartment, so I didn't have to watch Joel spin all day and all night. The sunny weather and the beach five blocks away didn't matter anymore.

It was month two and I had only managed to get a gig on *CSI: Miami* for two days. That's it, and that wouldn't be close to the amount we needed to get through another month.

The gig on *CSI: Miami* wasn't even that beneficial because that day Joel was out of town visiting Syracuse, which meant I had to pay a cab to get there. It cost almost as much as I made as a background actor to take a cab. But being booked for something just felt good.

On a golf course in the Virginia Key Beach Park, I mingled with the other Miami actors, they were different. I couldn't see their long resumes scrolling off their tongues. They were not as "ready to go on set," as New York actors were. I was also an alien to these other extras who only knew swamps and sun and didn't understand the term rat race. After my introduction about living in NYC, and listing a few of my gigs I felt advanced suddenly, I mentioned Coheed and Cambria and wanted a lead role again. We were portraying a high school student at a golf course murder scene; I look across the course and could tell I wasn't even in this shot at all.

At lunch I checked my voice mail and Gene had called for another shoe modeling job. It seemed all I ever booked from him were jobs for my damn feet! Still, it was a check. This time the show was in Vegas and since a girl had dropped out at the last minute, he said even though I was in Miami the shoe company would fly me to Vegas from here.

It sounded good to me—a Vegas vacation. Joel, who looked sad and distraught from being jobless, said that while I was away he would look into starting his own business, being a freelance graphic designer. I kissed his cheek. "Great! You can start with making me a website!"

The night before I left for Vegas I rubbed his back until my hand was sore. I listened to him change his position a hundred times during the night. The air mattress squeaking and exhaling air through the torn hole each time he moved. My deep breaths were getting deeper too. I spooned him and tried not to speak or have a fit over the fact that he was jobless and we were on the verge of eviction and he wouldn't accept a part-time job at Wal-Mart.

When I returned there was a website ready for me www.isobelladreams.com. It was perfect, including my modeling photos and my design photos. It was designed just as I wanted it to be. Only this would be the last gesture I would receive from Joel.

That week I ignored the stares from the rent envelope and rushed out of the door, I had a meeting with Michael, a photographer whose black and white photography grabbed me. I had admired him for weeks on Onemodeplace.com, and now he was waiting on Lincoln Road. I wore my tallest Two Lips high heels, I flicked away all the Hispanics that were fixing their cars, telling their kids to shut up or pushing a loud rattling shopping cart, and ignored the sounds of mowers mowing what was left of the yard side and yelling at me and my skirt.

I tried to be as ugly as possible on the bus, covering my legs with my denim bag, so that no one would look my way. I wasn't in the mood to fend off pick up lines on the bus today.

At a café off Lincoln Road, Michael didn't bring his portfolio, he went to the magazine shelve and whipped out two magazines that I recognized and wanted to be in badly, the shots on the open pages were his, this was his carefree way of saying "I want tear sheets too."

From the looks of his website, before our meeting at the café, I was already groping the idea of working with him. It looked like the Giraffes he shot didn't even know the camera was there, they were so calm, not trying, and just themselves. I hadn't been myself in a very long time, I thought now in front of him and the magazines.

He shot girls smoking cigarettes and every Giraffe was beautiful, ethnic. Giraffes with sheer scarves wrapped around their bodies, Giraffes with sundresses and beautiful silky legs, I wanted to be them all, and most surprising—he shot men as well. Each picture had an unplanned, natural vibe and most of his shots looked like they came out of a magazine editorial or they would be one soon.

I focused on the magazines he placed in front of me and also watching his lips as he spoke about living in Woodstock, New York and Aspen, Colorado, and while he did, my hips turned towards him. I let lose for a moment and my legs relaxed, my shoulders lowered, and as he spoke I quickly got excited about being another model that Michael shot. Especially after seeing those two magazines with his work printed inside.

His scruffy, long red hair looked soft and his wrinkled plain blue tee-shirt, laid back personality showed me he didn't give a shit or worry about a lot of things. We planned a shoot for a couple days later. The bus ride was worth it today.

When Michael picked me up in his Mazda pinto we went to a beat up but spunky restaurant called Jimbo's for the warm up shots, I kept my shoes on even though the water was near by. Then we jumped back into the car and got off near a deserted beach at the Virginia Keys.

I was nervous to reveal my short legs reassuring him that I was fine as I stumbled in my heels through the weeds and tripped over tree roots before we reached the beach. Once on the sand it was too wobbly to walk in my heels any longer. I had to give up my height. I surrendered to the truth of my puny self while keeping my distance from standing barefoot next to Michael; every girl he had shot looked tall. I was a midget compared to them. I knew this but he hadn't said anything about my height, so why should I?

He seemed fine with the real me and took a test shot. To distract myself from the lacking length of my legs, I wasted no time walking over to the water's edge with my back straight and my head high and kicked the water and twirled around in my purple mesh lingerie cami. After a few kicks it was getting all wet, it was easy now taking it all off, letting my little lingerie slip to the sand. I just did it myself, natural and without the moans and grunts of the amateur photographers of my past.

It felt good to be naked. I walked into the ocean and played for a moment and tasted the salty waves against my bare skin. I didn't understand my emotions or where it came from but I kicked the purple mesh fabric across the beach. Like trash or an empty can, it was in the way. I pretended the camera wasn't there for once and just focused on my footprints in the sand and as crazy as it sounds, a piece of my soul wanted to talk. So I spilled to Michael some of the assholes I had met along the way. I let him know that I wasn't like the agency models he had shot, with perfect teeth or with the industry standard height. I gave him a smile and my hair felt the golden sun warming the wet strands.

Michael was sitting on the sand, a little bit on his face; he was letting me do my thing. No one was around and I kept swaying and swinging my body, twirling slowly. taking my time, there was no need to rush while looking back at the camera with a little smile. I felt my breasts move and change shape when I jumped. I touched my ankles and forgot I was a college graduate and brushed some seaweed off my toes.

After the beach, Michael shot me again in a construction sight that we snuck into. I felt accepted, not a tease, not amateur, not as short, and I figured if Michael was giving me a chance then I was getting ahead.

Being naked again made me think of my mother. My birthday was coming and I thought of now calling her. Lara had already told me she was sending a gift certificate and I asked her to make it for Best Buy so Joel and I could finally buy a television. It was amazing how long we could live without television.

Joel's credit card was starting to look more and more tempting. It was supposed to be only for emergencies, and now we had one. The shoe modeling check from that Vegas show wasn't coming fast enough. The comfort of paying September rent was put on Joel's credit card. Then shortly after Joel moaned, "Maybe *you* should get a job." Like I was the one sitting in the goddamn apartment wasting the entire day, spinning in a used recliner. I thought about telling him to just go back to Syracuse. This was my dream; I never complained about eating rice and using dollar store soap.

The next morning, I woke up to the sound of the air-conditioner pumping dirty musty air out of the grate and peeled my face off the plastic bed. Joel was gone, probably on the computer. The bed sheet was wrinkled in a distressed ball on the floor. I had a gig today. It would be paying enough money to pay our rent and also his car insurance bill.

The photographer, Rod, had asked me on the phone if I

wanted to style an ad campaign for a real estate property. He explained that it paid five hundred. Well, considering rent of course I said yes. I had never been a stylist before, but how hard could it be? I brought all my own clothing and bikinis and heels to my shoots anyways.

I melted in the satisfaction of this gig; all my talking and research had paid off. I was the one who created this opportunity. It started when I had watched Michael scout out locations and borrow jewelry from shops on Lincoln Road. So I gave it a try. I recently scouted out handbags by Beijo and all I needed then was a photographer and a location. I walked down Collins Avenue in search of a spot.

I thought of Michael's techniques, and then I was a savvy little model with a plan, walking up into the Delano Hotel, but I immediately got a strong, "No."

I didn't give up.

I walked more. Soon landing upon a smaller, boutique hotel called The Whitelaw, I went in and asked for the manager there. In front of her I gave my gift of public speaking another try. "I am a bikini designer, new to Miami and I was curious if I could shoot in your lobby?"

Without question she said, "Sure, when?"

I thought it was the perfect pitch to a photographer. That I, the model, had handbags and a location ready.

I had found Rod on Onemodeplace.com and his work looked very conservative but elegantly done. I waited to contact him until I had something to offer more than my body and perky smile. I decided the handbags and the hotel would be something he was interested in. I wasn't wrong.

The day of the shoot, I sat on the white couches and posed delicately, with dignity, straight back, laughing with a Beijo bag slung around my shoulder, my neck tilted just right with a smile, playing with a chess set on the coffee table, all while in my hot little red dress. It felt good to know this shoot was planned all by me and when it was over I was a multi-model; I could put together my own little production.

Rod must have been impressed too with our first shoot

because here he was offering me new jobs. Jobs that paid five hundred dollars to style an ad campaign weren't a joke to me.

It seemed like I was on a roll, meeting some decent photographers, actually receiving a paycheck from a few Miller Light promos, and after a couple more hours on Craiglist, I booked another job as a promotional model for JLo Lingerie. I was out the door the next moment handing out beach umbrellas for one hundred bucks an hour and then in the evening I wore an oversize Eberjay bikini during a Sky Vodka party for another two hundred. Fuck Joel's demand for me to settle.

I woke up for it, I searched it, and I sought it out and created myself a job to do every day, and once I did book something it was all the proof that I needed to keep going towards the next month, and when the paycheck arrived, it was proof my modeling efforts had worked.

I was too absorbed in trying to book a gig and making it through the week to schedule in a damn hurricane blowing me away. We had forgotten about it all together. Now hurricane season was here. Finally before the winds really picked up, which meant all of Miami shut down, and no gigs would be available, the Vegas shoe money check arrived. Something to survive on. Happily, October rent was paid, but now who knew if the apartment would still be standing after hurricane season.

The most frustrating part was that the electricity and Internet were turned off because of the damn storm. All of Miami had evacuated, but we were here to stay, through it all, no matter what. I planned to be sitting in the dark, with all my shoes in the closet screaming for Jesus to save me but the floods and windstorms only left us bored and every bite of food in the fridge going sour.

I had just cashed my check for two hundred and fifty dollars from a shoot with a website called Girls of Miami. No Giraffe would have considered this type of job, where a bunch of girls that don't know better showed their asses on a website and got voted on by forty-year-old pedophiles, maybe. It was cash I told myself and took off my skirt.

Admitting to Lara these amateur moments that helped us

survived in Miami was too embarrassing. So when she visited I showed her our new television from Best Buy with a wave like one of the girls on *The Price is Right*. I tried to distract her when a roach ran by, and I didn't talk about any of my shoots or the thrill of eating anything that costs more than a dollar. I only talked about how much I loved wearing skirts every day and the beautiful weather, even though hurricane season had just ended.

Before she left her eyes asked, "Are you ever going to get a job in Advertising?"

It was terrible to have my dirty dishes, the grimy bath tub and the emptiness of our apartment open and available for judging eyes. I was glad when she was gone. Now my mother and sister wanted to come down for Christmas. I was unprepared and blurted out, "Sure! Of course, it would be great!"

Christmas was a few months away and the next holiday was Halloween. The children came with Spanish accents and didn't know how to say Trick or Treat. It was depressing to say it for them. Joel sat in his pink chair and I sat on the floor and ate the dollar store tootsie rolls for dinner. Then Joel asked, "Do you want to go to the beach?" I for damn sure did not want to go. I was getting sick of this so-called Paradise. And I was definitely getting sick of Joel.

Instead I spent the rest of the night cruising my new (and free) Yahoo email and Craigslist. I gave my full attention to the New York section. The very first gig I saw I submitted to. It was irrational and it was for a modeling gig at a new Japanese restaurant on the Lower East Side. If I could get back to New York I would be modeling for their website and flyer. It wasn't paying but it was in New York. The rate of the job didn't matter; I had to get the sand out of my hair for at least a few days.

I found a cheap flight on Jet Blue for about two hundred dollars round trip, and just like that I was heading to the North for this modeling gig.

When I got there, New York felt different, unmarked, and I imagined the possibility I hadn't considered before. It was instant, or maybe it was from walking alone in the streets of Manhattan again, but I was in control of my self again. I didn't need to bum a ride from Joel, I wasn't begging like I was in Miami. I missed running with the rat race.

Suddenly I realized it had been wrong to leave and while I was sun soaked in North Miami Beach with the geckos, I should have been scraping my heels against the pavement in New York. All it took was one gush of subway air to feel welcomed back and to know I needed to be in the city. The impulse would have to be halted though since our lease in Miami was for another two months.

As soon as I returned to Miami I was talking about leaving. Joel was pissed because he had just finally got an interview with the City of Miami Department of Parks and Recreation. I knew if he got it, we would stay. Or maybe I would just hitchhike back to New York. Every night I prayed against him getting that damn job.

Meanwhile Michael had emailed. I couldn't believe it. *Closer* magazine was doing a six page story from the images we took out on the Keys. It had to be a sign that my luck was about to change. I could show this tear sheet to agents in New York! It didn't matter that the magazine was only seen in Miami. It was a magazine. It was motivation to keep trying. I quietly hung onto the thought of being a model in New York.

On Thanksgiving, Joel and I gobbled down Boston Market like we hadn't eaten in weeks. Then that evening, I performed a fashion show at a club called STATE, on Lincoln Road. I was inspired from the styling job with Rod to do a fashion show, to end Miami with a bang of sexiness. So when the huge guy promoting the club with flyers on Washington Avenue, handed me a flyer, I knew what to do.

After a quick meeting with the manager at the club, using the words, "sexy, hot, girl, dancing, great bodies," a flyer was made. I was on the flyer modeling one of my suede bikini designs.

For the show, I crafted twenty garments for ten models to rock and rumble the runway wearing. I found all the models who would work for free, beginners, from Onemodeplace.com of course. At the show, inside my models were getting anxious and so was I, since there were only twenty-five people waiting outside. I quickly sent Joel and his credit card, to get some alcohol and magazines for the girls. The show was pretty terrible and I was just grateful at the end of the night for the twenty-five people who came out and left their families to see my bikini designs. Once again, I just fucking gave them all away. I should have promoted better, or maybe I should have planned to have a show on any day but Thanksgiving.

I started to wonder why I wasn't rocking the Miami clubs and parties more often especially now that I had done it once. I decided to set up more shows. A really hot club called Mansion was next. I walked in one afternoon in hopes that someone would be there to speak to about my designs. It was an actual mansion inside, really decked out for Christmas and a glamorous place where models hung, I was sure. Inside I saw a guy about my age, in baggy jeans and a wife-beater sweeping up the fun from the night before. I asked him politely if a manager was around. He suggested a promoter and gave me his name on a napkin.

In the shit hole I called home, I opened the crinkled napkin and googled the promoter's name and found his website. The promoter also worked at another hot spot called Nikki Beach and had an impressive reputation from what I could find. He planned all the parties; he had a huge table full of all kinds of Vodka most likely. He knew people, and he was my chance to be seen at Mansion. I carefully wrote him an email pitching my idea of girls wearing my sexy bikini designs standing around the Christmas tree and handing out my business card.

It was a genius idea; it would only cost me a few dollars in fabric and a visit to *Michael's*, the craft store. A few hours later I was ecstatic when the promoter agreed to my sexy idea and offered for us girls to drink at his table too, I quickly called some of the models from the Thanksgiving show.

At Mansion, on a busy Friday night, my girls would be petite and an ethnic artistic display of hotness. They *were* the hot spot that night in front of the tree, with their feathery, sequined, cheetah printed bikinis. They *were* The Exhibit and every guy that walked by took a picture with his digital camera.

I was excited by the potential of this new way to get my designs exposed at clubs. Both the promoter and club offered to let me do it again since it was so successful. This time he would pay *me* and the models, if I wanted after New Years. It sounded good but if my prayers worked, Joel wouldn't get that job and I wouldn't even be in town anymore after the New Year. So a few weeks later when my prayer was answered and I was New York bound, my second event at Mansion would have to be canceled. Still the promoter and I would keep in touch through email. I wasn't going to make that mistake again. I now knew the importance of not losing important names and numbers and emails.

My last Miami shoot would be with a photographer named Bo. He offered to pay me three hundred bucks to pose nude on the beach as a test shoot for *Playboy*. I took it. The money could be put towards our final rent payment in Miami. Bo picked me up at 5A.M. since he wanted to catch the sunrise. I had never been up so damn early but the rush and urge to get out of the despicable apartment made it easier.

Around 5:30 A.M. I was splashing and kicking the waves. The sun was peering out of the light gray clouds—a little pink was in the sky even though the moon was still out. It was perfect, I didn't wait. I rushed to the shore, more clothing coming off with each stride. In the water Miami was beautiful for a moment, as the water touched and kissed me. Being in the ocean again purified me. I felt all my failures wash away.

All the pressure and hate I had for Miami slipped into the sea. It would be the last photo shoot at the beach I would have there. I didn't care about not hearing back from *Playboy*. By then I had other things on my mind.

Like my loyalty to Joel.

During our last night in Miami, I laid awake thinking about only two things: how I had cheated on Joel with some stupid scrawny artist at an Art Basil promotion and how tomorrow I had to go back to the suffocation of Syracuse. Unless, I could discover a way to get an apartment in New York City, as fast as possible with barely a hundred dollars to my name and no plans of getting a real job.

With my bags and boxes loaded in the car, my body being poked by the television antennae and crushed by the cardboard box in my lap full of Joel's heavy Spanish books and a few seashells, I could feel New York City calling my name as I put on my seat belt. It was only ten states away. I watched Joel's hand turn the ignition and imagined being mobile again, and able to ride the MTA subway.

As we drove off I didn't even glance back toward our Miami chapter because just knowing I would never ever ride that fucking Miami bus again told me there was nothing to lose other than the chance that I would take for myself. I had to try again. Now all I needed was the cash to get there.

Chapter 13

A Real Chance in the Right City

February 2005: Astoria, Queens
I had stopped twiddling my thumbs and moved on to biting my pinky nail; I needed to chew up something, sitting in corporate situations, serious places made me restless. When he said, "You have a year to pay this off," I figured that was a long time away and my nerves calmed a little. All that mattered was that I would have my money. My mother sat next to me with a pen in hand, and that day, I didn't want to admit it but I needed her. As my mother signed her name on the dotted line I felt I owed her something, so promising her that when I got to New York City I would get a part time job made me feel better. Really I had no idea how the hell I would pay the two hundred and fifty dollar monthly payments for the loan. Putting that worry aside, the HSBC bank loan officer granted me a loan for $2,500 dollars.

It sounded like a lot of money and definitely plenty enough to get an apartment, along with a few hundred my mother had given me to pour on more guilt. Still I had money in the bank. I had to carry on. This loan seemed at the time the only way to continue to create my own reality and do what I wanted to do without getting a real job. Only of course, I didn't tell my mother that. She was barely off the brakes when I raced out of the car and rushed onto Craigslist.com, grabbing a pen. Now that I had money to spend and I scrolled for apartments.

Joel would of course drive the five hours it took to get to New York City from Syracuse for our one day of apartment shopping. It would be a miracle but somehow we wanted an apartment under $1000 a month.

In the car, his hand across my thigh, my eyes were staring out the window, dizzy from the spray of greens and white that rushed by on route I-81 South, or maybe car sick with knowing I was faking my loyalty. I was ready for my re-bound stage. I just knew I would cheat on him again, I couldn't trust myself that I wouldn't.

Yet, we, as a couple, holding hands walked into an apartment on the Upper East Side that was only $800 a month but Joel said it was too small. As if we had the audacity to be picky. Joel really wanted a one bedroom so if we had visitors we could "have *our* privacy." I thought a small studio would have been just fine and cheaper. This would have been a perfect time but I decided I didn't have the courage after all to break up with him. I wanted to say, "I want my *own* damn privacy!" Instead I agreed with him and we ended up going in circles trying to get in the right lane for the 59th Street Bridge, his hand across my thigh again. I was looking out the window again, tapping against the glass faster than a woodpecker. He was adjusting his glasses as I looked back towards the city.

The tall silver coated buildings, shimmering in the sun and smiling at me, the sight made me too wound up sit still and look at cozy apartments while imaging the next tear sheet and photo shoot I might have.

The one bedroom, in Astoria, Queens was only five or six blocks from Colleen's and it would be nice to have a friend in the neighborhood, although the apartment was a fifth floor walk up. I didn't plan my fate to be in Astoria but the skyline view, the five windows and the high ceilings sold us. It was amazing that two people without secure jobs could get an apartment in a matter of hours. Plus we had hit our goal; our rent was nine-hundred and eighty five a month. We drove back up to Syracuse to grab our shit, literally, and four days later on February 1st, we probably climbed the fifth floor walkup almost a million times, and moved into 30-78 34th Street with the same damn air-mattress and knife set. Joel's handy computer would come along too. I knew the skyline view out of our one bedroom window would be my inspiration each day. I had only a river separating me from modeling full-time in New York City, the greatest city in the world, where dreams happen, and I yelled to Joel to hurry up and plug in the computer.

We both didn't have to remind each other once again about how badly we needed money. It was all spoken by the atmosphere, by the things we still didn't have, there was no stereo, no paintings for the wall, no DVD player, no curtains, but the enchanting city view, we both agreed was worth the rent.

I got busy fast, and before we even unpacked, I ran to mail out my comp cards and maybe get with an agency that sent me on more castings. I felt that just by being back in New York I would book something big soon. I didn't care about exploring my new neighborhood in Astoria or having a coffee at the café with Joel and the locals. Colleen lived right down the street on Steinway Street but after a few days it didn't matter anymore. I told her to just meet me in Manhattan if we were to hang out. I didn't want to be anywhere but in the city. Based on what I saw, the sad looking street sweepers and the teenagers driving in circles in their loud cars, it didn't look like dreams happened in Astoria. I hated walking past locals, Greeks and Astorians. I didn't move to New York to notice the same old shit. My destination was over the East River. I quickly hopped on the next N train, a new yellow line. When I sat down it felt like home again. The above ground rusted train gave me a beautiful view of the East Side skyline and I was in awe looking out the window. The MTA must have given Astoria all the beat up, junky, loud and sad looking trains, because the brakes sounded like screaming witches as we pull in and out of a station. The first impression didn't bother me, it would be my new train, my main line, and I would call it "my train," proudly, if someone asked which one I took home. I felt lucky to be riding any subway again as we raced under the East River at the 59th Street bridge.

After the rickety ride, I got off by Penn Station and then

ran to Robert's studio on 29th Street to announce, "I'm back guys!" They were excited, too. After some chatting and a soda with the studio boys, I was off again. My next stop was Barnes and Noble to research some magazines and get some editors' names to submit my photos too.

I was alive, free, just as I knew I would be and Joel didn't need to know where I was or drive me there. The jerking of the trains, the bumpy sidewalks, and the sounds of the construction sights were running through me, every movement around me was a piece of luck. It gave me an appetite for becoming a New Yorker again. The street performers, and the screeching dump trucks, the sirens of the ambulance, the honking yellow cabs and swearing drivers, the whistles and cat calls I started to get again. Every single sound was hearty and spiritual, almost musical and seemed to seep up from the sidewalk cracks and from the gutters and out of the jazzy women's mouth and into my skin. Of course, to tease me and fire me up, the tall Giraffes I passed again gave me more motivation to continue to try even harder. To not get sucked into my old amateur ways and keep tear sheets on my mind.

Already, during week one, Gene at Flaunt Models calls for a shoe modeling gig in Vegas again, it would bring in a good check. I took the job but I knew afterwards there wasn't another show until June. I went to Craigslist hunting for more work. The website now had a schedule and by 1 P.M. there were new castings posted. Unlike the Miami market, I strayed from Onemodeplace.com. I knew photographers here already. I wanted to first give my shot at an agency again. I was a better model now. I had experience now worthy of being represented I thought. Especially since I had already booked a quick shoot with a clothing boutique on Staten Island, which was a long distance from Astoria. That day I had modeled for their online catalog wearing Juicy Couture jeans and made a few hundred bucks. Afterward, I really had my confidence back. I got an idea to just cold call a commercial print modeling agency saying I was a model from Miami and ask for a meeting just on the spot, right at that moment. I did, while standing on the corner only a few feet away from their door just in case. Surprised they said, "Yes, come by!" and gave me the address. Except I already had it, I was only about fifteen seconds away and just pretended to write it down. After waiting a few minutes I took the elevator up. It was then, in the elevator, that I realized Miami had a point. Besides those shoots with Michael; I now had the *sound* of being from a sexy place. This made me interesting, sexier, exotic maybe even fascinating I assumed, either way my phone call worked.

This random chance got me in front of an agent at Funny Face. Even though I had submitted to them time and time again and never ever got a call back. Today I was in. I gratefully took the offered cool water in a plastic cup and talked all about Miami like I had been born there. They dug my little story and took my comp card, but of course wanting it more commercial print looking and not so flirty looking.

Soon I was booked for a small spot on *As the World Turns* as a background actor. It sounded good because the agent said there were only going to be five or six other background actors, which meant I had a chance to actually be seen on camera. I would be in a bikini, for a resort scene, and it would pay a little over $100 after the agency cut. Posing in a bikini was pie to me, almost boring. The day of the job I had my own little dressing room in the background actor's area and felt quite full of potential while slipping on my green bikini. On set, even though one of the lead actresses' on the show said I looked hot, while standing with my partner, a tall black man, I was sure he took up any chance I had of a camera view. By then I had another job coming up for *Playgirl* magazine the following week. That was going to give me plenty of exposure.

The casting on Craigslist.com said, *"Looking for female to pose nude with male for magazine editorial."* My eyes got wide, it was a tear sheet, it also said "paying." It sounded very exciting; I had never posed with a male model before!

Before I met the male model, I met the photographer. That day I walked into a Cosi café on 7th Avenue and 13th Street, feeling naïve, and I could feel the eyes of the people sipping their coffee knowing I was really a Starbucks drinker. One of these "sippers" was a photographer I was meeting but didn't know which. I sat there and stared at my Cosi coffee lid. After a few sips and minutes, I caught eyes with a man, and smiled. It wasn't him though and I quickly looked away. Again, my mouth slowly hesitating started to bend into a crooked half smile when I saw someone that might be him. I called the magazine when I couldn't pinpoint the photographer and got too frustrated. On the phone I asked, as nice and quietly as possible, trying not to sound unprofessional, "I have a photo shoot for your magazine coming up and I am meeting the photographer but I don't know what he looks like?" I waited for help. I couldn't believe I just called and said that. The voice on the other end simply said quickly, "Long gray hair, a little overweight, Jewish." Then I was hung up on before I could whisper, "Thanks a lot!"

I looked around the café still clueless, considering everyone in the city could be Jewish, and suddenly everyone around me was overweight too. The man I thought, *Okay, definitely not him* turned out to be the photographer. Once we introduced ourselves, he got immediately concerned with my young look, but also said the other model was ethnic and that we would look good together. He added that he would have to convince the editor that I looked old enough and would call me at the end of the week.

Before the photographer left he told me that the male model had never posed nude before and that he wasn't a model at all. He's a painter. I almost laughed and joked that I would be pretty good at breaking in someone to their first time.

The day of the shoot I showed up way too early, down on the Lower East Side. I was freezing standing there in front of a graffiti-tagged building with a few dirty cats crying next to me. But any weather condition is worth a tear sheet. When everyone arrived, I saw that the crew was small, only four people. We said our hellos and introductions and once everyone settled in with coffee and bagels, I was made into a Bohemian Princess. I guess the male model was supposed to be the prince. While I sat on a little stool in my mesh thong with little pearls decorating it, I studied the naked painter and thought, *Wow. He has a lot of hair down there!*

He looked like a hairy Latin-Jesus or a cave man and hippie all meshed into one. While the fake eyelashes were being put on, a chain of stringed beads were wrapped around my neck and dangling down the center of my bare chest. My hair was put into a pony tail, pinned and plastered down, as a dark black short wig was adjusted to my head. I was too tired to be my usually chatty self, so out of the corner of my eye I watched the photographer and assistants decorate the dirty cobwebbed studio with pretty Egyptian and Bohemian ideas.

I crawled over the pink and blue pillows and settled next to Hairy Jesus, who looked a little uncomfortable on the tribal bed, a bowl of fruit between us. The set up was hand created, mocked up in Hairy Jesus' painting studio but with the lighting and beads and fruit it felt pretty real. Once we were in place and the lights were adjusted I started to like my role more and actually felt powerful, like a Queen, sitting on my pillow covered exotic throne. I was the seductress, giving the painter-turned-model a boner while I was told to touch his stomach and rub his leg.

He only had to hide behind a closet twice to get hard and asked politely to grab my ass while he jerked off a little. It was normal for everyone on set; no one seemed to think of it as weird like I did. The editors were standing by and everyone gushed at how cute we were together and how they were matchmakers. Although to disappoint them, I played with my beaded necklace uninterested in his hairy bulging cock.

After about eleven hours of shooting, I got paid. The check was for $640,

which was about $60 an hour. I was humble enough and thought it was a great contribution for rent. I signed the release, hugged everyone but as I headed for the door, I tried to convince myself it was also a shoot that would benefit me as a model and not just rent. I told myself that I proved again that being nude could be beautiful and not perverse. The editorial was mostly about "his crotch," not mine, and that felt good. I was a prop, the pretty seductress in the eight page spread of the "Man of the Year" July issue. I had had my crotch photographed before so maybe it was someone else's turn. At least a lot of gay people would buy it. Or women who liked naked hairy Latin-Jesus types. On the train back to Astoria, my thoughts took a turn and I wasn't sure if I really wanted the exposure at all or to be noticed from it by a stranger one day. It was *Playgirl*, it was nude, and it was his dick centimeters away from my hand. It was too late.

When I got home from the shoot it had already been two weeks living together in Astoria. I had to break up with him tonight. Only I still couldn't come up with the right words to say to Joel. When I walked in the door he ran to me and smothered me with a huge bear hug; it kind of hurt and it was weird to see him so happy. I let him keep his mood, it was the wrong time to break his heart, and he had finally got a job designing logos and product packaging for a credit card company. Ironically, he had over $5,000 in credit card bills from Miami. So that night I didn't mention much about the guy's cock that I had spent the afternoon near. Instead I ate the leftovers he reheated for me. It was some yellow rice and it had stuck really badly to the damn pot. For some reason I always made it Joel's fault.

After my meal, out on the fire escape, I looked at the skyline. I couldn't explain my day, or my ideas, or my fears without feeling like I was telling the wrong man. I felt alone for the first time in a long time and thought about writing in a journal. I had a meeting coming up in the Financial District about a lead role for jewelry commercial. If I booked it, I would have $500. It would be good considering the loan payment, rent, and the bills that were piling up each day. Also a job at a hair salon was on my mind; if I got the job they would pay me $100 to cut my hair short. I touched my long locks and I would miss them, I didn't know how sexy short hair would look on me, but these were the sacrifices I would have to make if I wanted to model full-time and be able to pay rent.

I knew Valentines Day was coming up and I would get us a piece of strawberry cheesecake for $2.50, just to be sweet and pretend Joel and I were fine. On the thousandth time he asked if I was okay, I said quietly, "No, I want some space." Now everything he did was annoying; how he combed his balding head, the way he spit into the sink, the way he chewed. When I just couldn't take it anymore I told him we were over. It happened two days before his birthday but I was too upset to care. After our explosion of swearing and throwing fists I was relieved, extinguished, and calm. I had been all jailed up, hot and tense but I simmered down, felt lighter, prettier, and cleaner when I knew the weight of him as my boyfriend and hiding my secrets were gone. I gave up on my thoughts about being with someone who knew me, the old me, as *Heather*, for sentimental value—when I wasn't a model.

Unfortunately to make it all more upsetting we still had to live together. On that same fucking air mattress each night, silent and sleeping as far away from each other as possible. Without any money saved he had no where to go, so the next day I had to create a plan to always be out of the apartment so we wouldn't run into each other. Ever.

So began my first day of single hood, the day started with a voicemail from the Consolidation College Loan Company. I hadn't paid a payment in two months and I owed big time. My credit was about to be effected they threatened. I had to shake this off. Even though it was freezing I still got out of the apartment and onto the yellow train, heading downtown towards SoHo. In college I had bought a ton of shoes there, but now it wasn't for shopping, it was for easing my mind.

I got off at Prince Street and wasn't sure what to do with myself or what way to go, but I wanted to do something. I couldn't believe how even on the coldest days there were street vendors, hotdog stands, coffee carts still brewing and selling on the street. I got a small coffee and continued down Prince Street, and only after a few sips I saw what I wouldn't know then as my future, but it began.

I walked in because it looked curious and kind of out of place. The building had been the post office but was now full of computers? I opened the huge glass doors slowly; they were heavy to pull open. Inside, what I learned to be the Apple Store, was busy even for a Sunday. I was greeted by a security guard's nod and then made a slow circle around all the computer stations on the first floor as if I was a shopping customer about to make a huge investment or ask an important question. Almost every store employee had said hello to me by now and asked if I needed help. It was weird. The friendliness in the store caught me off guard since I thought technology implied serious, quiet, and don't touch.

Except here, it was different. People were playing on the displays of computers and even laughing loudly, groups of teenagers were huddling over the screens and some were signing onto their email accounts. It felt clean and fresh, newness was everywhere.

I didn't notice anyone collecting money and children, mothers with baby strollers, old men with huge glasses were hovering over their computer of choice and absorbed. Everyone was staring at the screen in front of them. I got the feeling they were not meant to be bothered. That they were supposed to be here, playing, touching, and possibly even breaking these expensive shiny computers of all sizes. Still I was hesitant; it seemed too good to be true.

I waited until there was an open computer and I crept over it and played with the mouse for a few seconds. I was unsure of how to sign onto the Internet or if I really was allowed to. Curious, I walked over to the security guard, and he answered "yes, go ahead," when I asked if it was true that I could use the computers. I went back to the computer and wondered, *How could this be real?* It was unusual, it was perfect, a dream come true, and a free one. Even when nothing in New York is free? I thought the employee who came over next was going to tell me to not place my coffee cup near the new expensive computer instead he just asked, "Hi, do you need any help?" A part of my ears heard him say, "What the hell are you doing using our computers!" Only his smile said differently and I asked him how to sign onto the Internet. He gladly introduced me to Safari, an icon that opened the Internet on Macs and I clicked it and signed onto my Yahoo account. When he told me his name I almost wanted to hug him.

I couldn't believe it, I was in a public place checking my email and it was free. I felt like I was taking advantage even though it had only been a few minutes, I was too nervous to open up my website or go to Craigslist but I left with a plan.

On my way out the glass doors weren't as hard to open. I felt okay that rent was due tomorrow because I now had a place I could visit when I needed to escape Joel and the looks of Astoria. And it was free. I would be back tomorrow.

I took my *Playgirl* money and the $100 from that time on *As the World Turns* and the few hundred from the Staten Island Boutique and paid our second month's rent. I really don't know how I did it.

The next day, in front of a beautiful iMac computer at the Apple Store, I made a goal that I wanted another acting experience and another print job before the summer. I had three months. I stayed at the store for longer than a few minutes this time and extended past a whole ten minutes on the free computers. I downloaded an image of myself and I hurried to apply for another job on Craigslist. This time it was for an editorial for a magazine called *Jest*, it was a mockery of all things political, and including world issues and it was racist sometimes.

When the editor at *Jest* called me for a job that would involve some nudity I said was totally comfortable. I was on a roll since *Closer* magazine had come out and since *that* involved nudity I could handle more, as long as it was for a magazine and not some amateurs afternoon photo fling. The copy Michael had mailed me looked truly professional.

Before the meeting with the jewelry designer for the commercial, or the hair salon to debate if chopping my hair off was really worth it, I was already heading to the shoot with *Jest* magazine. That day I proudly strutted to the downtown F train with my portfolio by my side. On the train I had to hold back from opening my portfolio and looking at my new glossy six-page tear sheet tucked inside and ready to be showed off. I headed to a bar, the location, on the Lower East Side again, for the *Jest* shoot.

I was told that the shoot would be just of me and another male model. I had posed with a painter before so what could be worse. The story was a scandalous idea of a man obsessively stuck to his briefcase by handcuffs and how he meets a woman who is attracted to the power of his suitcase. It sounded a bit cheesy but in my little ten dollar red dress, I looked hot enough for the first shot at the bar. The male model, a French stuck up man in his early 40s, really like my dress and told me so over and over. When I stood in front of him with the suitcase between him and my pelvis bone, I had a feeling he really wanted to fuck me. I do as the editor says and reach for the silver suitcase delicately, seductively with my finger tip and look at the camera. With my flat hair now voluminous, I imagined the shot almost as stunning as something in *GQ* magazine. I thought about the tear sheet and felt proud of myself for making this day, getting this tear sheet, again on my own, as we packed and went to the editor's assistant's apartment around the corner for the next shot.

I knew this next shot was going to be a little risky and nude from get-go and as the French model took his clothing off casually, I flung my red dress across the room just trying to focus on the goal of the day. Get the tear sheet. I had tried to understand the drawings and storyboards that the editors brought but it just looked like two small circles and a few other random zigzagging lines. So when they said, "Get on top of her," I just sensed the position he would take and prepared myself. I wasn't here for porn. I waited for the camera to take this intimate shot of me pretending to make love to this asshole. I laid there, as the camera clicked again, with his breath so close to my face now, smelling kind of like seaweed, I thought, *How did I go from Coheed and Cambria to this?* I was pinned and besides that I had to stay; I figured we were almost done. The editors were then concerned to get the silver briefcase in the shot too.

When the suitcase was under the pillow, I tried to focus on the white walls and the goal of the day. Get the tear sheet.

I tried to think of where I was, somewhere among the Lower East Side. I had gotten myself naked in this same part of town only a few weeks before for the *Playgirl* shoot. Life sure fucking repeated itself lately but I needed work. I needed to feel like a model, I wanted the tear sheet, any tear sheet, for any magazine and I called this day diversity as I held onto the bed sheet and just kind of fell asleep.

Afterwards my hair was in a million knots, I brushed it imaging my hair short and the cut I would get by the hair salon and also modeling for the jewelry commercial. I was glad to have more plans that week. See, the classy jobs were coming, I told myself missing the shoe modeling gigs as I headed to 22nd Street. Colleen had just gotten a new job as a bartender and I needed a drink.

After the bar, later that evening, when I climbed the five floors I was completely drained and dehydrated. By now I knew the floors by heart and I could always count on the red marker stain on the stairwell and from the smells I knew what family lived on each floor. Some Indian cuisine lingered in the hall ways. I was hungry and beat when I turned the key. I found Joel on the computer, back from his day as a graphic designer for the credit card company, he turned to me. Before I could put down my bag he welcomed me with, "You have to move out."

He had a salary now and added, "Why should I leave when I can afford this place?" I was too tired to full out fight but with any energy I had left I roared, "No, fucking way!" I had taken out a huge loan for it that I was already having trouble paying back. I got on Craigslist again. The next day I took the train to Park Slope in Brooklyn to look at an apartment share. Who knew, maybe it would be better to just start over once and for all but Park Slope, with little shops and hip cafés and Slopians walking their dogs and whistling to themselves was like a little Astoria to me.

On the train I got a phone number from a cute blond ex-Marine but I wasn't in the mood for a hookup or a date. I dwelled on the loan I had taken out, the payments, the collectors and when I got back to Astoria, I started loving the apartment that I was never in but always busting my ass for. For an hour I started cleaning it with a ratty dish rag and considered buying some cleaning products, as if I had money. I used cheap soap instead and scrubbed the toilet. I was scraping the gooey stuff off the toothpaste rim and folding a towel or two. I hadn't cleaned in my whole life and now I almost felt that I could be a homemaker one day. I ignored Joel when he said, "So, how was the apartment hunt?"

Rolling my eyes was a normal facial expression now. I focused on my plans, licking a few stamps and crossed my fingers at the mailbox. I knew if I just kept trying, I would be able too pay for this damn apartment on my own, it had to work, I would get more modeling jobs, and I would stay afloat. I knew Craigslist could only give so much so I mailed a new agency I found, Lifestyles. They would receive my last comp card. This new agency booked commercial print jobs and lifestyle type print ads. Those ads that involve smiles and dogs and personality. They were not fashion at all. It would be perfect, I hoped.

Without a comp card to leave for someone's memory, I rearranged my portfolio book so all my tear sheets were in the front. I was meeting Alan today, the jewelry designer, and wanted to be in this commercial. It would be just the sign I needed to keep going. The commercial wouldn't be national or even on local TV, it would just be for his website, but it was a lead role. I hadn't had one in a whole year. The ad on Craigslist immediately caught my eye. It asked for "a female actress who had a great body, a fitness model, who was classy and well spoken." The ad also stated it paid $500. I applied with "Model-Fitness" as my subject to sound serious. I thought every female model in New York City would have already applied for it. I was on my way to Zetuna, a specialty food store with a café to chat with Alan in person after about four emails.

I recognized him right away since he was waiting outside in a brown jacket like he said he would be. After we got coffees he started talking about the commercial and I listened carefully. I wanted the job badly and already pictured myself starring in it. He originally said he wanted a girl in her mid-twenties. I was not this, but I could fake it, I thought to myself. She would have to be comfortable in a thong. That was easy for me.

He had a ton of details to share, "The first shot would feature the woman getting ready to go to an award ceremony with her husband, who is frustrated at how slow she is at getting ready." It sounded classy already and I told him how much I already loved the idea. He studied my body as I sipped my coffee and tried his chocolate doughnut. He liked my tan skin and my long hair. I felt this was a sign for, "You got the job." He went on to describe that "the model would be getting out of the foggy shower, putting on makeup and walking seductively down the stairs in a robe." I had a silk robe from Victoria Secret that I got on sale and I now dreamed of wearing it. Alan wasn't done. "At the bedside you will clip the jewelry to your panties and reveal your thong," he whispered it quietly and fatherly, and then with a little boy smile he said the music in the background would be "Smooth Operator." I could hardly remember the beat.

He talked about the power the jewelry had and got excited about it each time. It sounded like a bit of an exaggeration but he was passionate about his idea and I liked that. While we sipped our coffee he flipped through my portfolio. I hoped he would notice that I had a great ass but to make sure he knew, I stood up and turned around, did a spin and showed him the curve snug around my jeans. He laughed and looked around the café nervously. Just when I thought I got the job he showed me the photos of other models he had in a folder. One model looked about twenty six and she had blond hair and a good body. I tried to smile; it was hard while focusing on her huge breasts. He was talking confidently about her. I hated her. I wanted to be the lead.

The meeting ended and I thought of that blond model's face all the way back to Astoria. Waiting on Alan's reply was mind racing; I was feeling desperate for cash too. Each day was folding into the next day and I needed to start getting some rent money together again. Alan had liked my long hair but he hadn't called or emailed yet, and the hair salon did. The next day, I met with the hair salon owner on 13th Street and I watched my long hair fall like a blanket to the floor below me, my hair was chopped to my chin for one hundred bucks cash. At least I had a start towards paying rent, only $900 more to go. Then at the Apple Store, just as I was brushing my new bangs out of my face and settling into my new look, Alan emailed. I got excited because once again my great ass had helped me to get the job. I beat out the blond in spite of all the worrying. Now my first commercial was scheduled. I thought of my resume growing each day but then I remembered I had short hair now and Alan had liked my long hair.

About to blow my chance, I hid my hair in a silk scarf I bought for two bucks at Daffy's. I quietly sat in Alan's car heading to Westchester, to the rehearsal where I'd meet the male actor and knew I had to show Alan my pixie hair cut. I wore my tightest jeans and dressed up my eyes in dark gray with thick mascara to distract him from my head. Luckily, the sassy short hair look was a good look for me, or maybe he just liked my ass *that* much since he could deal with it. His eyes did get wider when I disarmed my bandanna scarf but he kept me as his lead.

After the commercial with Alan my next gig was with New York City Fitness Experts, on the Upper East Side, modeling with a personal trainer for their website. That same day I also had a gig with an aspiring lingerie designer Nilea, for her website, off the L train in Williamsburg. It felt good to be in demand.

After a long day of being at two places at once, I emailed my mother and told her about my roles, except the topless *Playgirl* and the naked *Jest Magazine* shoots. She seemed pretty proud of me or maybe she was just glad I hadn't needed to ask her for any cash yet.

Since I was getting comfortable with my new short hair style, I accepted more hair modeling jobs. The next few weeks consisted of hair shows at the Wella Salon in Rockefeller Plaza; and those shows made my hair a rainbow of colors and it was even cut shorter. In the lobby at the casting, before I was chosen, I stared at the Giraffes waiting too, all lined up, holding their books tightly, standing straight, some in heels, as if they were being judged for their height during a fucking hair show castings. I felt pretty honored to be picked. It was a good feeling to see these Giraffes again at the same castings. Especially when I found the casting myself on Craigslist and they heard of it through some agency and had to give a percentage from their paycheck away. While my hair was tussled and cut the agent's weren't on my mind. I wanted to be a working model and I was. Later, unknowing to me at the time, the paycheck for $350 for the day of hair modeling was just the safety net of cash I would need.

The next week, Joel's silver car was parked right in front when I came home after an Apple Store session. I wondered why he wasn't at work. I found him in the apartment packing and carrying his items down to his car. He was leaving and he did it without warning. There was no hug goodbye.

The night he left I went out. It was a perfect night to dance and I was going to a club called Marquee. The name sounded very posh and I thought it must be a place where every model was. I met the club's promoter through a casting advertising for hostesses at club events. Based on my photo and website, I suppose, he called and told me I could sit at his table and get in for free. I wrote back "Okay! Yes!" as if I was being invited to sit with editors at *Vogue*. I wanted to bring friends, unfortunately Colleen was working and Jac was too tired to go out at midnight. It didn't matter. I was going to enjoy it myself anyway and I could handle being by myself. Tonight I would go out, be seen, talk to new people, and make friends. The summer was coming and I slide on my shortest skirt and headed for the train. My reflection looked hot in the window when we went under the tunnel at the 59th Street Bridge, and I clumped on more mascara and some lip gloss. I planned to dance on tables and be drinking expensive Vodka all night.

There was a huge thing to celebrate.

Chapter 14

Surviving on a Dream

June 2005: Prince Street, New York City
Walking into the Apple Store, coffee in hand, knowing Joel's computer was gone it began to slowly hit me that the store would have to become my office. It might work because no one had kicked me out yet.

By now it felt routine as I raced down Prince Street, fondly messing up the street sellers displays and saying hello to all the bums and sidewalk singers along the way. Inside the store I felt a sense of security, and my day always started with an email check, signing onto my Yahoo account and then opening up a new window to open Craigslist.com, and then NYcastings. com, or Mandy.com. Next was downloading my images and my resume. Those sites had kept me busy so far and during the past few weeks things had gone good; I had worked another shoe show and the hair modeling check had come and of course, I spent some of it on new comp cards. So another round of fresh comp cards was sent to agencies and magazines but I was too busy to care when the phone didn't ring.

I had the Apple Store, and today I was booking a job with the network called Univision as the lead for the latest *Elvis Martinez* music video. For this I could stand without my fucking highest heels for once; finally a gig where the model had to be under five- foot-five.

The week before, I had worked as the lead again, this time for a Converse shoes commercial spec for a graduate student's project at NYU. The film director, an English man in his mid-thirties, had loved my ability to naturally just say whatever was needed. Or maybe he just thought I was cute enough for his project. Regardless it was a lead role. He said he was going to submit the job to Converse, too. Then about a week later I modeled ankle bracelets and handbags for an accessories company called Shoreline America, when I finally saw it in the print catalog, it was a job I felt any Giraffe would have been proud to get. I was getting jobs almost every single week and I had gained roles in music videos for an aspiring band called The Volunteers and also another band I never heard of called Yerba Buena. Each little job gave me confidence to get the next. In Washington Square Park, I had modeled for Minx Sunglasses and it was the same camera guy who filmed Alan's jewelry commercial, which was now airing on his website.

The gigs had paid a little over $100 or I did it just for the credit on my resume, to feel unstoppable. I could handle looking for work everyday and getting it, even if it wasn't paid, because at least I wasn't constantly naked and these were gigs I could tell my mother about. Yet whenever on the phone with her, I still always hung up quickly feeling guilty again; it was too emotionally draining confronting or explaining my choices.

I was also spending time in Robert's studio more than ever. His studio was now becoming more than a place to chat about modeling mistakes and make plans for shooting on random afternoons; it was a place to eat. My paychecks felt steady, but they weren't big and if I could save money on food, then I'd do it. I knew Robert's drawers were full of candy bars, granola bars, cookies. And if the studio was being used for a magazine or portrait that would mean there would be catering that day and I would nonchalantly come over and get a bite to eat.

Often I would walk from Prince Street to 29ᵗʰ Street just for the chance that no one ate the last granola bar out of Roberts's drawer. I had started eating the dollar menu at Wendy's, on Broadway before I went to the Apple Store. Usually the cheeseburger deluxe filled me up pretty well all day or else I would also grab a twenty-five cent banana from the fruit stand, it did the trick. Only I didn't care about eating. I just wanted to find modeling jobs and coffee would hold me over. I didn't want to sound ridiculous and desperate so I didn't tell Colleen, Robert, or anyone about my frequent visits to the Apple Store, or how badly I wanted a good meal; it was too embarrassing, it would bruise my ego and I feared being told to get a real job, to give up, to take a break. I didn't want to use Colleen's computer either. I wanted to be able to handle myself.

I had narrowed it all down to living on the basics, fifty cent toilet paper and Vo5 shampoo worked just as good. I bought food only when I needed it and never had a full cupboard. I told myself I didn't need anything. I tried my best to never get dirty. I washed my bras and underwear in the sink. Going to the laundromat was something that was now considered a splurge.

It made me a little nervous when the electric bill collector called threatening to shut it off; it made me think of the money I spent on fixing my high heels and buying more envelopes and stamps. I decided that I was only in the apartment at night and if I had to sweat in the dark, without a fan or electricity through out the whole damn summer, then I would. I said so to the evil collector, unafraid of having no electricity at all.

I went to bed thinking of the shoot I had the next morning, and I set my cell phone alarm.

Around 7 A.M. I took the W train to Rector Street to meet the photographer who was coming off his night shift as a security guard, or a Wall Street trader probably. When I got into his car, I was half asleep and he was hefty with huge bags under his eyes. He said he wasn't in the mood to talk about his job so instead I talked about me. We headed for New Jersey where there was a condo there; we would shoot for four hours. As we crossed the George Washington Bridge, the $600 he promised me was on my mind and then I followed him to the 8th floor. To think if I hadn't randomly opened my Onemodeplace.com account last week I would have never had this opportunity to make some cash.

Inside, the apartment was empty and he waved his hand

toward the bathroom for me to get changed. Before I closed the door he sat down in a folding chair in front of the fish tank, with only one little fish in it, and lit a cigarette. I debated my underwear choice for a few minutes and applied more blush and mascara; I used some of his hair products and focused on doing my task to get the money. I would be free to leave at noon.

He was slow, like a turtle, and definitely amateur by the way he held his camera, and he shot like a fragile old man, with nervous movements. Not smiling much, he had no opinion when I presented myself and asked, "Is this sexy enough?"

After each outfit I wore, he said we would take a 30-minute break which sounded great to me. I would get my $600 regardless of how many times the shutter clicked on his camera. I checked my voicemails in between shots and touched up my makeup, covering a few small pimples, and when he asked if I wanted to order food I said, "No it's okay" even though I was really hungry. I figured that eating might interfere with getting out of there by noon. I just wanted to stick to the plan and shoot for three more hours and get out.

I couldn't tell, as he smoked another cigarette in the kitchen, if he was just shooting to be turned on or if he was going to get a website one day for himself and try to become a professional. He stuck to his Onemodeplace.com account and talked excitedly about other models he worked with. They looked like shit, from what I saw on his laptop screen. With fake nails, fake hair color, roots showing, and a lot of bad makeup, they looked tired and worn out. Their stretch marks made me feel hot.

By the final hour I had only worn three lingerie sets. That is how slow he was, and I wondered how long it took to take a fucking picture, it was as if time stopped and disappeared and I was in a dark room in a sad never ending movie and I was stuck.

Some moments I felt my old self appear, the naïve 19-year-old girl spoke a few times, when I joked about how much I loved shooting lingerie and I giggled a lot to break the silence. If I hadn't had needed the money so fucking badly, I most likely would have never worked with this quiet creepy photographer.

I never got a CD of images, but in this case I didn't care to see the photos. I never even asked to see the shots and he didn't offer. They wouldn't benefit my book and I didn't really want to see him again.

For the final shot I bent over a plastic black stool. I couldn't stop thinking of how pathetic I felt, I had contradicted myself and it felt weird to suddenly be in the situation I had distanced myself from. I knew what I wanted to be. It wasn't a girl posing half naked today for a random photographer in his empty apartment. I would just forget about it tomorrow.

To convince my self I wasn't *that* girl, I also had a job scheduled for later that day on the Brooklyn Bridge with an aspiring fitness magazine. Another I found on Craigslist.

At the benches near the entrance to the Brooklyn Bridge I waited for the editors to arrive, and dug in my pocket to feel the six one hundred dollar bills, sitting in the bottom, more money than I would make during a week working at an Advertising agency. I wondered who had it so good. My eyes glanced over towards a black girl waiting on another bench, her hair was wild and huge, an afro, maybe she was the makeup artist, I wondered. I was glad if she was, since the photo shoot before in the smoky apartment had made my eyes tired and puffy. When the magazine crew arrived, I was hungry and tempted to take the bagel offered and water, but I knew if ate or drank anything I would have to pee and there really wasn't a place on the Brooklyn Bridge. Walking over the bridge it was windy, and the gusts were not stopping. My little-boy-short hair was blowing in a frenzy. While we fought the wind to the middle of the bridge, I realized the black girl wasn't the makeup artist after all, she was the main model, the girl who was going to be mostly seen in the shot. The editors and photographer for the magazine were suddenly ignoring me and thanking her and telling her how she would get credit in the issue. I had applied to the ad even though it said, "looking for experienced yoga model." I had never done yoga in my life.

The plan for the cover was to show three businesswomen in a yoga pose. I didn't have any business clothing so one of the editors gave me a shirt she brought with her and she also was going to be the third model. I felt pathetic, standing behind the black girl, who had never ending bouffant hair almost blowing towards my face. I stood next to the editor, who wasn't even a model, who was taller than me and while I balanced on one leg, I felt shorter than ever as the winds of the Brooklyn Bridge started to frost my barefoot body.

When it issued a few weeks later, my face looked stoned cold and pissed but I added to my portfolio book anyways. On a resume "cover model" would sound good. Even though the model standing in front of me was the real "star," if not her, then her fucking hair was.

That day after the shoot, before I went back to Astoria, I barely made it to the HSBC bank at 35th Street before they closed. I felt capable and independent, able to maintain my lifestyle when I deposited my $600 dollars. I felt rich and satisfied; it was pleasure to get my receipt. That was until I took a look at it. The bank had withdrawn all of the money I had just deposited? I felt tears starting to burn around my lower lid, but then reality hit when the teller told me that since I owed a few payments for the loan, all of the six hundred dollars (money I had shown my ass for) was taken immediately and was the banks money now. It had been a really horrible day and with only two dollars on me for the train, I walked directly to Colleen's new bar job near 48th Street and Eighth Avenue to get tipsy. It was on the way home anyways.

That evening when I got back I took a warm shower, I let myself air dry since there wasn't a clean towel and watched the five channels on the TV that Joel had left me. Then I called my mother while I boiled some elbow pasta and I got right to the point while I begged her to give me twenty-four dollars. I needed a weekly MetroCard, something to feel security from. Then I cushioned my demand with sharing my latest magazine exposure in that stupid fitness magazine, maybe the word "cover" sounded full of potential but thankfully she granted me the twenty-four dollars. It would be deposited into my checking account the next day so I could get my fucking MetroCard and carry on again for another week.

The next day on the way to the ATM I figured nothing could be worse than the events of yesterday so with my MetroCard money I was off to the Apple store. Once there, I really wanted to submit to a job I saw for background work on *The Sopranos*. At that second, I had to mail my headshot to the casting agency, this job would get snatch up quickly. It was a struggle to submit when I didn't have any supplies. The truth was I had no printer, no staplers, no paper clips, only a couple envelopes, not even a pen today. I had been going to the Staples store in Union Square to make copies of my resume for ten cents and using the stapler and tape provided and put together my headshots there. The thought of going to Staples again when I was already conveniently sitting comfortable at the Apple Store was a drain, so that day I asked a store employee for some help. This blue eyed, eager-to-help employee printed just one of my resumes and gave me a stapler too. I could now submit to the job. Maybe my little flirty smile helped but I bought the two stamps I needed and mailed myself to another agency, Grant Wilfrey. It felt good just to mail another agency.

That evening on the fire escape in Astoria, I was feeling like a broke slut, I had slept with four different men since Joel and I broke up and it made me think of the few real relationships I had experienced. It had been over two years and I hadn't said a word to Danny. Sitting there, I had an urge to call him and say I was sorry, but I didn't know his number anymore, I felt remorse for hating Danny so much when we were just too opposite to make "us" work. I now felt bad for thinking such terrible things about his mother. And I sort of missed Joel's arm next to me. Then another boy, writer, technician, auditor, or art director would call.

The next morning after another meaningless sex session, I had to get to a commercial job for the New York Auto Show; it would be shown later on a big screen at the entrance of the Javits Center. It called for attractive people to dance around and look glamorous. I could fake it. I had submitted a photo that Rod took of me in Miami, at the boutique hotel, in my little red dress. The photo had worked and I put on my trusty red dress again and walked through the Meatpacking District to a club called Lotus, where the shoot was. I was one of fifty background actors that wanted to be seen that day. I had asked Jacquelyn if I could borrow a bag. Later that day when the director told me that I was in every shot, I was happy again. I gave him my comp card and wrote my website on it then quickly blurted out that I was a full-time model, actress, and designer. I practically begged him to consider me for any future jobs. I had to constantly promote myself. The spec wasn't going to be aired at the Auto Show for almost a year but the one hundred bucks cash felt great.

Until the next afternoon when I woke up and counted my money and realized the money wouldn't go very far. So I spent it. It was just the amount I needed to buy a hot pair of Givenchy shoes on sale at DSW. I had never owned anything fabulous in my life. Colleen loved them too and every woman in the store probably wanted them. I hadn't bought myself anything nice in so long. I just wanted to own something that had power that had success behind the name. On the train, in front of everyone, I put my other ratty shoes in my denim bag and slipped into the Givenchy stilettos and I hung onto the pole balancing and standing almost 5 inches taller.

Back in the apartment, after I climbed the 5 flights in my new hot shoes, I wanted to ignore those voices in my head, the sounds of pressure terminating my modeling goals for the summer. I had wanted to be in a bikini shooting with Robert again, but I knew the terrible thing I had to do. The time had come, and there wasn't time this summer to be my own business when I had rent to think about. I had to surrender. Even though I was booked to work the Lingerie Americas show modeling Alan's jewelry and with a lingerie company he recommended me for called Level Eleven, this job wouldn't matter. It wouldn't be until August. All my money had gone to shoes and to the loan at HSBC bank. I was broke. What was coming was July and I needed hundreds, a lot of them, for rent.

With a grudge I deleted all my summer modeling goals from my mind and applied for a part-time job at the ritzy restaurant Jean Georges. Only I didn't know how stuck up the restaurant was and when the ad on Craigslist said "hostess with experience," I submitted without a resume only saying I had personality and was easy to work with. I hadn't worked a restaurant job since Friendly's in tenth grade.

At Jean Georges, the interviews were quick and I wore my tight denim dress and my new black Givenchy stilettos for good luck. Somehow my little getup worked but was a slap in the face the following week as I stood in my full black outfit, feeling stiff and constipated and corporate as a hostess for five days a week. To make me feel more like shit, my college campus was right across the street in Columbus Circle. I put aside my degree all over again; that was the past, as a hostess I was more ashamed to leave my modeling behind for 12 dollars an hour.

Some employees had worked there for years and were getting raises and went from hostess to Manager. The new manager looked like a young Spanky out of the Rascals. I told him my only profession had been modeling and later I found out that his girlfriend's sister had worked one of my fashion shows when I was in college and wore one of my sexy bikini designs. During the next month, all the cooks and wait staff and the other hostess's and even the dish boys knew all about my website.

It did affect my ego when I couldn't go on castings and be the model they saw on the website. I didn't have as much time to spend at the Apple store, and I was dying while making small talk with the other hostess's and feeling uglier by the second watching all the rich, beautiful people enjoy tiny morsels of delicacies' that I wanted to eat. Spending any money on large food purchases, like two Wendy's cheeseburgers, was analyzed more than ever. The first couple of paychecks at Jean Georges would go towards paying back what I owed of July's rent. I was a month behind now but if I could hack it a couple of more months at this shitty job then I might be caught up.

For my birthday my mother mailed me a DVD player, I wasn't excited though, I didn't want to pay more for my electric bill than I had to. Colleen gave me a gift of a book of stamps and envelopes which was so much more appreciated. I rushed to Staples to use the stapler and paper cutter and then stretched myself when I bought a new eight dollar Ross Reports and mailed out a ton of headshots. Yet while licking each stamp I just felt anything was possible as long as I could balance working as a hostess for a little longer and devote any other time I had to researching modeling and acting jobs.

Then just as I was thinking of a way to have it all, I got fired. Was it because I kissed the cook? Maybe I was too nice to the guests? Maybe I just wasn't prissy and bitchy enough. Maybe I just sucked as a hostess? I didn't care about the bullshit anymore and signed my release and was told to leave. When I walked out into the blue sky above the Trump Towers I was glad be fired, it was a beautiful day and I had not worked as a model in weeks. I was tired of wearing black and faking that I gave a shit about a restaurant I could never afford to eat at. I hated myself for trying. The summer was over and I didn't even get a damn tan since I was cooped up as a fucking hostess. So without anything to do I raced to the Apple Store.

On the way back to the dumps of Astoria, I calculated my savings. When my last check arrived from Jean Georges I would finally have enough saved to pay August rent. It was a beautiful thought even though it was the first week of September. This was still a huge accomplishment for me.

The next night I called the promoter from Marquee and put on my cheap little halter dress and I went out to dance on tables and drink a lot of free expensive Vodka again. Forget September rent, I would figure that out later all that mattered was that I would never again work as a fucking boring hostess.

The next morning, with the phone against my ear, dodging video cameras and the clicking shutters of cameras from people who had never seen Times Square before, I thought about how many times I had worked promotional events in Times Square and how much I hated the area. I ignored and darted around people, listening to a voicemail while applying lip gloss and some blush, a mirror in hand. After a night of drinking I had wound up with another boy I was about ready to stop seeing but somehow I was still tangled in his sheets when the sun came up.

I was planning to head back to Astoria to change my clothing and then come back to the city and, of course, go to the Apple Store. Only I got this voicemail from Lifestyles. I hadn't heard from the commercial print agency in three months and it shocked me yesterday to find out that they were still in business. They had sent me on a casting that same day involving a fitness print ad which I knew I didn't get the moment I walked in and saw the abnormally buff Giraffes. I was surprised to hear from them again so soon. Finally checking the voicemail two hours after it was left, I was too tired to even think about talking to anyone at the seemingly ungodly hour of 11 A.M., since I usually didn't start my chatting until at least noon.

The message from the agency said to bring a bikini and then asked if I had tan lines. The casting was for an ad campaign with a product involving shaving. My photo would be taken at the casting and I needed to wear something that showed my body and skin tone—I didn't have a bikini with me, or even a bra, since I was out partying and dancing on tables all night. All I was wearing was a thong and the olive colored halter dress I had worn out to the club, which had a toothpaste stain on it from when I missed the sink. I had to be at the casting in less than thirty minutes or I'd miss it. I scratched down the address with six-year-old handwriting and raced to the A train.

I had two pairs of shoes with me, and I can't remember why, or what I had done with them while I was at the club. Regardless, I had on my version of flats, which was actually a kitten heeled Aldo vintage inspired tan and brown shoe. They were easier to run in. I stood outside the building and buzzed. Waiting for an answer I took off my kitten heels and placed my tired feet into one of my tallest heels and then took flight, hauling myself up three stories.

When I opened the door to the casting, the room was an office with people typing away and working attentively, like they were oblivious to the casting call going on in front of them. I stayed quiet and when I walked in I saw that there was a Giraffe in her bikini hiding behind the door. She had cellulite on her butt and although she was about six inches taller than me, I felt confident. The woman taking the photos of the Giraffe's front, back, and side, for this body part print ad casting didn't even look my way to say hello. The photographer instead sat at a near by table and gave her full attention to the Giraffe who was towering next to me and even gave the Giraffe her personal business card. My doubt seeped in as the photographer barely flipped through my book. I started to take off my dress, openly and unashamed. I mentioned that I had body part modeling experience and that she could find my body photos toward the back of my book.

She didn't look at me when I said I was comfortable posing in just my thong. As I stood there, already half naked, she finally looked up, a bit shocked, and she said I didn't have to. She suggested I just pull my dress up and show my legs that way. I wanted this job. I needed this job badly, rent was ten days late, and there was no way in hell I was not going to show my whole body. I knew if the art director later saw the photo of me prudishly holding up my dress and scarcely showing my body, I wouldn't get it. I whipped my dress off completely, and covered my breasts with my hands, I couldn't fake that I was tall but I could show I had a nice ass.

I woke up on September 14th, knowing I would be able to finally pay rent, feeling overly excited and anxious; more importantly my first legit print modeling job from an agency awaited me in a little less than an hour. It took three years but the day finally came. I laid in bed for a few extra moments to remember how even though this would be a significant day in my modeling career, I had worked before. I wasn't new to this, I had shot more times than most models I met at castings, and a shoot was no new news for me.

I took this confidence and got out of bed, I gave myself only ten minutes to get ready because I knew being rushed would wake me up. The apartment floor felt cool and depressing and I almost stepped on a dead roach by the doorway. I walked to the kitchen where there was nothing in my fridge but butter, hot sauce, and lemons. It didn't matter, I just needed coffee.

I had already shaved the night before with my cheap pink shaver and added cream to my legs, trying to remove any presence of hair and unprofessionalism. I had toweled off hoping my roller-skating accident scars wouldn't show under the studio lights or on film.

I had just enough time to grab my bag, brush my teeth, throw on a skirt, and get some coffee from the guy on the street. I was singing to myself in the mirror saying "Oh my god, this is a body job for Braun Razor. It could be National. It could be nothing, but I got it."

The thought that in a few months, the photos taken could be part of a print ad campaign released the tension and questions and tears. It all made sense suddenly and the moments I had posed in silence in dead empty creaky living rooms, the realization of how broke and hopeless my life looked dissolved.

Finally all the meals off the dollar menu, having only five television channels, my lack of curtains and clean towels, and the days I unplugged everything before I left the apartment to save even the tiniest amount of electricity, were all worth it. I wasn't just amateur, I was capable and this day would define that I was considered good enough. It was proof that I wasn't wasting my time or fucking around with some "pipe dream." I had a tickling orgasmic feeling in my stomach, the anxiety and the pleasure of knowing I had a shoot. This time the difference was I had a person to call after the shoot and a voucher to be signed. The door to be professional was opening, slowly, but it was opening a little bit.

Now the potential was in my face and I was booked by another modeling agency. I was working not just to get attention or to flaunt my ass, I was working for an actual paycheck and a legit brand. Maybe it did still involve using my ass and legs but I was aiming for a better life where I wasn't whoring myself out for tear sheets.

I left my apartment and ran down the five flights of stairs, questioning myself if I should really be as excited as I was, because "it was just a test shoot" as the agency had stressed. I couldn't help my nerves and the tingles inside; I was bursting and hopeful and I had to be. It was a job, a moment, a booking that was a ticket to the train of acceptance into the modeling world. I wanted to melt into this moment and remember it.

I pushed open the front door and walked into the complacent world of Astoria, Queens, where no model lived on my block and no one with a dream seemed to be breathing. I didn't have any makeup on since I always applied it while I was en route to wherever I was going, and as I reached for my lip gloss I realized that my weekly MetroCard was about to expire. I had four dollars on me and I was going to spend one of them on a coffee. Going to the ATM to get a twenty and getting to the shoot on time was more important then getting my needed coffee, I argued with myself. Considering I was eating nothing that ever cost more than a dollar every night and living my current lifestyle meant every penny counted, this MetroCard was a crisis. I started to sweat. It was making me even more nervous. It sounds crazy but buying this MetroCard was now holding me back from the simplicity of just being on time. It was forcing me to be late and run in heels down one of the most animated streets in Astoria. The street was the same everyday, active but always predictable. Mothers with carriages, old ladies with broom sticks, and men with little coffee carts all mumbled as I started to run. There was no time for "Excuse me." Aggressive fruit vendors and teenagers that appeared to have never left the block, gawked, even though it was only 8 A.M. I guess being in a short skirt didn't help to prevent the noise of their lips air kissing me, or old men looking over their glasses to see me more clearly followed by a simple, "Mmm."

I almost made it to the ATM, and I was only a few steps

away from the subway stairs, when suddenly something didn't feel right. It was right in between my vagina and my underwear and it felt uncomfortable. Instinctively I shoved my hand down my skirt and slide my forefinger into my vagina. I didn't care who saw. Of all the moments, God chose this fucking one to pour more guilt on me for being such a dreamer. It was like he let my body go to hell that morning. There was blood on my finger. I had my period. For Christ sake, it could have come the day before, the next day, but not on the day I had my first real print modeling job with a known brand, from a real New York City agency waiting for me. The words "Fuck, fuck, fuck, fuck, help me, me, me please!" birthed out of my guts and groin. I didn't care who heard as I stood still, in the mess of Astoria morning foot traffic. Then I had an urge to pray, I had to ask some God out there who I knew was watching and hating me at that moment. "Why me? Why couldn't this morning just be simple?" Was it because I should be using my education? Was it because I didn't pay rent this month?

Astoria felt lazy to me, the same old Italian and Greek life, everyone knew everyone and everyone's story but me. It was like a TV show, seeing and watching the simple life that people wanted was purely innocent. I would listen out my window and watch like a tourist from the roof. It hurt to see it. Seeing that simple life right in my face when I wanted something more killed my focus. Smelling barbeque only upset me more; I had to be out of there as much as possible, it was just a place to sleep. If I was in Astoria, I wasn't in Manhattan, which meant I wasn't working, wasn't earning money so I could survive. Astoria meant I was going to wither away and die.

I couldn't handle seeing the smiles on teenagers driving their pimped out cars. I didn't want to see the kids playing jump rope or with a rigged out basketball hoop or a ripped soccer net on the sidewalk. It all reminded me of the blue collar man, the working young adult, the entry level job that I refused to settle for. I wanted to do what I loved and looking at them made me feel selfish.

Most people appeared happy just buying fresh fruit and drinking creamy Cafe Mocha at Athens Café. I never wanted to buy fruit or get a fancy coffee while watching the neighborhood go by. I wanted to survive. No, I wanted to do more than survive; I wanted to escape Astoria and this life that was being pushed on me by everyone here. Whether they knew it or not. Just by existing in their daily lives, I could feel it slowly stealing my ambition. Getting my period was also a reminder that another month went by, that I had made it another month. The summer was over and I didn't know how I made it alone. How did three months go by, my birthday, I was a year older and my period reminded me I had another month on the record of living and still without a stable paycheck.

I had only a few seconds to think of a plan to deal with the blood. The day was beginning; the bodies were moving rapidly passed me. A few girls my age rushed by in their suits and bumped into me. I hated Astoria, even more than my bed ridden cramps that would follow my period later that day. Watching my five pathetic television channels, eating worse than the homeless, sleeping, cleaning the few items I owned, it all made me feel very guilty for being so stubborn for refusing to live like a normal person. I didn't own a calendar or a nice cooking pot. It was emotional to see them eat on *Friends* or *Seinfeld*.

I was thinking of all of this as I stood on 30th Avenue and 32nd Street. And how I didn't have a tampon. I only bought things when I needed them, and usually I got fucked over because of it. Like now when I didn't have enough cash to go to Duane Reade, not that they were open anyway. My next option was obvious because there was an ATM at the Subway sandwich shop, and I knew most fast food places had bathrooms. I needed to get some toilet paper and clean up a little, and make it to the photo studio before I ruined my underwear and skirt.

I could feel the wet and sticky disgustingly gooey feeling of blood about to drip down my leg through my underwear and splat right onto the floor. It wasn't spotting blood; it was a flood of biblical proportions coming out of me. It was mushy and at any moment I could have gushed and exploded all over the tacky,

soda stained tile floor. I started to push my pin number into the
ATM while yelling frantically to the Spanish or Greek teenager
who was opening the sandwich display. "Do you have a bathroom
I can use?" He said no in a deep and unfriendly devil voice, and I
swear he had horns growing out of him. I told him, "It is kind of
important," and he still said no. I wanted to ask him "Where do
you pee?" Everything around me fell and cracked, and I blamed
myself, like in some way it was my fault that Subway didn't have
a bathroom. I was still in fucking- happy-go-lucky-let's-prance-
around-because-we-love-Astoria land and I had 40 minutes to
get to the Meat Packing District.

Then the nightmare really began—the desperation, the
dripping, and the twenty bucks I had to withdrawal. I would
be left with almost zero in my account again. Each second
reminded me that I was going to a shoot that would give me
an opportunity to grow as a model. To be in a different league
but my dream was dying with each bloody step, and I wondered
how long I could go on. How do people do this? Do people do
this? Do they live for this and only their dream? I had no savings,
I had no support, no sugar daddy, no funds, and my stubborn
passion wouldn't allow me to hostess again.

I didn't have a tampon because I couldn't afford to buy
them. I had been out of college for just over a year and it was
moments like this that I had to remind myself of my strength,
my focus, and how much I wanted this. Thoughts of my mother
came to me while I waiting for the ATM to spit out today's
survival in the form of green recycled paper. How she really
knew of nothing I was doing and how it seemed I only called
her when I needed money and usually the most she could give
me was forty bucks.

Amazingly it was all I needed some days, amazing that $40
could put me at ease. Knowing I could be purely saved, fed and
happy from that $40 was a joy, it was so simple but also it was a
kick in the face like I was unable to take care of myself. I tried
to only call her once a month at most, and only if I *really* needed
it.

But 8:14 A.M. was too late to call her, she was already on

her way to teach children how to read, I needed someone to teach me how to give up. I could turn around and go back to the apartment, lie on my mattress and curl up, forget about modeling, about my dream, and just accept Astoria's fate for me. But I couldn't give in and give up, even with my period, without a tampon, running late, and with no money in my bank account.

I just couldn't give in, because my plans were always to self serve and

I owned all I worked for. I was already too deeply affected by my past, and all I worked for would whisper to me and I would fall back to being grateful and feeling lucky that I was doing something with value, self worth, and I was exactly what *I* wanted. A piece of me didn't mind that I was bleeding down my leg, like a bitch in heat, because at least I was my own boss, and I was making my own problems, not getting them from some one else. Maybe I was in denial of seeing my own desperation.

All that mattered as I stood on 30th Avenue was that at least I wasn't working a 9-5 job. My face must have made five different expressions while I thought of all of this and I wanted sympathy from someone about my shameful secret time of the month on 30th Avenue. Calling my mother might threaten my resolve to make it to the shoot and it would force me to be vulnerable to her words, her nail scratchy, convincing motherly words: "You need to get a real job." I desperately wanted to call her, to have the kind of mother I could cry to, wishing she would reassure me that everything would be fine, that she would encourage me. Instead I knew that phone would only make me feel like shit. So I didn't call. And I felt in control again when the twenty bucks came out of the ATM. The dollar service charge could go to hell.

Before I left, I wanted to yell at the Subway boy behind me, "Fuck off bastard," but I didn't. I just kindly asked him for a few napkins, and I stood with my body close to the ATM Machine, hiding my next action of folding a napkin in a narrow rectangle and shoving it down my underwear. I said thanks to the teenager

who noticed nothing, and I left in rage, I had my MetroCard money and I could go to my shoot. I felt bitchy and
materialistic even though I had nothing impressive. As I waited on the platform for the N train, blood started to drip down my leg from all the running and movement. There isn't anyplace to hide waiting for the train, and the unstable napkin didn't do justice. I was trying to keep my cool and not lose my mind, not let anyone see my truth and blood. I grabbed the other napkins out of my bag and did my best to clean up my leg without making a scene. I was pretending to fix my shoe but I was really crouched down by a payphone feeling myself up again through my skirt, adjusting my Subway napkin sanitary pad which by then was almost completely used up.

I stood on the train even though there were seats open. Any movement could cause a river of red, and I was too afraid to move and make more of a mess on myself, or leave a puddle on the seat. My hands had blood on them, and there were not enough napkins to also clean them. I hoped no one would notice my bloody fingers. I watched people on their way to work, thinking I just came out of a murder scene. They were all very tired, it was quiet which made the ride very slow and my heart was racing to escape the entrapment of the train. I didn't own an MP3 player to allow my mind to slip somewhere else, I missed music. Everyone was listening to iPods, while I looked out the window at the skyline. This city was really starting to make me fucking emotional.

It sounded simple but it seemed I always did things the hard way, or hard things followed me. I couldn't just wake up and go to my shoot, and get the credit on my resume. It couldn't be a sweet, morning glory moment, it had to be a damn circus of heart racing madness, and the words "I just want to model, I just want to model" didn't make the train go faster.

I transferred at Times Square to the A train, and by this time I had asked about ten women from the train and platforms if they had an extra tampon or sanitary pad. Of course they didn't. I was the only female in New York City that morning with her period. Some women got as personal as to tell me they didn't get their periods anymore or telling me how they just finished their periods. I hated them all with a passion, but I gave them understanding eyes and I just couldn't figure out why in a city of over a hundred thousand women no one had a tampon to spare.

I even managed to get off the train with eight minutes to spare. It wasn't a comfort though because I knew the girls in *Vogue* didn't have to run in heels with their periods down the street at 9 A.M. They had a town car pick them up, or cab fare given to them, or they could at least afford another way other than running. Hell broke lose as the train slowly stopped and I impatiently tapped the train doors with my finger nails, saying out loud, "Hurry, hurry you fucking door." Emphasizing the "fuck" every time I said it. Saying it made me feel better because I was pissed off and I was dripping sweat like Niagara Falls. I found it to be a good thing though—it was evidence of my effort. The sweat on my forehead would prove that I wasn't walking gracefully through the Meat Packing District, sipping coffee, noticing the sunny day above.

I was running as fast as I could through the subway station even though I hadn't worked out or stepped on the track in years I suddenly felt like a marathon runner. The adrenalin built up from the Subway shop, to the MetroCard machine, to the warm suffocating air of the subway, and my need for coffee took over. I had this impulse to run. Like if I didn't literally chase my dream, it would disappear in the distance.

Or maybe I just felt like I had to run to try to make it on time.

My eyes were still heavy with no sleep and I hadn't fully applied my mascara, this pissed me off even more because if I was going to be late, I at least wanted to look good. I stopped to fix my strappy shoes that annoying came undone. I had to get them ready because the real race happened as soon as I broke the surface to the street. That's when the gun really went off, right when I heard the cars screeching and honking at each other on Eighth Avenue. I was off. I might have made a world record racing across town on Fourteenth Street. Or set a record telling over five men to" fuck off" in a forty-five second span. I was, of course, not able to run without confrontation. There was not even a moment of peace while I ran. The bums just had to say hello as if I had candy and cash coming out of my bag. It was the worst moment to get spoken to by anyone, I was fending off random walkers who were saying "Slow down little lady. Do you need help with that bag? I'll carry that for you." I told each man I hated them personally without guilt or shame and they each got the finger, too. It was like dominos, one man would say hi, I would say "fuck off" and then I would get called a bitch and the sound of "Bitch, bitch, bitch" charmed through the air with a Motown melody.

I would have taken the compliments of my sexy legs and about how well I ran in my heels on a day when I didn't have a modeling job that would change my status waiting for me. Any other time than when I wasn't late, hungry, tired, and bleeding out of my vagina. I couldn't believe it, I needed this opportunity many months and years before and I was late for it. There couldn't be one moment of calm to enjoy this pre-experience. Even my big black bag was trying to slow my pace and I almost wanted to drop it and just give it to the bum that I passed by. He would wake up and find a portfolio of a girl who was trying to be a model and maybe he would try to sell the photos for a meal. I would end my career on 14th Street and the last person to see my book would be some lost, reeking dreamer himself. Everything was slowing me down and testing my patience. The sun was too bright, the air too chilly and making goosebumps pop up on my hairless legs, and nothing was on my side, not even the wind. I really had enough of the bullshit as I jay-walked across to Ninth Avenue and hardly noticed as an old lady with a huge cart full of bottles slammed right into me.

I was abusing my body, I had been racing and pacing, and my heart had been athletically working hard for the past forty-five minutes of this journey. Even when I was on the train, I was still running in my mind. Now I was almost there, the whole next five minutes would be insanity. The final was about 400 meters of non-stop run.

I was dizzy by then, dehydrated, and hot, then cold, tired, and then full of spunk. A desert formed in my mouth. The cobblestone pavement was hitting my feet so hard; my poor heels were crying and whimpering for me to just give them a break. I felt so exhausted, pushing my heart this early in the morning to wake up and run. I was sweating, without deodorant, scrunching my face like I was battling every Giraffe in New York City, like I was fighting Goliath. I was making my own history, transforming that second, morphing into a "professional model." I could barely stop to look at what street I was on, blinded by the sun, with my skirt twisting and turning all the way around and falling, slipping off my skinny hips. My hair was like overcooked spaghetti in my face, damp and limp from sweat, and nothing wanted me to be on time. Nothing wanted me to be one of the first people there with a smile. The morning wanted me to run, to remember my roots, the days when running was passion, not regretful and annoying.

There were no cheers or flags waving from the side line or sidewalk. The morning wanted me in heels, in a skirt, bleeding my innocence, breathing heavily like a psychopath, or a woman panicking in labor. Sounding like a stuttering airhead or a straight talking TV host asking women embarrassing questions, while revealing my own tragedy to them all. I gave in, I let the morning win, and I asked one more lady if she had a tampon when I was on 12th Street. Lost and late I said, "It's okay" when she replied that she didn't have one, and she also couldn't tell me where to go. It hurt to know how nothing might ever be simple. I wanted so badly to not have my period and pinching cramps. I wanted so badly to be on time.

I lost feeling in my legs right before I got there and I almost forgot that I had my period as I ran down Washington Street, trying to stride out my legs a few more inches. I was almost there, but being there wasn't a comfort. By the time I arrived, I just wanted to die right there on the glorious entrance steps and collapse and forget about all this modeling. I actually thought I could collect myself and pull together whatever was left of my face and not look like I was screaming and dripping "bloody murder."

I knew time was of the essence but I just had to swipe on a little mascara and wipe away the snot and the crust on the corners of my dry lips. Then, I was Dorothy entering Oz, but the doors to the production studio took all that was left of my might to open. Even that had to be difficult. I was not myself, I didn't know who I was, I think I was Martin Luther King internally screaming, "Free as last" but I still needed coffee and a tampon and I wasn't free at all of my uncomfortable, war beaten bloody body. I felt nauseous and had hot flashes as I stumbled in like an elephant, I couldn't breathe or speak clearly. A daze took over; I swore I saw fairies cheering me on. I was looking and feeling like a pothead and I needed another hit. I was the Big Bad Wolf huffing and puffing and with cotton mouth choking my words at the reception desk. Could the girl sipping a soda at the desk not realize that I could hardly feel my body and I needed a drink? How could they not see that I was on pins and needles, beaten by the cobble stone, beaten by the Subway Sandwich guy, beaten by the ATM, and there was even sweat behind my ears and in places I didn't even know I could sweat. They stared like I was a street urchin, a dirty, crusty-eyed, and smelly, uncombed raga muffin.

The slow blink of their eyes told me to hurry whatever I had to say. I took a deep breathe and I spoke a mile a minute asking where the bathroom was, where the shoot was, if there was coffee near by, and if anyone had a tampon. Then I managed a smile and gracefully and gratefully reached for the one tampon I was offered by the women who looked like she ran the place. It was clear she didn't feel any mercy for me and wasn't happy about my disheveled appearance. I went to the bathroom with my coveted tampon and as I hurriedly shoved it into my bloody vagina, I wished I could tell her to fuck off.

Nine hours later my naked body had just about enough of the brutal lens probing and scrutinizing my body from every angle. I wasn't getting paid any overtime and I was craving a beer so badly. I needed something to ease the fact that we had shot fourteen rolls of film and I still had in the same tampon. It would have been a great day if it was a Tampax commercial shoot but I was tired of bleeding and hiding my tampon string during the nude shots of my gushing body. By 6 P.M. I was literally dripping and asking for a tissue, I was battling my mind, spirit, and crotch all at once and then the photographer wanted some video too. Before the video shot I actually left a little blood on my robe but no one seemed to question that it was anything but "just some lip gloss."

I felt like I was in a Nazi camp for nude models. An hour later my body was speaking slow and, almost in a whisper, telling me to sit down and enjoy the quiet subway ride back to Astoria. My mind was chanting at me that I should walk as fast as I could to Colleen's bar. It was over forty-four blocks away. At the end of it all the photographer had photographed almost everywhere skin covered. I said goodbye to him with an awkward hand shake and politely didn't take the Polaroid I was offered, a keepsake that most models would have taken with pride. I just wasn't sure I would want to remember this day. I didn't even care about the potential ad campaign anymore. He signed my voucher and I could still smell the fertile blood on me as I walked out of the studio. I had to walk and clear my head and suddenly forty-four blocks seemed like the perfect distance. Colleen looked shocked when I wandered in. She offered me a Cranberry and Vodka and was startled when I said "No!" All I really wanted was a fucking tampon so I could go back to Astoria. I felt broken and oddly triumphant.

The five flights to my apartment weren't as mountainous that night when I got back and my legs felt longer as I escalated, my body felt transformed, as if I grew a few inches taller. My muscles were tender and sore and I was hungry but what filled my stomach and eased my mind that night was the thought of how I had made it through the day and no one but me really knew the secret tolerance of it all.

I knew this day would keep me full of ambition and it

proved the point that I needed and would never forget. I now had another story that would shock people, but it was proof that I was capable of anything. The day rewound and repeated itself as I got ready for bed and laughed a little when I used the last sheet of toilet paper and then found a forgotten five-dollar bill in my bag. It was just the sign I needed and I said my prayers and then said, "Fuck you" to all the doubts given to me along the way. Then I regretted not taking the Polaroid.

Maybe nothing would come of the photos since it turned out that they didn't run nationally in an ad campaign, but still the day proved how I couldn't be beaten by the ATM, by the wind, and the cobblestone; it could be my time of the month and I could be gushing with blood, sweating and running late, with cotton mouth and still I would efficiently, just as good as any Giraffe, get the job done.

Chapter 15

Nothing Left to Lose

October 2005: Apple Store, Prince Street.
By mid-October paying September rent was impossible. I knew coughing up the money for October would be even more impossible. I still hadn't gotten paid for that Braun test shoot. But I was confident; I thought of that day now whenever I needed a pick me up. I sure of hell hadn't bled for sixteen hours on the same tampon for nothing, and modeling wasn't over. After that shoot, it had just begun in my mind. Getting a real job or another part-time job wasn't starting. I would never relapse and settle. I would stay in Astoria, in the apartment until I was kicked out.

I had considered being an egg donor. It paid a whopping $8,000 and I was willing to give up a few eggs for the cash. Except my father's alcoholism would prevent me from being accepted into the program. Something I didn't find out until after about three visits to the offices way over on First Avenue. I was pissed.

At least I would be soon in magazine called *Mac Directory*, to be one of the Mac users whose faces are featured at the back of the magazine with their name and little comment about computers. It was something.

I hated fucking working promotional modeling jobs but I had found one that was paying cash. It was a promotion for the Independent Film Channel. Perfect. Afterward I would be able to go to the bank and mail my landlord a check. It sure wouldn't cover the full September rent I owed but it was something. The morning of the promo I was given only a white pair panties and a set of pasties to cover my nipples; I had never worn pasties before and looked ridiculous because they almost covered my *whole* little tit. For thirty minutes I was spray painted and the blue paint was so cold it stung my bare skin. In a row we stood, twenty other girls getting airbrushed as a character from the Quentin Tarantino movie, *Reservoir Dogs*. While I was getting painted, I checked out the competition. The other girls had plenty of boobs and I felt not as attractive when my group of three rode around in a convertible through Union Square, my tits shivering in the cold while yelling about the Independent Film Channel.

I felt a little better when the tourists and men in suits by Wall Street were taking photos and waving us on as we flew by, basically naked since the paint was peeling off by mid-day. In the *Metro* the next day, there was a small photo of me and two other spray painted girls. None of us in the picture was a fucking Giraffe. The day got better when I was picked along with three other girls to go to the Opie and Anthony radio show.

After the promo I took my four hundred dollars and went right to the bank, and then spoiled myself with buying a jar of tomato sauce. I had to mail my landlord a check but first I called him. Recently I purposely missed his call, avoiding facing that I now owed about five times more than the four hundred I had.

Even with my Craigslist gigs I doubted I would be able to catch up. So suddenly waiting to be kicked out of Astoria wasn't my plan anymore. I offered a plea to end my lease, spur of the moment, leaving a message, "I only have about four hundred dollars but I will give you everything I have...The deposits I made when I first moved in, please use that to cover October...I need to get out of this apartment!" Before I hung up I even said, "I will help you find a proper tenant by November 1st." I knew if I left the apartment and Astoria good things would happen.

Still it felt pretty pathetic when I hung up and rubbed my arms to make them warm again. I had shaken through out the whole message. Then I cried really hard but I cleaned up my face with some rough toilet paper and went to bed hopeful.

When Monday came there was a message on my voicemail. He must have pitied me when he said I could leave at the end of October. I had gotten my way. I would be able to leave in two weeks. He would take my deposit. I didn't even have enough to give him September rent. I never would. I couldn't believe that I was free to leave my lease three month's early.

I quickly thought of where to go. I had only gone on a few dates with the skinny, blue eyed art director who I met at the Braun shoot and it was too forward to ask to already move in. Plus I wasn't sure if I really liked him and he said he already had a wacko roommate. I needed to find a place to stay, with someone who wouldn't ask too many questions about my choices would be best. I thought about my options for a couple of days.

The handbag designer, Jac, came to mind. Maybe I could stay with her for a couple weeks. I started to throw out my life. Everything had to go. Everything. Handbags, shoes, a dresser, a table set, two chairs, all thrown out the window and into the garbage five flights below. I had just modeled during the Fashion Coterie Tradeshow at the Piers on the Hudson River for Jealousy Jeans, but now those beautiful three pairs I got as part of my payment for the long two days would have to be thrown out, too. By mid-afternoon I had most of it out of the apartment when the landlord told me to stop throwing things out the window. Apparently it was making too much noise and it was dangerous to throw chairs and boxes out the window he said. I told the neighborhood boys they could have any of my DVDs and while I threw out my life, random boys would knock on my 5th floor walk up door and ask to see what else I was willing to part with. One boy almost took one of my nude modeling CDs and I grabbed it back but then threw out about ten CDs from my past amateur days an hour later. I was taking only what I could carry. I had to be selective on what would stay and what would have to go into the trash.

When I walked to the trash, I almost tripped over a smashed pumpkin and I realized it was almost Halloween.

The orange guts flung everywhere and pumpkin seeds were splattered all over the sidewalk and now this shit was all over my shoes. Fucking perfect. After a few more trips to the trash, I ran for the train to work promotional job in Times Square. Even without rent anymore I would still need money later for a MetroCard. Since Jac lived in Hoboken the Path train would now cost me more money just to get to the city. At least it wasn't Astoria I told myself as I chucked more, jeans, sweaters, coats, purses I didn't use, pots, forks, and the knifes in the trash. There was no time to give things to charity or have a street sale. I tried for five minutes, and left some of my favorite jackets and shoes on the street, but they sat in the sun. No one wanted them.

On the last night there was nothing in the apartment but a mattress and a few garbage bags. The apartment looked just about as empty as when Joel and I first moved in. I loved it then, it was paradise, a new chapter, another chance, it was hope. Now it was all I needed to get rid of. I threw the mattress out the window and left the apartment with five bags. I got only two blocks down the street, when I just couldn't even carry it all. I dropped a few bags and thought of a plan. Every ounce of strength inside of me didn't want to call Joel for help. I had no choice. He lived right down the street and he had a car. When he arrive though, he didn't have his car because one of his friends was borrowing it. He still agreed to help me carry my bags to the train. I hesitated as he reached for the heaviest one, wanting to say, "No it's okay, never mind. I don't need you." But I didn't.

With my bags at my feet on the train, heading to 33rd Street to get the Path train, Joel didn't look at me during the ride to Hoboken and I didn't let him into Jac's apartment when we finally arrived. I sort of thanked him but it was too painful to look him in the eye.

As I plopped my bags against Jac's white walls, I felt like the book *The Things They Carried* without the machine gun and ammo. Jac was her southern comfort peppy self. I tried to be cheerful too but it had been a long fucking dramatic day of promotional modeling and throwing out more clothing and after seeing Joel and now being in fucking Hoboken, with no modeling jobs coming up, I wasn't really in the mood for chatting when she handed me her spare pair of keys.

That night, I tried to sleep on Jac's black leather couch. It was difficult thinking that all I owned fit into five medium-sized tote bags. I fell asleep thinking about chasing my dream and I realized how much it meant for me to call myself a model. No matter how hard or difficult it would be. I knew trying to be a model would fulfill me more than having a home.

I couldn't fail now.

I spend the next couple of days using Jac's stamps and mailing more comp cards and contacting all the people I had worked with and asking for a copy of the music video or proofs. I had to collect all my hard work and hard copies of it. Proof that I was on my way to being a professional and serious model. The film director from that NYU Converse commercial had submitted late to the contest and no one at Converse had seen it. I was disappointed but he still said I could meet him in SoHo and he would bring me a copy of the video. We set up to meet in a couple weeks. Then I contacted the director from the Univision music video, it was already airing on Univision and I was anxious to get my copy. The next days were spent preparing for a photo shoot I was very excited about. An Australian photographer had posted an ad on Craigslist looking for models to test. I first scoped out his website and then emailed my own to him. He had mentioned submitting the photos to fashion magazine in Australia. Suddenly our little test photo shoot could become a published piece and I would get a tear sheet.

He didn't have clothing for our shoot, but I was beginning to think of doing some of my own art directing and styling. I remembered a small lingerie company called CLO which I discovered when I worked that Lingerie Americas trade show back in August. I emailed the designer to see if I could borrow some of the designs for a photo shoot. Now I was borrowing lingerie and looking for jewelry designers and posting my own ads on Craigslist.com, I grabbed a couple of Jac's bags too. I wore my own sexy *les tropeziennes* shoes that I bought at Daffy's months before for only twenty five bucks. With all of these accessories I was trying to create my own concept of an editorial for our shoot. (A year later when it is published in an Australian fashion magazine called *Curve*, it would prove that I had the vision for this fucking industry.)

After a week at Jac's, I heard from the agency Funny Face and I was sent to a casting for Oxford University Press for a book cover. When I got the job, it wasn't the money that only made me happy. I didn't have to worry about rent anymore. I looked at my five bags against Jac's white walls; this was another credit of modeling experience to keep me assured that everything would be okay.

Then reality hit when I woke up ready for my day at the shoot, and realized I had only a couple of dollars on me. I dug in Jac's couch and found some extra quarters for the train. Three bucks was all I needed to get there and back. The next day I took the train to Christopher Street and walked the rest of the way to SoHo and the Apple Store, even using Jac's computer wasn't the same.

During those next weeks in Hoboken I wasn't just bumming off of Jac; I was earning my keep. I had run errands for her and become her gopher for her handbag needs. I picked up leathers and hardware and went to the engraver. At night, while Jac sipped a diet Coke, I gave her some ideas to shape her simple handmade handbag line into a higher end handbag collection. We became very good friends during these meetings and seeing her succeed was now important to me. I wasn't just her model anymore, I was becoming her sidekick.

Each night she had bought me sushi or I stretched myself to get just one roll and we would go over patterns and leather swatches together. I had asked Robert's assistant Larry to shoot some of the new bags. I offered to write press kits for Jac, and help market her bags to magazines, kind of like how I was trying to market myself. It worked well, since I was in all of her photos, I would also get publicity when she got in a few magazines. We became very good friends but after thirty one days of sleeping on Jac's leather couch, it felt like too long.

When I went home for Thanksgiving, I tried to be normal.

I tried to not mention where I was living, what I was doing and why I was doing it to anyone. I saw my father and I waited in the car while he went in for an interview at the Salvation Army. I had recently got myself a Macy's credit card, for when I needed to buy someone a birthday present or get myself some discounted high heels, and now wanted to buy him something nice, he looked so old and tired, he needed something new. I didn't know how I would even make the Macy's bill payment but as I watched him cough his way out of the car wearing, most likely, a fifteen-year-old baseball cap, I felt he at least deserved a new hat. My sister had traded in her American Eagle days for her new wardrobe at New York and Company and she already looked like a college graduate. She even had a pair of heels and I wanted to get to know her again, but I just couldn't care, I had to think about where I was going to live next. I had to find someone fast or else I might have had to come back to the slug life of Syracuse.

That thought scared the shit out me. When I got back to the city I met the film director from that NYU Converse commercial contest, I had told him we should meet to talk about working together again but while we sipped coffee at a small café on Prince Street I calmly asked this film director, who I hardly knew, "Would you mind if I stayed with you for a little bit?"

And that's how I found myself with another place to sleep and put my bags. Before I left Jac's and went to live with this English NYU grad student, I did another shoot for a fitness book, this time for a small publishing company in Long Island City. At the shoot I felt very weak and out of shape pretending to lift the weights properly and balance on the exercise ball. The fitness book was for a professional trainer who had been seen on national television talk shows and working with him, being a model for his book, was just more hope to continue on. I didn't need a home or my own apartment; I could bounce around until I got enough money to try to hack it in another apartment again. Rent was what had held me back, held me down, made me worry and without it I was better I believed. I still owed HSBC bank three months of payments for that damn loan. It hurt. I hated still paying for an apartment I wasn't even living in anymore.

I prepared to leave Jac's throwing out yet another whole bag of clothing and a pair of pink shoes I really wanted to keep. I had now gone from sixty to six pairs in about four weeks.

One day while standing in one of my highest heels during another Apple Store session, shit really went down when the Internet had been abruptly shut off. After about a minute of waiting for it to be turned back on, I felt a slight dryness in my mouth form. Soon I couldn't take it as I was staring at the frozen screen. I said "fuck" about a thousand times under my breath as if it would help. My fist hit the table and people stared with puzzled looks, a fucking boy about my age even laughed at me. They didn't understand what I had been working on.

The document I was writing couldn't be saved into my email. It was the beginning of a memoir I was writing. I had always saved every writing session to my Yahoo email account. When an employee said, "Just go buy a CD and burn your document onto that" I almost wanted to laugh. *Didn't he know I could barely afford my MetroCard and I was sleeping at some middle aged English film director's apartment soon because I had given up my fucking apartment in Astoria?*

After clicking the Safari icon a few more times to open the Internet with no luck, I asked each employee that grazed by once again, "When will it be turned back on?" I couldn't just re-write what I had written, it was honest, and from the heart, I had spent an hour on it. It wouldn't be the same if I had to start over again.

I looked to the right and the left, everyone around was so calm. I looked to the ceiling, then up towards the second floor. The store was very busy today. I wasn't giving up my spot. The employee had said, "Sorry, it's free Internet."

It was free, but it had been my life line.

I had used the Apple Store every single day or just about for the past eight months. Now I was feeling the desperation of my choices and lifestyle. I realize how much I wanted to model and all I had given up. I had sacrificed my ego, for it. Standing there, empty, broke, without my email, without the Internet, without my document, with nothing to do, my stomach felt weak, butterflies fluttering in my stomach ached impatiently to be free.

I was having an epiphany, right at the fucking Apple Store. A moment of truth appeared and I saw myself. My nose looked bigger reflecting on the screen and my forehead had lines creased out of frustration. I was so involved with what I was pursuing I didn't see my own desperate lifestyle. The store had become the means to do my dream as I stood there waiting for the Internet to be turned back on. It was a choice to be there every single day.

I was vulnerable. I wouldn't leave until I got my document.

All around me were people shopping and trying out new gadgets and iPods. People on their lunch breaks, students preparing for college, parents and corporate professionals asking very intense and important technical questions. Then there was me; I was using the Apple Store as a source of survival and I needed my goddamn document.

Tapping my foot at the computer I started to question my dream, my plans, the fact that I was giving up simple things like the Internet and a good meal some days. I thought of the stable life I could have tomorrow if I wanted it. But I couldn't, I couldn't give in. I had to prove I could model no matter what.

The store had been so good to me up until this point. From my research on the computers I had recently scored an editorial lingerie gig that wanted a girl originally over 5'7 for a magazine called *Accent*. It didn't matter today. I had posed as a butt double to cover the lack of an ass on the tall Giraffe who was the main model for the *Level Eleven's* lingerie catalog. But that didn't matter today either.

I wondered who else would allow themselves to be this fucking desperate. Was this crazy? Did this make sense? But I had to do this; I was already too deeply emotionally affected by this challenge to model. I looked at my jeans and the stains were just baffling, how did so much coffee not get in my mouth? I looked like shit too. And I was late for a job.

The only person I knew near by who would have a blank CD for free was that English film director. I hated asking for help. I hadn't moved my bags in yet and I was already asking for more favors. Once he arrived I downloaded my document and was off after a huge hug of gratitude.

I grabbed the N train and zipped up to Times Square to the QT hotel on 45th Street to the job for Fuji Television, a Japanese Television program. Once again, Craigslist. The segment was for live TV and for the job I pretended to be a hotel guest as I swam in the pool that had a "wet bar," which was the featured story. The host of the show spoke about it while I sucked down a martini with another model who was too prude to go in the pool and wet her bikini. Then Fuji called again and this time I was pampered at the Cornelia Spa on 5th Ave for their segment of hot New York City spots, these quick hour long forty to fifty dollars gigs wouldn't help to put a down payment on a new apartment but it would help to get me a MetroCard.

The next day I moved into the SoHo apartment with the English film director and plopped my five bags down on his wood floor by the television to announce my arrival. There wasn't much room to spare in his narrow apartment. He bought me some dinner and I thought maybe this would work for a while. But then the following week he left a note near the stove that said, "Success came by, but you were asleep and missed it." What a bastard. I had been motivating his old ass to get more creative with his filming and even cleaning up a little and here he was making fun of me for sleeping. I was pissed that I shared with him any of my dreams and ideas, and I went to Robert's studio for some comfort snacks.

I had complained about the rude comment from the English film fuck to Robert and he had said if things got bad I could sleep at the photo studio for a night or two and I considered that if things got any worse living in the narrow SoHo apartment. My little dates with the skinny blue-eyed art director I met at the Braun shoot had got me a few good meals but besides that, he didn't have anything to offer me. And I certainly had nothing to offer him. My father tried to understand me and I felt the more desperate I was, the more we had in common. But he couldn't give me much encouragement either when he was having just as hard of a time finding work himself. I did have Robert's studio, it always made me feel better. I had asked him if I could make the studio my permanent address and now I went there to collect my mail almost every day.

Colleen now was a regular too since I had introduced her to the Studio boys. In turn, she had introduced me to her next door neighbor who was an agent at another modeling agency called R&L models. If only my next door neighbor when I lived in Astoria was a fucking agent. It didn't matter, knowing Colleen's neighbor was good enough. I got a meeting out of it.

The meeting with R&L was quick and even though the sassy young agent said I needed a new comp card, I was sent to *Cosmo Girl* magazine a couple weeks later. I waited with four other girls for my turn, seizing up the competition. They all knew each other, and they all looked alike with similar clothing, shoes, even their faces looked alike. The job was for a fitness editorial. A stomach shot. I imagined that when it would be my turn I would mention I was a track scholarship runner and I would get the job on the spot.

I focused on my journal, pretending to be very engaged in my schedule but really listening to the Giraffes' conversation. They talked about the housing they were living in and about their modeling agency. It's an agency that would never look my way but I considered stopping by anyway next week. I looked at my comp card which had suddenly transformed and tricked my eyes. I saw what the R&L agent saw—how ugly and stupid it was. When it was my turn, I walked into the glassed in room and lifted my shirt and had my Polaroid taken. I felt all the Giraffes in the lobby staring at me and the editor of the magazine didn't even flip all the way through my book. But she smiled at me when I left, which I thought might mean something. Only it didn't.

After the letdown, I wasn't sure R&L would send me out

again, but when Flaunt called and sent me to see a shoe company called E.S Originals, I felt capable again. Even the agency Funny Face had called too. They sent me to an audition for a Spanish teen magazine called *Quince*. The casting was in Brooklyn Heights and I had to lie and say I was only seventeen. I didn't care, I would tell all the lies I had to. It felt good to be sent out to a casting by an agent again. It wasn't just about booking the job anyways; it was about getting the chance to go to the audition or castings. It was about being given the chance.

By now the English film director had gone to England for a vacation and he wouldn't be returning for about six weeks. His apartment would be all mine. He wouldn't be back until after the New Year. I had plenty of time to think of a new plan of a living situation before that.

But I wasn't too concerned with finding a home. I kept on pushing any modeling I could. After a mailing to a commercial print agency that had never accepted me, I finally got a call. When they sent to me a casting at Wella, not for a hair job but for a makeup job, I was sure I'd get it. If I did, I would finally get to meet with the agent. It was kind of weird but after I booked the makeup job I did meet with the agent at the Abrams Artist Agency. When I left the agency I had five New York City agencies that knew my name and I would have a check for the makeup job of $75 soon too, I hoped. I had wanted to buy some boots to stay warm but I really dreaded the thought of having to carry anything else when I moved out of SoHo sooner or later.

I took a Greyhound to Syracuse for Christmas and while I was home my sister and I tried to bond over the movie musical *Rent*. She handed me a tissue during the song "Seasons of Love" and I don't think she wanted to realized how much I could relate to the movie. I never wanted to pay rent again. After the holiday I took the Chinatown bus down to Washington D.C to visit Maryam for the New Year.

Around New Years, I was starting to think of living in a commercial space, it would be a lot cheaper even though it would be illegal. Plus I called the YMCA and it was more expensive to live there. All I needed was the money for a down payment.

I still had a few days to think until the English film director returned from England; I needed to get something together fast. I should have worried about it sooner because now it was tiring, draining, thinking of where to live and the thought of carrying all my bags there when I finally figured it out. I was also constantly at the Apple Store hounding Craigslist, looking up jobs and the apartment sections too, running to castings, trying not to give in or give up. I feared my future would have nothing to do with modeling if I didn't find a place to sleep soon. I'd be forced to return to Syracuse. I could almost smell the chili grease and thick creamy macaroni salad. I was desperate enough for a modeling job to walk to Midtown, on the coldest day of winter, during the MTA strike, just for a stupid modeling casting call.

Only it wasn't stupid at the time, ironically it was a print ad for the Independent Film Channel and it would involve an ass shot. I had to go.

Up on 38th Street, I sat on a wood bench waiting for my name to be called. There were only five other models waiting to be called so my chances were higher because of it. I was so glad that Gene at Flaunt had called me.

As I sat and eyed the Giraffe next to me, I picked at my fingernail. The Giraffe had ugly, tight black jeans and when she stood up I saw she had no shape to her ass. This was a modeling job for a *butt*. I knew my ass was better than hers. It paid $2,000 and considering I walked over 40 blocks to get there, I fucking wanted the job. I really needed some new shoes. Plus this money would basically save my debt and get me into stability again.

Secretly I also wanted to be part of an ad campaign. To be "the face" of a product and I was hoping this shoot would be it. Looking at the pale, milky, freckled face of the girl next to me, I couldn't stand the idea of her getting the job. Her voice irritated me; it was low and sounded like a man. She was confused and flipped through her day planner, not even sure what the casting was for. She was obnoxious enough to ask, "What is this for anyways?"

She looked right at me, so I had to be the one to tell her.

I could tell she was with a big agency from the logo on her modeling portfolio book. I looked at my bent, wet, old and dirty portfolio. The photo I printed at Robert's even now has some slush on it from the hike.

I always wondered who got the butt casting job, who got the $2000 bucks, who had the perfect ass they were looking for. Actually, I didn't want know. I just hoped to god it wasn't the idiotic Giraffe who had the flat ass. I hated myself for being so desperate that I would walk from Spring Street to 38th Street to only be dissed by not getting hired.

That shitty day I walked back to SoHo sleepy and the fluffy snow looked more comfortable than the fucking couch I was sleeping on. I had a long walk back. On a sunny day the walk would have been pleasant. I was freezing, with no mittens and I hadn't eaten in over 15 hours.

I took a different route back, and made it up as I went, purposely making the walk longer even though I was tired. I needed to think and clear my head; cold air does that. The streets were bare, almost *Twilight Zone* scary, too quiet. Less than a few times, random colors of blue and red hats would pass by, and sleek leather gloves, puffy coats all black, wandering, hurrying like little city socialite mice.

The sidewalks weren't shoveled. It was sad how the world ended in a city when it snowed. Knowing it was only me making small tracks in the snow was a strange freedom I didn't want. I could scream and no one would hear or notice. I could steal someone's mail, or bash a car window in and run; only my footprints would give me away. It was a feeling of danger and risk I had remembered from my amateur shoots. I inhaled the cold air, it burned the back of my throat a little, and when it did I was grateful to be alive. My stomach was making noises and they started to annoy me. I knew I wouldn't be eating anything high quality anytime soon. Plus I was beginning to get sick of dollar menu and it was starting to be not worth the dollar. By the time I got back to the English director's apartment, I was too tired to even wonder when I'd have a bed of my own.

When the English film director returned, he looked paler than usual and we went for drinks at the Grand Hotel around the corner. During my second apple martini we got into a heated fight and it didn't matter what it was about, by the morning I swore to myself I would be gone. I had enough of his shit.

That night I pretended to be comfortable as I lay on the couch again but when the apartment was quiet, I got up. I threw out more of what little I owned. I even had to trash a few thoughtful Christmas presents my mother had just given me.

I only had a twenty dollar bill on me but it might be enough to get me to Brooklyn, I thought. The last thing I wanted to do was call Jac or Colleen or cry to Robert. I had cried enough to them it seemed. Suddenly the Corbis casting I had the next day wasn't on my mind. All I cared about was getting to Brooklyn and going to sleep. I would take my four bags and get in a cab and call my sometimes boyfriend, that skinny blue eyed art director from the Braun shoot. Maybe he would have some food in his fridge. Twenty minutes later I left him no choice when I arrived at 3:00 A.M. interrupting his sleep, I suddenly felt like the nag and burden I never wanted to be but had obviously become. It was still snowing out and my bags and I were soaked. As I was waiting to be let into his apartment, I noticed a broken umbrella in the pile of rubbish. I wished I had a damn umbrella when I saw the grumpy, pissed off look on the art director's face as he opened the door. He grabbed my bags and threw them under the stairway.

The next morning I didn't show up for my casting for Corbis, a stock agency. The art director had left for work at his big shot advertising agency job and I focused on my new goal. Getting an apartment again. I just wanted to try to get a place to live again. I needed a quiet place to live. Or at least something cheap.

I applied to four potential apartments. My estimate from my Craigslist.com search was $1500 dollars. While I waited for a reply from the tenant I called my mother. Only, to my annoyance, there was no answer. Then she answered twenty minutes later and said she was at Wal-Mart. I was pissed that she had something to do while I was sitting here, practically homeless. Again, my lies about trying to get a "real" job helped me to get more money from her. Even though she was already paying my college loans, phone bill, and the Victoria Secret bill (well, she didn't know about that yet). But it's time to find a new home.

This time I actually will go to an interview at an advertising agency so I won't feel so guilty about my lies. It was a job I didn't get, but that wasn't the point. At least my lies had some truth to them. After the interview, I took the 2 express train up to Harlem. I get off at 141st Street. I walk a few blocks and the brick building on the right side will shortly become my new home. As I walked, I thought of my father, he had told me during our last phone call that he had moved thirty times from the years 1997 to the year 2000. He had lost a lot of important memory's along the way too.

My new rent was $650 a month. I convinced myself it was doable. I had three roommates and even though it might be a loud and scary neighborhood at night, and I could probably hear out my window children screaming and crying, it was a freshly painted apartment. The Hispanic girl who was looking for a roommate didn't need a copy of my ID or any proof that I was not a criminal. She was sold on my smile and she only asked for $1300 to move in. There was no lease to sign.

I used the left over $100 bucks to buy a roll bed at Urban Outfitters and the other $100 I saved for food and MetroCards. My first night I slept like a baby on my new roll bed and even drooled a little.

The next day, I got a weekly MetroCard and went to see Robert. I told him about my new apartment but ask him, "Do you think it is all just a dream?" He looked at me with a sad, confused look and said, "You are a dreamer, that is what they do, they dream."

I knew I had to pay back my Macy's card or give something to HSBC for that loan, and I wanted to give at least fifty bucks towards my college loans. Yet for some reason, I felt like spoiling myself with a really big juicy turkey and tomato and cheese sandwich. I didn't know how in the world I would ever pay everyone back as I took the first huge bite of hope.

The rest of the day I spent at the Apple Store, checking my email and sipping a fifty cent coffee. Once I got a few smiles from the employees, I was back in my zone again. Afterward, I hopped on the subway, transferred a few times, and took the 2 express train back up to Harlem with my half eaten sandwich. On the bumpy ride, I did my mascara carefully as possible, even though there was no one to see, and no one to impress. When I thought I looked good I tried to remember everything that had happened in the past six months. I still felt there was a chance out there if I kept pushing and trying something would happen again and again. I had chosen a line of work that involved a lot of bullshit and stress and had been emotionally damaging at times but it had always been worth it.

It all made sense now. I had forgiven myself for letting that first photographer photograph my crotch, then I remembered my tear sheet with *Women's World* magazine, all those shoe modeling castings, that lead role in the Coheed and Cambria music video, then graduating college, all those fucking promotional jobs, all that sand in my ass crack in Miami, every visit to the Apple Store, everything had brought me to this day. I had only been a tenant in Harlem for one day and I already knew I would be leaving after the thirteen hundred I paid for two months were up. I knew myself better now. I knew I couldn't fake handling stability. I had used my mother; I had lied to her again. It wouldn't be long before my bags would have to be turned into one suitcase, and without an apartment again, I would then rely on Robert's studio more than ever as my home base, a place to breathe, a second home to the apartments I would stay at. Robert's studio would be my safety net whether he knew it or not, a place to collect my thoughts, to get my mail, and most of my belongings would be stored in the back of the studio underneath a wood table and between his photo equipment.

Around this time I told the Apple Store manager about my visits, about my memoir. He was amazed and I found myself preparing for a reading at the store. I wouldn't get the job for Jockey underwear at Macy's, or the body double job for the movie *The Girls Guide to Hunting and Fishing*, but I was still trying.

During this period everyone and anyone was a potential place to stay for a night or two. It started to feel normal being homeless, carrying what I needed with me like a soldier, and now not only Colleen and Jac, but a new guy I was seeing for a few weeks, a photographer I had just met, the camera guy who filmed me for a little gig with the Biography channel, a gym manager I met at a dance club was an option, or I would gather any cash I had and spend a few days with Maryam in Washington D.C, or when there was really no where to stay at all I would call my mother and pretend to miss Syracuse and she would give me enough money to take the Greyhound back home for a few days. It hasn't killed me yet and just last week I booked another shoe show and I am hoping that fit modeling job with *Teen Vogue* comes through.

After five years of creating myself, I can finally be honest with myself. I might not carry glitter cream and thigh highs in my bag anymore but I have become comfortable with my past, with my height, with myself, and my real name. What had grown from that very first photo shoot in Syracuse to where I was standing as I wrote a book about it, all gives me more reason to not give up and I am still trying.

Some people know exactly what they will be doing and who they will be in five or ten years. For others it isn't as simple. The only thing I know is that I won't be any taller and my mother might not be any thinner and my father still might not have himself fully together, but I know I will love them and myself more than I ever have.

Because over time my shame has dissolved, and now I want to learn my mother's thick macaroni salad recipe and after I have eaten a couple of bowls I will go for a nice long run and this time I won't just be chasing the Giraffes.

Isobella Jade is a petite model living in New York City and *Almost 5'4"* is her first book.